MW01169019

Dear Sweet Girl
A Memoir of Fear and Faith

Jenny Radler

ISBN: 9798668893294

Credit for Cover Illustration: Sarah Nicholson
Photo Rights: Jennifer Radler

Printed in the United States of America

This book is dedicated to
Grandpa Tep and Caren Atieno Owade

Prologue

Dear Sweet Girl,

I know you've waited a long time for me. You've imagined me a million times and wondered what I'd have to say to you, if I ever had the chance.

You're probably also assuming that I am not qualified to give you advice, or to console you in times of paralyzing fear and uncertainty. You probably don't expect to hear me cheer you on, or tell you that things will get better, because feeling better is usually only temporary for you, isn't it? So much of your time is spent waiting for the "next time," so how could I possibly talk you into feeling differently after all of these years?

If you think about it, I'm really just a stranger to you. I've spent years getting to know every piece of who you are, but I've only ever existed in your imagination. You actually happen to have a wildly creative imagination, and you always find a place for me in there, but you still can't quite put your finger on who I am. It's okay, though, you aren't supposed to at your age. You'll get there.

I do have some things that I want to share with you. I realize that you aren't able to hear me from where you are, but I still owe you these words. I owe you the time and attention and the endless amounts of love that you've always deserved from me, but that I've not always been capable of giving you. I think now is a good time to start trying.

The story that I'm going to tell you is a truly beautiful one; filled with unexpected adventures and people who are going to change your life. Perhaps some of them will even help to save it. They are going to alter your perception of the world and everything you thought you knew or wanted from it. You're going to be stretched and challenged in ways you never thought possible, and you'll come to know a power and a love that is greater, stronger, and wiser than all of us. I think that's my favorite part.

The truth is, I used to think that life works better for me when you stay hidden. I do tend to feel lighter and freer when the enormous weight of your burdens is nowhere near my tired shoulders; so, I pushed you away a lot. I don't feel good about that, but for someone so tiny, you sure can be heavy sometimes.

It wasn't until recent years that I began feeling the desire to pull you out of the dark. I began wanting to hold you and nurture you, and to let you experience this crazy life alongside me, the way that you deserve

1

to. It's because you were who you were, that I am who I am. I wish we celebrated that more often over the years, but at least we can do that now.

So, buckle in, Sweet Girl, because I'm about to flip your world upside down more than once. I know how scary it sounds, and how desperately you'd want to run away from everything that I'm going to share with you, but I'm going to do it anyway. For the both of us.

Chapter One

Today should be a fun day in class.

We get to look through another one of those children's news magazines, and I really love those. I love when they have fun pictures of places like under the sea or outer space. And I love when there are stories about animals in there. I've always loved learning about animals. I wonder what story we are going to be talking about today?

My fourth-grade teacher walks around to each group of desks and lays down a pile of the magazine copies; one for each of us. I lean over to grab mine from the pile, and when I see what's on the cover, my heart does that thing where it feels like it's going to jump out of my body. It's a fast and sharp pain that I am used to by now, but I hate it every single time. I hate the way it feels in my body and I hate what that feeling means: I am about to feel anxious again.

There is a boy on the cover of the magazine, standing in a field. It looks like he wants to run from something, but he only has one leg. He has light-colored jeans on, that are rolled up on the side where his leg is missing. He is dirty and skinny. He looks scared, and really, really sad.

My heart keeps giving me those sharp pains and I feel like I want to throw up. It's a good thing I didn't eat a big lunch today, because if I saw this picture after my stomach was full, l would throw up all over my desk, in front of my classmates. Then I would be so embarrassed. No one likes to see a person throw up, and I know that my classmates would shout and run away and make me feel bad, even though it isn't my fault. I can't help it when I do that.

The story in the magazine is about a country in Africa where there is a war going on. Bad guys hid some kind of bombs under the ground, and regular people, like this little boy, had no idea if they were going to step on one by accident.

My mind starts moving really fast, like it usually does when I feel anxious. I want it to slow down but I don't know how to make it, so I get tangled up in it instead.

Is this boy scared?

How can someone live with one leg?

Why do we live in a world where some people have to live without their legs?

Where are this boy's parents?

Do we have bombs hidden somewhere near us?

3

What if we do but we don't know it?

Why is the world so scary?

How can we know where the scary things are so that we can stay away from them?

Is there anywhere in the world where scary things don't happen?

Who is taking care of this boy?

Where is he now?

I want to erase this picture from my mind. If I can't then that means I am going to see it over and over again. I'll never forget it; I'll never not be sad about it. I'll never not be scared. I wonder if that little boy is always feeling scared, too. I wish I could help him.

My teacher reads through the story with us, but I am not paying attention. I can't hear her words and I can't keep up with my classmates. I am too busy thinking about that boy and wondering if he is scared. Then I wonder if I might step on a bomb someday, just like he did. They can be anywhere, can't they? We don't know for sure that they're not.

Our lesson finishes and now it's time for Art. We are learning how to draw 3-D shapes and all of my classmates feel really cool now that they know how to draw them. I'm doing my best to draw, too, but I can't stop thinking about that boy and his scared face. I don't know what it feels like to live where he does, but I can feel him being afraid. It feels cold and lonely, and I wonder who is there to comfort him, the way my mom comforts me when I feel scared.

My classmates are chatting away while they draw. I can be pretty shy sometimes, but I have some good friends in my class, and we are sitting together at the art table. They are talking to me and I talk back, because I know I can't let them see how I'm feeling on the inside.

One of the things that I've learned since being a really little kid, is that I am not like the other kids. They don't get scared or upset about the same things that I do. And, even when they are feeling scared or upset, they calm down easily and then they forget. That's not how it works for me, though. It takes me a long time to calm down when I am upset. And, also, I never forget anything.

Back at home, I tell Mom about the story in the magazine. I tell her about my fear of stepping on a bomb somewhere, and she tells me that we don't have to worry about that where we live. She tells me I am safe. Then she and Dad try to encourage me to eat my dinner, so that I don't go to bed hungry. They ordered in pizza from my favorite place, but just looking at it makes me want to throw up. I can never eat when I feel this way.

4

After dinner, I try to do my homework. We have to answer questions about another article in that magazine, which means that I had to bring it home with me. I don't want it in my house or in my brain, but here it is, so I keep looking at it. I keep going back to the front cover and staring into that boy's eyes. Sometimes I test myself, and try to see if I can look at something long enough that it won't bother me anymore. It's really hard for me to do that, though, so I just feel like I'm torturing myself.

Eventually I get up from the desk in my room and go into my parent's bathroom. I bend down over the toilet and make gagging noises until I throw up. It takes a while this time because I didn't eat very much today, but something always comes up, eventually.

Mom walks into the bathroom behind me. She rubs my back and tells me I have nothing to worry about. Then she tells me to brush my teeth and get into bed, and that she will meet me in my room. Minutes later, she comes in and sits on the edge of my bed. She starts rubbing my back again, and telling me happy stories until I finally fall asleep.

All my life, I've been afraid of things. Well, that's what it feels like, anyway. Even when I'm doing something fun, and am supposed to be feeling happy, there is always a part of my brain that is waiting for a bad thing to happen. Sometimes, that part of my brain is the loudest, and sometimes it is almost completely quiet, but it always exists somehow.

I'm starting to think that I was born this way, like maybe I was born with a brain that doesn't work like other people's brains. I go to a special type of doctor called a Therapist, and I talk to her about how I feel. I know it's her job to try and fix me, but so far, there hasn't been much of a change. I do like talking to her, though. Her name is Rachel and she's really nice.

Besides talking to Rachel, I don't really talk about my thoughts and feelings with anyone. Mom and Dad know that I feel anxious a lot, but that's only because they're around to see me skip meals or throw up when something that I see or hear upsets me. They listen to me cry when I tell them I don't want to do things away from our house, or without them. If they weren't around to see certain things, they wouldn't really know.

The doctor I used to see before Rachel, said that I have "separation anxiety." It's common, we were told, for young kids to struggle with being away from their parents, even if for a short time. It's just a phase, he had said. Kids outgrow separation anxiety with age.

I never outgrew mine. And, also, I don't just feel anxious about being away from my parents. I feel that way about so many things, but *since I don't know how to explain why, I usually don't want to talk about it. I don't think that anyone would understand me or have the same feelings that I have, so why should I try?*

The best way I can explain it is like this: I know that bad things happen in this world. Even though nothing really bad has ever happened to me or my family, I know that it is possible. The world is full of bad and scary things; things that I hear people talking about or see on the news and stuff. There are accidents and diseases and people who hurt other people. Countries go to war. Parents fight and get divorced. My parents fight a lot, so I think if something bad is going to happen to us, it's going to be that one.

Some kinds of foods are unhealthy and can make you sick. Sometimes breathing in the wrong air can make you sick, like adults talk about germs a lot. How are we supposed to know if we're breathing in the clean air or the sick air? And even the weather is dangerous sometimes, too. The weather can actually be dangerous enough to kill you, and that is so scary. I don't understand how anyone on earth can feel safe, if they know that the very earth itself can betray us like that.

There are also things that we don't know could be bad yet. Once, maybe a year ago or something, I was sitting on the floor in my parents' bedroom, watching a game show on TV. The contestants had to answer questions about a bunch of different things, and I wondered how one person could know so much about the world.

"How do they know all of the answers?" I asked Mom. "Are they told the questions before the game starts?"

"Well, not exactly," Mom answered. "But they know the different types of questions that will be asked, so they just study each subject really hard."

I thought about what she said for a minute, and then my mind started to do that racing thing.

How could one human brain hold so much information?

What would happen if someone studied too much or too hard and their brain broke?

What if their brain exploded?

What if my brain explodes from worrying about their brains exploding?

I sat and watched the game show for another few minutes before I couldn't take it anymore. I couldn't look at those people, who may have accidentally overstuffed their brains without even knowing it. The more I thought about it, the more my own brain began to feel overcrowded. My heart was beating really fast, and my hands started to sweat. I stood up and ran to my parents' bathroom, and Mom followed me in there to ask what was wrong. I told her, and then I lost control of myself and threw up. She rubbed my back as I bent over the toilet and threw up my dinner. I had worried myself sick again.

"Sweetie, learning new information is great for your brain!" Mom reassured me. "It is so healthy to learn new things, as children and as adults. The more you learn, the better!"

I kept throwing up in the toilet, wondering if someday a group of doctors or scientists would discover the opposite to be true. It seemed like that type of thing was always happening: something we thought was good for us turns out to be bad, or the other way around. Sometimes I even wonder if what I'm doing right now- like the way I am walking or talking- could turn out to be bad for me. But how could I know that for sure, until someone else figures it out?

I can't. And that's what makes everything feel so scary.

~ ~ ~

Dear Sweet Girl,

It's hard to know where to start, so I guess I'll start with a short story...

When I was in my mid-twenties, one of my best friends, Sarah van Edema, and I went on a road trip. We were to drive half-way across the country, and decided to get an early start so that we could make the entire drive in one day. I don't remember the exact time that we left her family's house in Connecticut, but it was somewhere in the wee hours of the morning.

We were driving and chatting endlessly, when Sarah turned to me and said, "Jenny, why hasn't the sun come up yet?"

I was the one driving, but I hadn't been paying attention to the timing of the sun. When Sarah asked me that, I looked up into the darkness, and I couldn't find the slightest hint of a sunrise.

"Oh yeah," I said. "It definitely seems like the sun should be up by now."

"Doesn't it feel like we've been in the car for hours already?"

"Yeah, it really does."

7

There was a brief moment of silence, and then Sarah continued.

"But seriously...what if the sun just doesn't come out today? What if after the entire history of the world, today is the day that the sun doesn't rise?"

My weary eyes struggled to stay open as I forged ahead in the darkness, suddenly contemplating what it would be like to do the whole drive in the dark.

"Great, Sarah! Now that's all I'm going to be thinking about until we start to see the sun!"

There was another moment of silence before Sarah spoke again.

"Okay, Jenny, I'm actually starting to freak myself out here! What if it's really going to be dark for this entire drive?"

"I don't know Sarah!" I shouted, fighting back the slap-happy laughter that comes with waking up in the wee hours of the morning, jumping in the car with one of your best friends, and knowing that you have an entire day of driving ahead of you.

"Now I'm not so sure it's going to come up, either!"

We both burst into laughter. We were exhausted into borderline delusion, as we both admitted to each other a fleeting moment of panic over something that was clearly so absurd. Less than an hour later, after a quick stop for coffee and a pee break, we found ourselves driving into the sunrise that we thought may never come.

I tell you this story for a couple of reasons. First of all, it's a great example of where most of your fear sits. You don't realize it where you are, but at the root of all of your fear is the question: What happens if the world turns on me?

You know that it's possible; bad things happen. People get sick, houses fall down in storms, drivers crash cars into trees. There's "good" food and "bad" food, "kind" people and "mean" people. "Safe" fun and "dangerous" fun. How can we tell the difference? How do we truly know what's good and bad, safe or dangerous? And what happens if the good, safe, fun life you're living suddenly becomes bad or sad?

What happens if the world turns on you?

What happens if the sun decides not to rise?

I also tell you this story, because that road trip is one of my favorite memories. We drove for sixteen hours and laughed almost the entire way. Yes, there were some moments where Sarah and I had to take a quick survey of our sanity; but the more fed up with the drive we became, the harder we laughed.

If you had been in the car when someone asked: "What if the sun doesn't come up today?" that would have consumed you. For the entirety of the road trip, you would have obsessed about it; torturing yourself over whether or not that was actually possible. If Mom had been in the car, you would have asked her, and she would have told you that the sun always comes up, of course. But how could she really know? How could any of us really know?

You and I are alike in many ways; there's a lot that you've passed on to me, and I've had to figure out how much of that to keep, and what to throw away. Like anyone else, the ability to figure a lot of this stuff out comes with time and maturity. Sometimes, though, we have to put in a little bit of extra work, and luckily, you started doing the work long before I did. You may feel like what you've been doing hasn't helped you, but it has; and that's why I was able to laugh about the missing sun.

So, let's move on and get to the bigger story here. When I was eighteen years old, well before that road trip was even a potential thought, I went to college away from home. Yup, against every fiber of my being, and whatever shred of decent judgement I thought I had back then, Mom and Dad forced me to apply for college.

As you can probably guess, I was dead set against this, so I initially tried to fight it. I suggested to them that I attend a community college, rather than go to a school in another town- or God forbid another state- where I would have to be far away from them, and from the few precious things that made me feel comfortable and safe. Community college made perfect sense to me, as I would be continuing my education like they wanted me to, but I also wouldn't have to leave home. It truly felt like a win-win.

But alas, Mom and Dad weren't having any of that. They believed that me spreading my social wings was just as important as furthering my education, so living at home while attending college was never going to be an option.

I suppose it should have helped to ease my anxiety knowing that my best friend, Sas, was looking at some of the same schools as me. Since you knew Sas first, you can imagine what a huge source of stability and comfort she became in my life; and how could I not want to begin this exciting new chapter with my very best friend by my side?

Well, you know exactly how. I didn't want to go because even though Sas was familiar, college was unknown territory, and I didn't do unknown territories. I had never experienced the joy of "stepping" outside of my comfort zone, because I always needed to be "pushed." Stepping was for brave people, and I sure as hell wasn't one of those.

To be fair, I had made some progress before I left for college. Being back in therapy got me to a place where I was able to finish my senior year of high school without skipping days based on my anxiety, like I had been doing in years prior. I was eating well and getting sick less; I participated in activities both in and outside of school. There was still a bit of you left in me, but I was surviving in my little bubble of life, and that was good enough. As long as I was functioning on a daily basis, and not talking or thinking about college, everything felt just fine.

The problem was, thinking about college became unavoidable. The closer I got to the dreaded days of packing my bags and saying goodbye to my family and friends, the further I fell back into those anxious ways. I couldn't eat, I didn't want to get out of bed, and I even threw up a couple of times. Every time Mom brought me to a store to shop for dorm stuff, I would cry or lash out at her; telling her over and over again that I couldn't do it.

When it came to knowing how to deal with me, Mom and Dad struck a fantastic balance. They may not have gotten along with each other, but their ways of combatting my anxiety complemented one another quite well. Mom was the one who assured me that I was safe, and Dad was the one who encouraged me to be brave. You know how they are; and it is that combination that pushed you through some of your darkest moments. In all of the uncertainty that you feel about…everything…you can be sure that you will never live a day in your life without an extremely solid support system. And while many will come to build upon that support system over the years, don't ever forget that it started with Mom and Dad.

Anyway, did you know that not everyone has the opportunity to go to college? And not everyone who does go is gifted that opportunity by their parents. Did you know that? Some kids have to pay their own way through college, or borrow money that takes years and years to pay back. Meanwhile, our parents simply handed the gift of an education to me, and I was too busy pushing it back to be thankful. I would get so tangled up in my own emotional distress, worrying about all of the "what if's" I can think of, that I missed what is actually happening around me. I can't tell you how often I've missed the gifts in life because I've been waiting for the curses. I know you do that, too, and that is just no way to live. You don't ever want to get so caught up in fear, that you miss out on the gratitude.

As it turned out, I absolutely loved college. Sas and I stuck together the whole time, but we made some amazing, life-long friends along the way. I developed a love for Psychology and Sociology, and a passion for helping some of the most vulnerable populations in our community. I served as an intern at a Suicide Prevention and Awareness agency, where a huge part of my role was answering their Suicide Hotline. To answer your question: yes, it was really sad listening to other people's deeply-rooted pain, one after another. But because of you, I never judged or shied away from them. I only ever met them with compassion.

At the end of my senior year, I worked with a professor of mine to develop a community research program, which addressed the challenges that our town's homeless population was facing. Again, it was sad, but I pushed myself to do it because they needed and deserved the help. I was finally starting to learn how to harness my compassion and empathy and use it for good, rather than let it take me down.

The summer after we graduated, my friends, Jackie, Kellagh and I decided that we wanted to experience a change. All of us had grown up in New England, our college was in New England, and we thought it would be fun to give another part of the country a try. We moved all the way from New England to Tennessee, and although it took some time to adjust to a new place, I did successfully start a life there. I found a job as a Mental Health Case Manager, and made new friends. That move was huge for me, and I was so proud that I had been "brave enough" to do it. I was an independent woman, finally starting a life that I could claim as my own.

Eventually, I decided to go on to earn my Master's in Clinical Psychology. In order to save my money, I moved in with Mom and our Step-Dad, Paul. You haven't met him yet, but you'll love him when you do. Just like you'll love your new Step-Mom, Sharon. I'm so proud of you for getting through Mom and Dad's divorce, by the way. I know that was something you were most afraid of.

Anyway, Mom and Paul moved to Tennessee about a year after I did. Mom says that me being there had nothing to do with that decision, but that's still up for debate. Either way, it worked out perfectly because I was able to enroll at Lipscomb University. Once again, I was making strides in building a life for myself, and I was loving it. The anxiety was still there, but it was manageable, and I felt like I was thriving in a way that I had hoped for, but never expected.

One day, less than a year into my Master's program, I was sitting in my Counseling Theories class and a friend of mine said, "Did you hear about the trips our department is offering this year? We have the option to go to Moldova, or to Kenya, I think. We should totally go to Moldova together!"

After discretely using my phone to look up where Moldova is, and deciding that was an instant "no," I let the idea of traveling to Kenya linger in my mind for a second. *That would be kind of cool,* I thought. But then I let it go. Even in all of my progress, traveling to somewhere as far as Kenya seemed to be too big of a leap for someone like me.

It wasn't until a few months later, when a close friend of mine traveled to Israel on a Jewish Birthright trip, that the idea of Kenya came back up. Julia was at the airport in New York, waiting to meet the strangers that she was about to travel to another country with. We were texting one another while she waited, and she admitted that she was nervous, but mostly excited.

As a Jewish person, I was also entitled to take a Birthright trip. I'd be able to travel to Israel, all expenses paid, with other Jewish people who had an interest in exploring the land of their ancestors. But even in my new-found "bravery," I never considered doing it. I didn't want to travel to a place so far away with people I had never met before.

I know, you'd never consider doing that trip in your wildest of wild dreams. And to be honest, I didn't consider it, either. I didn't even really know what it meant to be Jewish; other than having lots of family traditions. But there was one of my friends about to go on this trip of a lifetime, and I sort of envied her. I was jealous of her bravery and the anticipation of such an adventure; it was something that I never felt capable of until that very moment.

Maybe it would be exciting to go to Kenya, after all. At least I'd be going with people that I had sat with in class before. If we got to know each other a little bit better before the journey, it wouldn't be so hard.

The day after Julia left for Israel, I asked my professor, Dr. Douglas Ribeiro, if it was too late to sign up for the Kenya trip. He told me that there was space available vand time until the deadline, so I put my name on the list and never looked back. Not once.

The months leading up to our departure were blissfully, and surprisingly anxiety-free. Each week, my Multicultural Counseling class would gather to discuss the obstacles that are presented when counseling across different cultures, and how to combat those challenges in order to meet the goals of a client. We talked about our own cultural reservations and the potential challenges specific to our upcoming time in Kenya.

None of us had ever traveled to Kenya before, and for a lot of us, our collective knowledge of the country was limited to what we had grown up hearing about it, or seeing on television and in magazines. Although I was ashamed to admit it, I had always lumped all of the countries in Africa together, in terms of my preconceived notions about that area of the world. When I thought of Africa in general, I thought of AIDS, orphans, war, and safari animals.

Do you remember the little boy from the magazine? The one from Africa who was missing a leg? He was your very first frame of reference when it came to that part of the world, and it stuck for a really long time.

In our discussions as a class, although some of my peers had those same preconceived notions about Africa, we realized our mutual desire to see Kenya for the country that it is beyond this "worldview" that had been presented to us as Westerners. Although our primary goal for the trip was to conduct a Psychological Needs Assessment for Orphaned and Vulnerable Children, who had been effected by loss attributed to HIV/AIDS, (I know, it's a mouth-full), all of us agreed that tuning into the beauty of the Kenyan culture would be equally as important as the work that we were going there to do.

Given that we were a group of aspiring Counselors and Psychologists, my classmates all bore a high level of sensitivity, just like me. The thing that set me apart from the rest of them, was their varying levels of faith. Lipscomb University is a Christian School, and all of my classmates, Dr. Ribeiro, and his wife, Vanessa, who was joining us on the trip to Kenya, were all raised Christian.

As a Jewish person, who never truly believed in God, I did feel like somewhat of an outsider. None of my classmates ever made me feel that way, I just didn't know how to relate to them when they talked about anticipating all that God was going to do through our trip. I was honest when I disclosed my lack of faith, and my inability to share in their quest to see God work in Kenya (mostly because I didn't know what they meant by that), and my classmates were all respectful of that.

Together, we participated in group activities that allowed us to get to know each other better. Then, Dr. Ribeiro broke us off into the pairs that we would be conducting the Needs Assessment in, so that we could spend time bonding with our partners. He felt that it was important for each pair to spend one-on-one time together; familiarizing ourselves with the material, and with each other. We were encouraged to learn the working style of our partner, and to practice running through the assessment as many times as we needed to feel comfortable with it.

As a whole class, we continued to bond over discussions on what to pack and where to receive our vaccinations. When you are traveling to a country in the developing world, there are certain vaccinations that are

13

available, based on the illnesses that are most prevalent in that country. Some of the vaccines are required, some of them are simply a suggestion.

For me, receiving the Yellow Fever vaccination was a defining moment, in terms of travel preparations. Unlike all of the other shots that can be administered by a General Care Physician, the Yellow Fever vaccination is only given at designated travel clinics. Along with the shot itself, they also provide you with a five-minute consultation, where they hand you a packet of information about the country that you are going to, and tell you everything that could go wrong there in terms of your health.

Don't eat raw fruits and vegetables.

Don't drink the water.

Don't let your skin touch any natural body of water.

Apply bug spray and sunscreen constantly.

Failing to comply with any of these guidelines may result in the following: extreme nausea and vomiting, diarrhea, fever, body aches and/or severe pains, extreme weight-loss, minor skin rash or flesh-eating virus. Death.

Oh! But don't over-do it with the bug spray, because it causes cancer.

The irony was clear to me, as I sat and listened to the nurse give me a brief summary of my impending death, that I had spent my entire life fearful of pretty much everything, and I was about to throw myself into a situation that required shots and a consultation by a medical professional. I was shocked by your silence during this time, but I very much appreciated it. If there was ever going to be a time during my travel preparations that I would second-guess myself or back out, it would have been at the travel clinic.

On departure day, I woke up feeling fantastic. Not only was I not afraid, but I was *excited.* I was all packed and had loaded my electronics with plenty of entertainment for the travel. I received calls and texts from loved ones, filled with well-wishes, and I was ready to go. I met up with the rest of my class at the airport, and was just as excited as they were to get our trip underway.

To this day, that departure to Kenya is one of the most surreal moments of my life. I thought about you often, throughout the entire process of getting ready, and at the airport as I prepared to leave all that was most comfortable and familiar behind. You were with me, and I felt you, I just desperately hoped that you would stay quiet. I wanted to soak up this experience for everything that it was worth; and you, Little One, are the girl who never wanted to leave the house.

Chapter Two

We were really excited about our sleepover.

Sas and I only live a few houses apart from each other, and our families even went to Disney World together, but we've never had a sleepover at one of our houses. We're six now, so our parents said that we're old enough, and even though I don't like being away from Mom and Dad, I love being with Sas. Our families spend so much time together that it's almost like we are one big family. I've been to her house a million times; I just haven't slept here yet.

I picked my favorite pajamas to bring, and also my favorite stuffed animal. When I was born, my parents got me a teddy bear that has a red t-shirt, and on the t-shirt, it says "I Love Jennifer." I never sleep without him.

Playing at Sas's is so much fun. Her little brother, Andrew, always wants to play with us but Sas doesn't like for him to. He's so cute, though, and I like when we play "House" and he gets to be my baby. We always play that game, or we play "School", and he gets to be one of our students. My favorite is when my brother, Jake, is with us, too. Then we can all play Pretend together. He and Andrew are the same age, and our parents always talk about how perfect it is that Sas and I have each other, and that our brothers have each other. Jake isn't sleeping over tonight, though, because he's too young.

After we play for a while, it's time for dinner. Sas's mom, Dayl, made us beef stew, which is one of my favorites. Tonight, I even finished my entire bowl, and I was so happy because I'm not always able to finish my food. If something in my mind is bothering me, I can't eat anything. I hate it when that happens because then everyone stares at me and asks why I'm not eating.

"Are you sick?" They ask sometimes.

"Did you eat already or something?"

"What kid doesn't like pizza?"

I think even Mom and Dad don't understand why I can't eat sometimes. They know it's because I get anxious, like the doctor says, but I don't always know how to explain what I'm anxious about. I really hate when I can't explain it.

Tonight, I am so happy that I finished my beef stew. Even though Sas is my best friend, I don't think she understands what happens to me when I get anxious. She is always really brave and never gets upset about

15

leaving her parents. It seems like she never worries about anything, and I wish I was more like her. I would be embarrassed if she knew how worried I feel all the time.

After dinner, we get into our pajamas and Sas's mom takes a picture of us so that we can always remember our first sleepover. Then she tells us that we are allowed to play a little bit more before bedtime, and that's when I started to feel bad. She said, "before bed," and it reminded me that I'm not going back home for the night.

I'm trying my best to "tough it out," like Dad always tells me to do. I don't want to tell Sas or her mom that I'm starting to feel homesick, or that feeling homesick is going to make me start feeling sad about other things. Usually when I get sad about something- especially missing my family- I start to worry or feel sad about other things, too. I can't explain why that happens to me; it just does.

I know that this would never happen to Sas, and I also know that she would be really sad if I went home. All day at school today we talked about this sleepover and I don't want to ruin it, but I'm starting to feel like I have to.

"I miss my mom and dad," I tell Sas, just when she is taking out supplies for us to do a craft.

Sas stops pulling down the package of Pipe Cleaners that she found in the toy closet and looks at me.

"You can tell my mom," she says. She doesn't sound mad, and that makes me feel a little bit better.

I go into the kitchen to find Dayl. She is cleaning up from dinner, and now thinking about the beef stew is making my stomach hurt. I wish I hadn't eaten so much of it because wanting to go home is making me feel like I might throw up. I REALLY don't want to throw up in front of them here.

"Dayl?"

Dayl turns around from the sink to look at me. "Yes, Darlin'?"

I know that once I tell her I want to go home, there's a whole thing that's going to start. She will ask me questions, and then I'll call home and talk to my parents. Then, after asking me a few questions, they will try to get me to stay. Then I'll cry and beg them, and then one of them will come and get me. I will have ruined the sleepover and Sas will be sad.

"I'm feeling really homesick and I don't think I want to stay here."

Dayl puts down the pot that she was drying and walks around the counter to stand closer to me.

"Okay, well, what can we do to make you feel better?" She asks me.

"You and Sas were going to make a craft, weren't you? That sounds like fun."

I don't say anything, and the pain in my stomach gets bigger. I want to throw up.

"Would it help if you talked to your parents before bed? Would that make you feel better?"

I know that the only way they could make me feel better is by coming to get me, but I don't want to tell Dayl that. I just say that I would like to talk to them, and she dials. When Mom answers, Dayl talks first, to tell her that everything is fine, I am just feeling a little bit homesick and want to talk to her. Then she passes the phone to me.

At the sound of Mom's voice, I want to cry. I know she is just down the street, but she feels really far away and I want her to tuck me in. I want to be in my own room and in my own bed.

"Sweetie, you've so been looking forward to this sleepover with your best friend! And you can come home first thing in the morning," She tells me.

My eyes start burning like I am going to cry. I don't want Sas to be sad, but I also really miss my own house and my own family.

"I'll tell you what," Mom says. "Why don't you stay and play for a little bit longer and then see how you feel."

I liked that idea. Sometimes it helps when I know I have a choice. Mom told me to try staying for a little bit longer, and she didn't say I could come home after that if I wanted to, but I knew that's what she meant. And I can do that; I can stay a little bit longer if I know Mom will let me come home after.

I give Dayl the phone back, and go to find Sas. She is laying in front of the toy closet, where she dumped all of the Pipe Cleaners on the floor.

"Wanna make 'thing-a-majigs' with me?"

I sit down on the floor next to Sas and pick up a couple of pipe cleaners.

"It's easy," she says. "You just take the pipe cleaners and bend them and attach them however you want. Then we have to guess what each other made."

Sitting next to Sas and playing around with the pipe cleaners makes me feel better again. I twist them into weird shapes and we laugh at each other when we try to guess what we made. When Dayl tells us that

17

it's time for bed, I don't feel sad. I know that I'll see my parents in the morning. I know that my house will be right where I left it.

Sas and I jump into bed and each grab on to our stuffed animals. We giggle so loud that Dayl has to come back in and tell us to be quiet; she doesn't want us to wake Andrew.

I'm happy that I decided to stay, but I already know that I'll never sleepover anywhere else.

~ ~ ~

Dear Sweet Girl,

I don't know how best to describe it to you; the way it felt when we first arrived.

Including a twelve-hour layover in London, our total travel time to reach Kisumu, Kenya was about forty hours. We had each accumulated a few hours of sleep over the course of our four flights, but a long journey like that doesn't exactly facilitate adequate rest. Clearly, we were running off of adrenaline, because whatever exhaustion our bodies felt was overshadowed by excitement and disbelief. After months of planning, and imagining what that very moment would feel like, we were finally living it.

I stood at the top of the airplane steps- the *final* airplane steps- that brought us from Nairobi to Kisumu, and breathed in the air with such intention. I was determined to remember every single detail about our time in Kisumu, starting with my first deep breath off of the final plane. The smell of freshly cut grass, combined with the sunbaked pavement, and a small hint of body odor, seeped into my nose and trickled down into my soul.

I felt calm and present and ready for whatever was waiting for us at the bottom of those airplane steps. I couldn't believe that I was in Africa, thousands of miles away from home, and that I wasn't feeling desperate to turn around and run. The only person who truly understands how unlikely this was for me, is you.

If I'm being honest, I could feel you stirring inside of me a little bit, and begging me to remember what it feels like when I'm thrown into a tailspin of fear from the unknown; when I feel trapped with no option to run or retreat to a safe place. I'm sorry I couldn't be more nurturing to you

18

in that moment, but all I wanted to do was push you back into the dark, where I couldn't see or hear you. I craved freedom from those burdens, and you represented the opposite of that to me.

My classmates and I took turns posing for pictures in front of the bright blue sign that read, "Kisumu International Airport," and then we walked into the tiny building to collect our bags and meet our host family. Our class had been told about Chris and Sarah Nicholson, the missionary couple who Dr. Ribeiro and Vanessa knew from church when they all lived in Atlanta, Georgia. Eventually, Dr. Ribeiro and Vanessa relocated to Nashville, and Chris and Sarah moved to become full-time missionaries in Kenya, but the two couples followed each other on social media.

When the prospect came about of taking our department from Lipscomb on a mission trip, Dr. Ribeiro got in touch with the Nicholsons to see if their program in Kisumu would be a good fit for our class. The Nicholsons agreed to have us, and that was the extent of what we knew about them.

As we walked into the "Arrivals" entrance of the airport, we saw dozens of children in school uniforms, pressing their faces against the metal fencing that separated the parking lot from the runway.

"I wonder if those are students from the school that we will be with," one of my peers contemplated.

Tired as we were, all of us were hoping that those were our kids. We were so excited to finally meet them.

We collected our bags and headed for the glass doors that would lead us into the main airport. The automatic doors slid open, and standing right in front of us were five beautiful children. They had soft dark skin, big brown eyes and smiles that were bright enough to make the rest of our surroundings disappear. They wore matching school uniforms, but not the same ones as the children we had seen outside. Each one of them was holding a small bunch of yellow roses.

These are our kids, I thought.

Our entire group shed tears as the children came up to greet us, handing each of us one of the yellow roses as a "welcome gift." As they handed us the roses, they shook our hands and introduced themselves in sweet, soft voices. I received my rose from a little girl named Nissi Patience, who was the tiniest of the group, but her eyes were the biggest and the brightest.

Standing off to the side, so as not to interfere with the children's greetings, were Chris and Sarah Nicholson. Sarah was carrying a baby girl on her hip, and as a family of white-skinned blondes, the three of them naturally stood out among the sea of dark brown skin that surrounded them. They may have looked different from everybody else, but they still looked like they belonged there. I got a sense of their belonging, and their "ease," before I even had a chance to introduce myself. Kisumu, Kenya was definitely their home.

We all walked out to the parking lot together, each of the children offering to help us push the trollies that were piled high with our suitcases. When we told them they didn't have to, Chris said, "It's okay, they really are happy to help you."

With that, we handed over our trollies, and were taken aback by how much joy the children seemed to find in something that was so simple, and something that most children back home, would never offer to do. They pushed the suitcases across the parking lot, while not-so-discreetly stealing glances at us, almost as if they couldn't believe that we were actually there. The smiles never left any of their faces for a single second.

Once our bags were loaded into the Nicholson's vehicle, we divided into small groups for the ride to the guest house that we would be staying in. A couple of people rode in the car, while the rest of us got to experience our very first tuk-tuk ride. We piled into the loud, tiny, brightly-colored, three-wheeled, gas-powered vehicles that serve as a main mode of transportation in Kisumu, and hung our heads out of the open sides, for the entire journey. All of us seemed to be torn between wanting to take as many pictures as possible, and wanting to stay present enough to just enjoy our surroundings with our own eyes. Like the rest of my group, I ultimately opted for a little bit of both.

What struck me most on our drive to the guest house, were the bright colors. The tuk-tuks, the clothing, the painted buildings- everything was so colorful. There was an energy in the air as people went about their daily lives, and even though Kisumu looked nothing like home, my heart ached with the possibility of feeling at home there. I knew I was meant to be exactly where I was.

We arrived at St. Anna's Guest House, where we were welcomed with more smiling faces and helping hands. The staff greeted us warmly and assisted us with our luggage, as we were each given our room assignments. The rooms were tiny and simple; our bathrooms had both shower heads, and buckets for bathing, and instructions on how to access hot water. There were tied up mosquito nets hanging over our beds. It didn't matter that I was thousands of miles away from home, or that all of my surroundings reminded me of this. My desire to be in that moment, overcame all fear. I wish so badly that you knew what that felt like; or at the very least, I wish you knew that someday, you would.

Anyway, once we had a few minutes to settle into our rooms, it was time for lunch. I flashed back to my consultation at the travel clinic, as I scooped rice and vegetables onto my plate. The vegetables were cooked, so I knew that it was okay to eat them.

Chris and Sarah had lunch with us, and then they educated us a little bit on Kisumu, and what we could expect while working with the students of Ringroad Orphans Day School. We were told that Ringroad is located in the Nyalenda Slum, which is the second-largest slum in all of Kenya. Due to undocumented births and deaths, along with the constant moving around of families (or individual family members) who had been displaced, it is impossible to get an accurate census of just how many people are living in Nyalenda at any given time.

We were told about the students at Ringroad, most of whom were either "partial" or "total" orphans. This meant that they had lost either one or both of their parents, leaving them to reside with guardians. Chris let us know that while many of the students looked healthy, we should be prepared to see some students who were malnourished or suffering from physical ailments, such as fungal infections on their skin.

Sarah reassured us that while we cannot change the circumstances for these children, we can brighten their day, simply by interacting with them. She explained that Kenyan children tend to stay focused on the "present," because their lives can change so rapidly from one moment to the next. They don't always know where they will be sleeping or, if they will be eating, or whether or not their loved ones are going to survive illness, but if we could give them moments of happiness to live in- even if just for a little while- we would be a blessing to them.

I thought about this concept of staying "present," as we finished up our meeting and prepared to walk to Ringroad for the first time. Every single therapist I ever had, some of which you know, talked about the importance of "staying present." Like you, I always understood how that would be a useful tool in managing anxiety, but I was really bad at it. Constantly worrying about the "what if's" in life tends to pull you away from all of the moments that you are living in real-time. I remind you of this, while also acknowledging that I haven't fully mastered it, myself.

Our first walk through Nyalenda forced my eyes open wider than I had ever allowed them to be. We walked down the muddy road, houses made of mud and stones crammed together on either side of us. Women were cooking and selling food, and men were working on repairs, or transporting people and goods on their motorcycles. Children played with toys they had made out of sticks and bottle caps. There were smiles and laughter and people chatting among themselves in Swahili. Chickens and pigs and goats and cows walked freely right alongside of us, and large trees offered fresh food and scattered spots of shade.

I was mesmerized by the flurry of activity, and the creativity and resourcefulness that surrounded us. I had been expecting to feel sad, when walking through an area that is so infamously tied to poverty, but it was much easier to see Nyalenda outside of that lens than I thought it would be. I don't want to diminish their hardship by telling you that, but I do want you to know that beauty can be found everywhere, even in what is perceived as broken. I wish it wasn't going to take you so long to see that for yourself.

It took us about fifteen minutes to walk to Ringroad. When we arrived, the children were waiting for us; assembled in a perfect horseshoe in front of the school building, and organized by height. You could tell that they were instructed to be quiet, but were fighting the urge to giggle and whisper to each other as we made our way to the front of the crowd. All of them wore uniforms, and all of their heads were shaved- even the girls- but each of their features were so distinct, and so incredibly beautiful. We had spent so much time referring to them as "the children" or "the students," and we were finally about to learn their names and faces.

Our first day at Ringroad was just a Meet-And-Greet, as it was already mid-afternoon and we were exhausted from our travels. After we introduced ourselves and were treated to some songs, dances and prayers, we were given the chance to mingle with the kids and play with them a little bit. Some of them were eager to get to know us, and asked a lot of questions about our families and America. They asked how many siblings each of us had, if our parents were still alive, and what foods we liked to eat.

Other students were shy, but intrigued none-the-less. They would listen as we spoke to the chattier kids, and giggle when we smiled or waved at them. Lots of the kids wanted to touch our skin and our hair. I felt funny about it at first, being someone who appreciates my personal space, but there was too much joy in the air to be bothered by anything, so I let them do as they wished. It was such a perfectly beautiful afternoon.

Unfortunately, we did encounter a little bit of a setback, when it came to executing our Needs Assessment. After consulting with Chris and Sarah and realizing how challenging it would be to issue consent forms to the children's guardians, we decided that it would be best not move forward with the assessment. We floated the idea of having the school director sign the consent forms on the children's behalf, but since

Ringroad was only a school at the time, and not also a "group home" or an orphanage, the staff didn't have any legal rights over their students.

We scrambled for a bit, as we tried to put together a new itinerary for our time at Ringroad. A group of us worked through a good part of the night with Dr. Ribeiro, to come up with a program that would utilize our counseling skills and encourage the students to become familiar and comfortable with their emotions. We came up with a song, a coloring and writing activity, and a simple presentation that we would give to each class, and adapt as we needed to for their different age groups. Each person in our group was assigned a role, and we all felt confident in our new agenda.

As a Multi-Cultural Counseling class, half of the fun in creating this new itinerary, was trying to determine which activities and lessons would make sense in the context of their culture. Just because we believed in the importance of expressing one's emotions, is that something that makes sense in all cultures? Is that something that is even possible in all cultures? We'll get to more on that later. But for now, just know that the students thoroughly enjoyed the activities that we prepared for them, because they enjoyed having us there with them. Like Sarah Nicholson had encouraged us to do, we were bringing them joyful moments, and that's what mattered.

About a week into our trip, I hit an emotional wall. Our sessions with the kids were going great, and when we weren't teaching them, we were playing and getting to know them. It seemed like each one of us had a specific group of kids that gravitated to us, and I was having a blast getting to know the group of fourth and fifth grade girls who had flocked to me from day one.

The day before I "hit my wall," my roommate, Brittany, shared with the group that she witnessed a little girl get bullied during lunchtime. The child was eating her lunch, which was a plate of beans and corn, when another girl came up and grabbed the plate from her.

"Did she say anything or get a new plate?" I had asked Brittany.

"Well, I didn't see if she got a new plate," Brittany replied, "But she definitely didn't fight back."

I was so distraught by this. I wanted to think that in all of their daily struggles outside of school, these students at least had one another as friends and allies. Bullying anyone is never okay, but for a child who already has so many obstacles to overcome, this felt like too much.

When we returned to Ringroad the next day, I asked Sarah what the process was to start sponsoring a child. Through a non-profit organization that is based in America, students at Ringroad receive sponsorship in order to ensure that all of their school needs are met. This includes school fees, meals, new uniforms, books and medical care. Many of the children were already sponsored, but there was a list of students who weren't. I was in a place financially where I could afford to sponsor, and I felt it was important to offer help beyond what my peers and I had come to do for ten days.

"Actually, my mom is here with us for a couple of weeks, and she has the sponsor list," Sarah told me. "You can go ahead and let her know that you are interested in sponsoring and she will let you know which children are still needing one."

Sarah pointed me in the direction of her mom, who was sitting in a tiny office at the end of the school building. I was excited to talk to her about sponsorship, but I didn't want to choose which child to sponsor on my own. All of those children were deserving of a sponsor, so if there was one in particular who was more vulnerable than the others, I was hoping that Sarah's mom could help connect me to him or her.

Maurine Jones welcomed me into the tiny office with a big smile. She and Sarah looked so much alike and, like Sarah, Maurine seemed to be perfectly at ease in this environment that wasn't her own. It felt nice to see another American there who looked so at-home, and I wondered how much time she had spent in Kenya since her daughter and son-in-law relocated there.

I told Maurine that I was interested in sponsoring a child, but would like help in choosing one. If there was something she knew about a specific child who had specific needs, that was the one I wanted to hear about.

"We do have one little girl who is without a sponsor and has a lot of need," Maurine shared. "Are you willing to sponsor a child who may have some needs outside of typical sponsorship?"

I didn't even have to think about it.

"Yes," I told her.

Maurine smiled and sent someone to find Joan, the little girl with "extra needs" and no sponsor. I was nervous to meet her, but so excited that I would be able to hopefully improve this child's life somehow. I wished I could sponsor more than one, and as I stood in that tiny office and waited for Joan, I pushed away the guilt that was starting to cloud my brain.

Focus on the one you can help, not the ones you can't, I told myself.

Joanie walked into the office, small and timid, and I knew she was meant to be my sponsored child. I had fallen in love with all of the students at Ringroad relatively quickly, but the instant pull I felt for Joanie was different. She had extremely gentle eyes, that appeared to be wise beyond her years; like she had experienced more life than a person who was almost triple her age, like me.

When she was told to greet me, Joanie stuck out her hand to shake mine, but only looked me in the eye for a second before she quickly shifted her focus to the ground. Even though her head was slightly bowed down, I saw her sneak a smile when she was told that I was going to be her sponsor. I asked her for a hug, and Joanie wrapped her tiny arms around my waist.

According to her records, Joanie was in the third grade, but her age was unknown. She lived with her mother and her siblings. Her mother did not have a stable income, and her father was not around. Aside from living in extreme poverty, Joanie suffered from a number of chronic medical conditions, including HIV. She also had a learning disability.

After we finished meeting each other, Joanie was sent back to class, and I rejoined my peers, who were in the middle of teaching a lesson.

"Did you find a child to sponsor?" Brittany asked me.

"I did and she is so sweet. I'll show her to you at lunch."

When the bell for lunch chimed, I found Joanie and called her over to officially meet my peers.

"That's the little girl who was bullied yesterday," Brittany said, after Joanie had walked away. "She is the one."

Well, Sweet Girl, for the first time since we arrived in Kisumu, you managed to peak your head out of the darkness. Small but mighty, you forced me to recoil back into your world; a place I had worked tirelessly to grow out of. In an instant, I felt incapable. I felt unable to take the joy and the beauty we found in those children and use it to wipe away the sadness that came with getting deeper glimpses into their lives. For the first time since we arrived, I felt like I couldn't do anything.

The heat suddenly became unbearable, the schoolyard chatter, too loud. I went to sit down on a half-broken bench that was propped against a wall outside one of the classrooms, and stared blankly at a group of little girls playing jump rope with some of my peers.

What is wrong with us? I thought as I watched them jump and giggle and cheer each other on. *Why are we acting like what we see here is okay?*

I felt dizzy and nauseous.

Why are we pretending that these kids' lives aren't that bad? Or that we are somehow making any sort of a difference?

I thought back to what Sarah had said about giving the children happy moments; about their ability to stay present. But then I thought about little

Joanie getting picked on at school, and the idea that she doesn't truly have a safe place. My heartsickness grew, and, in a way that felt all too familiar, it cued physical sickness. I thought for sure that I was going to throw up, and I desperately wanted to get out of there.

One of the things that you and I have in common is our fierce hunger for a "safe place." I suppose this is true of most humans: a desire to feel safety and security in another person or in whatever environment we find ourselves in. But for people like you and I, experiencing the lack of a safe place is beyond paralyzing; it makes us feel sick and sad and afraid of the world. For what it's worth, I have gotten better about managing my expectations when it comes to seeking safety in something, somewhere, or someone, but that desire remains a common thread between us. We do seek it differently from one another, though, and that's something I'll get into later.

For now, follow me back into this moment of pure emotional unravel. As I sat on the broken bench at Ringroad and watched the children play, I continued to spiral into your world, where everything feels dark and cold. I locked in on Joanie and what it must feel like for her to wake up and go to sleep in complete chaos and uncertainty every single day.

Does she wish she had more friends at school?
If she doesn't get to eat her lunch, is there any food for her at home?
Is she ever asked how her day was?
Does she ever feel scared? Alone? Hopeless?

Two of the fifth-graders, Lintalian and Beryl, walked over to the bench and each grabbed one of my hands.

"Jen?" Lintalian whispered my name in the form of a question. "Will you come jump rope with us?"

I couldn't look either of them in the eye. I didn't want them to grab my hands, and I wasn't in the mood to play anything. I wanted *out*. Someone had to help me get out of there.

With shaking legs, I stood up from the bench and found Dr. Ribeiro, who was playing football with a group of boys.

"Dr. Ribeiro, I'm really not feeling well," I told him, willing myself to stand upright.

"I think I need to go back to the guest house."

Dr. Ribeiro didn't ask me a barrage of questions, and I was extremely grateful for that. There were a few people in our group who had experienced stomach issues by this point in our trip, so it was easy for Dr. Ribeiro to assume that I was experiencing the same. And, to be fair, I *was* experiencing stomach issues…mine just weren't induced by the meal we ate the night before.

26

Dr. Ribeiro located a man named Jared, who was the school's Director, and he called over one of his staff.

"This is Onesmis," Jared told Dr. Ribeiro and I. "He can drive you back to the guest house."

After confirming with me that I was okay to go back alone, and that I just needed to drink water and rest, Dr. Ribeiro bid me farewell with Onesmis. It was only a five-minute ride from Ringroad to St. Anne's, but I was thankful to be in an air-conditioned car. The cold air gave me a bit of temporary relief, along with the knowledge that I was on my way to a "safe place," where I could hide away and comfort myself. As we emerged from the slum and headed down the main road, I found myself wondering if Joanie ever longed for a safe place.

Upon reaching St. Anne's, I thanked Onesmis and climbed the stairs up to my room. I unlocked the door, walked my shaky self to the bathroom, and bent over the toilet. With each hurl came increasing relief, as I untied the knot in my stomach.

It's funny, because even though it had been years since I made myself sick like that, it didn't take me long to remember why you've always done it. The release of the physical pressure immediately helps to alleviate the psychological pressure, and back in your day, I don't think you could tell the difference between the two. It started as something that you had no control over, but became something that gave you a sense of control, amid your chaotic thoughts.

And so there I was, caught in a moment of relapse, crouched down on the bathroom floor with my forehead resting on the toilet seat. At home, the coolness of the porcelain always helped to wind me down, but the toilet seats at St. Anne's were plastic, and I didn't get any soothing vibes from that.

I took a moment to collect myself, then stood back up and walked over to my bed, where I spent the remainder of the afternoon. I didn't eat lunch, nor did I have a desire to sit with my peers as they ate and recapped how their morning went. I knew that if I heard one person talk about how inspired they felt after the day's sessions with the kids, I was going to lose my mind.

I thought about that little boy from the magazine, on the day I met Joanie. I obsessed over whether or not she felt safe, just like you had with the little boy. I cried a lot. Like, really, really sobbed. My heart broke for Joanie and the many injustices that were stacked on top of her innocent little life. My hurt for her made me want to crawl out of my skin, but I didn't know where I would go from there. I wanted to find a way to make

27

her life better and to help her not feel so scared. But you know what, Sweet Girl, I didn't even really know if she was scared, I had just assumed.

Then I thought about you, and the deep, unbridled distress you carry with you but can't quite put your finger on. It's so sad to me when I think about what a wonderful life you have, and how much of it is spent tangled up in your fearful thoughts. You're missing out on so much, and you don't even realize it. Well, I suppose you've become used to missing out on things, but if only it wasn't going to take you so long to realize that you didn't have to.

Chapter Three

I have an appointment with Rachel today.

I like going to talk to her because I can tell her how I'm feeling and she doesn't make fun of me or anything. She just listens and asks me questions, and I answer them as best as I can. Sometimes I don't really know the answers to her questions, but she doesn't make me feel bad about it. Like one time she asked me if there's something that I am most afraid of, more than anything else, and I told her I didn't know.

"I'm afraid of something bad happening that will make me or other people feel sad," I had told her.

"So, do you think what you are most afraid of is feeling sad?" She had asked.

I told her I didn't know, and she said that was okay.

Whenever I go to Rachel's office, Mom and Dad make me bring my homework so that I can do some in the waiting room. I usually get here early and have a few minutes for homework, but it's so hard to concentrate. I always start to imagine my classmates doing their homework at home, and wonder if they would think I'm weird for doing mine in a therapy office. I bet none of them even know what a Therapist is.

Today, I have a packet to finish with my Spelling Words in it. I like to write, and I don't think this packet will be hard to do later, so I put it away and walk over to the table of magazines that Rachel has out on a table. Some of the magazines are for adults and some are for kids, but I've never seen another kid in here. I'm always sitting in the waiting room with adults.

Before I even have a chance to sit back down, the door opens and Rachel pops her head out.

"Hey!" She says to me with a big smile on her face.

I put the magazine down and follow Rachel through the door to where all the offices are. There's a little machine on the ground, right outside her office door, that sounds like a fan and keeps people in the hallway from hearing what you're talking about. Every time I see it, I wonder what other people talk about when they come here. I wonder if any of them feel like me.

We go inside her office and I sit on the couch. There's also a chair that I could sit on, but I like the couch because when I feel tired from talking, I can relax on it. I like talking to Rachel, but it also makes me feel tired.

"So!" Rachel says, as she sits down in her chair across from me. She smiles at me again, and her teeth look perfect and white. She has curly hair like me, but hers stays in perfect curls, instead of getting all frizzy, like mine does. Her eyes are big and kind of grey, and I think they're really pretty. She always looks like the happiest person in the world, and I like that because it means she is good at her job. If she knows how to be happy, then she can help other people feel happy, too.

"What's new?" She asks me. "How was school today?"

"It was good. I ate my lunch."

I tell Rachel I ate my lunch because food is usually the first thing she asks me about. I've told her that when I feel anxious, I don't eat, and we talk about that a lot. I think Mom has mentioned my eating problem to her, too, because sometimes Rachel knows that I haven't eaten anything, before I even tell her. I think Mom calls her and tells her things on the phone sometimes.

Rachel tells me she's glad I ate my lunch, and then she asks, "What was it about your day today that made you feel good enough to eat? Did something happen that made you happy? Or you just didn't feel anxious?"

This is one of her questions that I don't know the answer to. "I don't know," I tell her. "I think it was more I didn't feel anxious, than me feeling happy."

I think about it for a second and then I keep talking. "When I'm not anxious, I'm happy. So maybe both then? I wasn't anxious, and I was happy?"

"Is that what it feels like?" Rachel's grey eyes are looking right into mine. "Does it feel like you are either happy or anxious?"

It takes me a minute to answer again. "I guess so. I hate feeling anxious, so I guess when I don't feel that way, it makes me happy."

Rachel writes something down on her notepad, then looks up at me again. She is quiet before she asks me her next question, and I know it's because she's about to ask another one that I might not know how to answer. I've noticed that she is extra careful about finding her words when she is about to ask me something that I might have trouble with. I like when she's careful like that because I know she cares about me.

"Do you ever identify how you're feeling as sadness? Or does it always feel like anxiety?"

This is the second time she's asked me about feeling sad. Usually when we meet, we only talk about my anxiety.

"Umm...I don't know?"

I think about it some more. "When I feel anxious, it makes me sad, I guess...because it makes my life feel harder. It especially makes me sad when I see other kids around me having fun and laughing and I know I should be doing the same thing. But sometimes I don't know how to, and I feel like I can't help it. I want to be happy like the other kids, and I wish it wasn't hard for me to be like they are."

I stop talking for a second, but then I keep going. "The world feels sad to me. Even when I'm doing or seeing a happy thing, I know that it could end up turning sad."

I've explained this to her before, but I guess I need to explain it again. Rachel writes something on her notepad, and I keep talking.

"I think sometimes maybe when I feel anxious, I feel sad, and then when I feel sad, I find more things to be anxious about. It goes around and around in a circle."

Rachel listens and writes, I talk.

"I feel sad about the way the world feels sometimes, but I don't know how to explain what the world feels like; my world, I mean. My parents love me and they give me and my brother a really good and fun life. And they are always trying to make me feel better when they know I need them to. So, when I do feel sad, it feels like it's for no reason. Nothing is really bad in my life."

Rachel listens and writes. Then she asks, "Do you think part of the reason you feel sad sometimes is because you don't know where the sadness is coming from?"

"Yes," I answer, without having to think about it this time. "I don't think other people understand me, but I want them to. So, when I feel bad, and I can't tell why, it makes it worse. I feel stuck in my own world that no one else understands."

Rachel doesn't say anything yet and I know it's because she is waiting for me to say more first.

"Even when I'm doing something that makes me feel so happy, like when I play with my friends or when we go on a family trip that's really fun, it always ends with me feeling sad again, because I don't like when fun times are over and I have to wonder what to do with myself next. What toys can I play with or TV show can I watch that will keep me happy when those fun times are over?"

"And you're afraid that when you aren't doing something that brings you lots of happiness, you're immediately going to go back to feeling sad."

"Yes. Or start worrying about things again."

31

Rachel nods to let me know she understands what I'm saying.

"Do other people that come here tell you they feel that way?" I've always wanted to ask her that.

Rachel looks into my eyes and nods her head again. "Yes, lots of people experience the same feelings that you do."

"Really?!" I'm surprised to hear her say that.

"Yes, they do. A lot of people tell me exactly what you just did; that they feel sad, but they don't know how to explain where that sadness is coming from."

I think about this for a minute, and it reminds me of something.

"One time, when my family went for a bike ride, my brother rode over a rock and toppled off his bike. He scraped his knee really badly and was bleeding a lot. He screamed and cried the whole way home, and kept screaming when my parents were trying to clean up his cuts. I felt so sad for him, that I went to my room and cried. And then, for a long time, I couldn't stop picturing it in my head. I could hear the screams he made, even after he was done making them. I think he probably forgot about what happened before I did, and it didn't even happen to me."

Rachel keeps listening.

"But when my parents were putting medicine and bandages on him, and asking him what else hurts besides his knee, I wished it were that easy for me. Like, when I feel bad, sometimes I wish I could point to a scrape on my knee and tell them, 'This is what's hurting me.' And then they could put a bandage on it and I could go back to feeling good again."

Rachel looked into my eyes, and smiled. "Jen, do you know that you just described what makes your feelings so challenging, in the exact way that I explain it to my other patients sometimes?"

This makes me feel proud, even though I don't really know what she means.

"When people feel anxious or sad, but they don't have anything to point to that explains why, there is an extra challenge there. It feels harder to fix."

That's right! I wanted to shout. But I didn't shout. Instead, I told her, "Yeah. When you can't show someone what hurts, how can they fix it?"

Rachel's smile got even bigger. "You know, sometimes I forget that you're only nine years old."

She says this and it makes me feel proud again.

"You, my dear, are wise beyond your years. Did you know that?"

I didn't know that, but I like that she told me.

"You just expressed something to me that I try to explain to patients who are much older than you. And you figured out how to express it all on your own."

"Because I'm wise?" I asked, feeling more proud by the second.

Rachel was still smiling. "You are," she says.

And I believe her. For once, I don't feel different or weird; I feel 'wise,' and I know that makes me special.

~ ~ ~

Dear Sweet Girl,

You may assume that I'd be crying for home by now. To you, my sadness over Joanie and the world that she's living in, should have rattled me enough to pack my bags and beg Dr. Ribeiro to put me on an early flight back to the United States; where Mom is, and everything else that makes me feel safe. It's always been your tendency to run and hide from the situations that make you the most uncomfortable, so it makes sense that you'd expect me to do the same.

But this is the thing: even when I felt sad and helpless, and made myself sick to my stomach over the pain I felt for Joanie, I never felt the desire to leave Kisumu. I did need some time to be alone, in a place that I felt safe enough to process how I was feeling. But I never, ever, ached for home.

If anything, my strongest desire was to figure out a way to manage my emotions better, so that I would be able to continue engaging with the kids. I didn't want to leave them; I wanted to help them in any capacity that I could, because I had such a strong feeling that I was "meant to be there." I mean, think about it…how crazy was it for someone like me to end up in Africa in the first place, right? Even with all the work I'd done, over years of therapy, I was still surprised by this most unlikely journey that I suddenly found myself on.

Now, let me get back to sharing it with you…

After spending the entire afternoon lying in bed and crying a fairly excessive number of tears, I decided to join the rest of the group for dinner. Thankfully, this was one of the nights that we stayed in and ate dinner at the guest house, rather than going out to a restaurant. Even though I was feeling slightly more social than I had been earlier, leaving the guest house would have required more emotional energy than I had left.

I was able to eat a little bit, which felt good because I hadn't eaten anything since breakfast. I remember all the nights you went to bed hungry, and how sick and weak it made you feel. Sometimes, you waited so long to eat, that you developed sharp hunger pangs, and those made it physically impossible to eat because they were so painful. Even after your anxiety had subsided, if the hunger pangs were there, you didn't have a choice but to wait them out. They always went away eventually, but sometimes it took a while. When I think about what you put your little body through, that's when I wish the most that I could hold you in my arms.

Not wanting to slip back into your world for the second time in one day, I forced myself to eat just enough at dinner that night. The kitchen had prepared beef stew with rice, and I happen to love beef stew. I was also really starting to love the group that I was with, and sitting with them at the dinner table helped to bring my spirits back up. It's amazing how quickly you bond with people when you're thrown into a completely foreign, highly emotional situation together, and I found myself leaning into that bond more and more each day.

Once we finished dinner, it was time for our nightly Processing Session. Every night, we gathered in one of the conference rooms at the guest house, to share our thoughts and feelings with one another. We would reflect on how the day went, and then Dr. Ribeiro would throw out a question, or a theme, for us to go around the room and comment on.

Before we began on this night, I had already decided that I wanted to share what I experienced in the afternoon, with the hope that someone might be able to give me advice on how to manage my perspective. I was beginning to feel afraid that after my emotional breakdown over Joanie, I'd wouldn't be able to look at any of the kids the same, ever again. What if I spent the rest of our trip grieving over their hardships, rather than celebrating their strength and resilience? What if I couldn't identify their joy anymore? That wasn't what I wanted, and it sure wasn't what the kids deserved from me.

The conference room where we held most of our sessions had tables set up in the shape of a square; which was perfect because no matter where we sat, we could all see each other. Once everyone had taken a seat, there was a palpable stillness in the air, as we prepared to share our hearts with one another.

Dr. Ribeiro's question for the night was: What is one thing that has surprised you most so far? He gave us a moment to think about our answers, and then we began going around the table.

"For me, I've been in awe of how I see God working here," One of my classmates shared.

Oh God, here we go, I thought. No pun intended.

As she spoke, my other peers nodded in agreement.

"I was expecting to have trouble seeing God's goodness in a place where there's so much suffering, but being around those kids...God's presence is just so evident to me."

"Mmm," others expressed their agreement again, as I looked around the room and secretly hoped that I wasn't the only one who had no idea what she was talking about.

"What do you see in the children that makes God's presence evident to you?" Dr. Ribeiro asked.

Yes, Thank You, I thought, as I suppressed the urge to shout it out instead. This was a question I needed an answer to, myself.

"I see God in their smiles. And in their strength."

More nodding.

"What does that mean?" I heard myself asking, before I had a chance to stop myself.

"I'm sorry, I just don't get it. How could you possibly think that God is anywhere around here?"

There was a silence that fell over the room, but not the awkward kind. I could tell that my peers wanted to give me the time I needed to express myself, while also taking their own time to find a thoughtful response.

"I kind of had a breakdown today," I continued. "I signed up to sponsor a child, and then I found out that the child I'm sponsoring is the one that Brittany saw get picked on at lunch. She has a broken family, lives in extreme poverty, and is HIV positive. And, apparently, she also gets picked on at school. Who knows if she even has any friends? Or anyone that she can trust or feel safe with?"

I looked down at my hands, as my eyes burned with tears. The rest of the group remained silent, to give me the space I needed to process my thoughts.

"So where is God in Joanie's life, then? Why isn't His 'goodness' protecting her?"

We all sat in silence for another moment.

35

"Do you sense God in Joanie's strength?" Someone finally asked me, gently. "To me, it seems like Joanie is a really, really strong little girl. Where do you see that strength coming from?"

Herself.

"I don't know. She's strong because she doesn't have a choice."

I was exhausted, and could tell that this conversation was about to go around in circles. They saw God in the children, I saw God's absence in the children. They saw beauty, and all I saw was pain.

And then there was you, screaming at me to run as far away from the pain as possible. After all, what choice could I have had but to run away and let myself grieve it until I couldn't anymore? I would never forget the people that I met in Kisumu, but eventually they would become a distant memory that didn't evoke such emotional distress within me, just like that little boy from the magazine. I could move on from this if I wanted to; that's what you were telling me.

But I ignored you. I didn't want to move on. There were names and innocent little faces attached to this pain, and all I wanted to do was lean into their world and find a way to fix it.

In fact, I was so determined to bring them joy, that I talked myself out of focusing on their pain. For the rest of our trip, I taught and played and laughed with the children, just like I had when we first arrived. It's amazing to witness what happens when love truly conquers fear.

Chapter Four

I've been feeling bad again.

If there's one thing that's making me anxious, I usually feel better by the next day because I've had time to think about that thing over and over, until it doesn't feel so bad anymore. Whatever upsets me will stay with me, it just won't feel as bad. But when I don't know why I feel anxious or sad, that it takes longer to go away. That's what's happening now.

I haven't had an appetite in a few days. Mom keeps trying to get me to eat, but I can't because I know that if I do, I will throw it up right away. The bad feeling that I have in my stomach will make me throw up without giving me a chance to try to stop it. I wish I knew where the bad feeling was coming from this time, but I don't.

My body feels sick. Mom tells me that when I don't eat, I'm keeping my body from getting the energy and the nutrition that it needs to feel good and healthy. I don't want to do that to my body, but I also don't know how not to. The stomach aches I get from my anxiety make eating way too hard sometimes. I don't know how to explain to Mom where that feeling is coming from, so I won't try.

Today for lunch, Mom offers me a sandwich, and I tell her that I don't want it. Even looking at that stupid sandwich is making me feel sick, and I don't want it anywhere near me. I love turkey and cheese, but not today.

Mom lets me put the TV on because she knows that it helps me. When my mind is distracted by a show that I love, sometimes that makes it easier for me to eat. I especially like TV episodes that I've seen before, because I know how they're going to end. But, when I know the end is coming, I get sad again because I don't know what I'll do with myself once it's over. I want it to keep going so that I don't have to think about what to do next. What's another thing that I can do to keep my mind busy once the show is over? I always think about that.

After I refuse my turkey and cheese sandwich, Mom brings it into the kitchen and then comes back with something else.

"Well if you aren't going to eat your lunch, will you at least try one of these delicious chocolate-covered cherries?"

I shake my head.

"Oh, they are the BEST!" Mom says. "How could anybody possibly turn down a chocolate-covered cherry for lunch?"

I watch her bite into one of the pieces, the cream and the cherry juice oozing out the middle. I love chocolate-covered cherries, and could have probably eaten the entire box of them if I was feeling better. But just seeing them, like the sandwich, makes me nauseous. Mom must really want me to eat, though, if she's trying to give me sweets for lunch.

After I refuse a couple of times, Mom puts the piece she's holding back in the box and looks me in the eye. She looks serious, not like she just did a second ago when she sounded so excited about the cherries. She seems kind of upset now.

"You know, if you can't start eating by yourself, we're going to have to take you to the hospital, where they will feed you through a tube. Is that what you want?"

I don't say anything.

"You can't not eat, Jen. You just can't not eat."

I've never gone to the hospital to be fed, but Mom has told me before that I may have to. She says that when people can't eat through their mouths, they have to get nutrition through a little tube. I don't ever want to have to do that, but I can't force myself to eat the normal way. I'm not going to put food in my mouth if I know I'll throw it up right after. It's embarrassing to do that, even if it's only in front of Mom.

The next day, Mom and Dad offer me a drink. Mom says it's a special drink that has a lot of the same nutrients as food, and thinks that it might be easier on my tummy. Dad pours the drink into one of my cartoon cups, and tells me that I can sip it as slowly as I want, as long as I finish it. The drink is vanilla flavored, but Mom tells me that they also got strawberry and chocolate.

I try a sip, and don't really like it, but Mom was right about it being gentle on my tummy. Dad tells me that if I finish it, I can watch one of my shows, but I can't get up from the table until the drink is gone.

"It doesn't matter how fast or slow you drink it, what matters is that it gets into your body," Mom says.

I don't argue with them because I know I need the nutrients in my body. I'm tired of feeling sick. So, I sit at the kitchen table and drink my nutrients, wondering when I'm going to feel like a normal person again.

~ ~ ~

Dear Sweet Girl,

As I sit here and write these words to you, I can feel myself slipping back into your world. I don't see things the way you do anymore, but it isn't hard for me to remember what it feels like. It's dark where you are, even though you're surrounded by light. You are not burdened with tragedy or injustice, but your inability to see the world without those things is what keeps you where you are.

You have an extreme ability to put yourself in the shoes of other human beings and feel what they are feeling. This ability is called "Empathy," and it's both a blessing and a curse. It's a beautiful gift, that often masquerades itself as a nightmare, and you're going to have to learn to find a balance between the two.

Now, don't get me wrong here. I know that finding the gift in what you're feeling is not an easy task, especially for someone so young. You're tired from constantly trying to figure out how the world works, and seeing life as a game that you can't quite figure out how to play. I also know how frustrating and saddening it's going to be for you when you encounter people who wonder why you can't just "get over it," and enjoy your present moments. *"Life's too short to worry all the time,"* they'll say to you, as if you're choosing to spend so much of your life sitting in a place of fear.

Sometimes I actually picture myself stepping in and scooping you up from that place, where you torture yourself with "what if's" and try to make sense of how life seems to work. I want you to hear me when I tell you that you don't have to live in that place of fear, and that there will come a day when you won't. But you can't hear me, so all that I can do is continue telling this story, with the peace I have in knowing that you will get to live through it someday…

Before we left Kenya, I knew that I would be back.

I remember standing at the gates of Ringroad Orphans Day School, hugging the children goodbye, and sensing that this was no longer a "once-in-a-lifetime" experience, but rather the gateway to something much bigger. At the time, I didn't know where that feeling was coming from, but I knew it was there.

About a week after we returned home, I met with Dr Ribeiro and asked for Chris and Sarah's contact information, along with the name of

39

the travel agency that he had used to book our trip. My plan was to travel back to Kenya alone, to spend more time with Chris and Sarah and get a better idea of what their daily lives looked like. I wanted to know what it felt like to be a part of the actual work that was being done there.

I justified my trip to Dr. Ribeiro, my parents, and everyone else who asked me why I needed to go back to Kenya so soon, by explaining that I wanted to write my Thesis there. Since our group from Lipscomb hadn't been able to complete our Psychiatric Needs Assessment of Orphans and Vulnerable Children, I figured that I could conduct this research on my own, at an orphanage, and use it as my Thesis. I was genuinely excited by the opportunity to complete this research, but to be honest, I really just wanted to get back to Kenya as quickly as I could. There was something waiting for me there, and I needed to go figure out what it was.

As you would imagine, family and friends were hesitant to offer me their blessing. I think most of them were concerned for my safety while traveling alone, but I assured them that I knew perfectly well how to navigate the travel, after doing it just a few months prior. Others were curious as to why I needed to travel all the way to Kenya to write a Thesis, when there were plenty of topics I could research from home; research that would impact our own communities, rather than a community so far away. I understood the questions and concerns, but I was relentless in pursuing my desires. We returned from our group trip on June 30th, 2013, and by the second week in July, I had a trip booked for October.

Preparing for my second trip to Kenya, was just as blissful as the first. Being able to picture where I was going and who I would be seeing, made for the most exhilarating anticipation I had ever experienced in my life. There was absolutely no fear, just slight disbelief as I tried to wrap my mind around the fact that I was actually about to do this. I was about to travel to Africa for the second time in four months, and I was doing it alone this time.

Shortly before I left, I went out to dinner with my peers from Lipscomb. They wanted to send me off with prayers and encouragement, and I let them know that I would carry their hearts with me, every step of the way. I promised that I would shower the children with love on behalf of the entire group, and as we sat and reminisced about our time together in Kenya, a part of me ached with the desire to experience it with them all over again. Nevertheless, our dinner together helped me to feel strong and confident, and I was ready for my journey.

After thirty-two hours of travel, I touched down in Kisumu, Kenya, once again.

I cried tears of joy and relief as I headed down the airplane steps and walked across the tarmac with the rest of the passengers. I gazed up at the "Kisumu International Airport" sign, and didn't want to go inside the airport just yet. I wanted to soak up the moment and breathe in that familiar smell. Everything felt good and right.

I know this place, I thought to myself.

I rode that high pretty consistently for ten days, but there were definitely more challenges with me being alone. While I had Chris and Sarah there to guide me and show me the ropes, I really missed my classmates, and the conversations that we had as we discovered this new world together. I missed swapping stories and sharing meals together. I missed the power of our collective love for those beautiful children. It had been like Ringroad belonged to all of us as a group, so there were moments that it felt strange making memories there without the rest of them.

Even so, I was hanging on and falling deeper in love, as I got a fuller taste of what life is really like there. I spent my first week helping Chris and Sarah in the office, and the teachers in the classrooms. I graded papers, helped children write letters to their sponsors, and sat with sick children as they waited to be seen at the school's clinic. I helped prepare bags of food that the children got to bring home to their families, I read to them and I served them porridge during their mid-morning break. I did anything that I was asked to do, and I never wanted to stop.

Once, when Chris and Sarah brought me to visit another school, I stepped in a thick swamp of mud and got stuck. After they helped me pull my foot out, I fixed my flip-flop and worked through a brief moment of panic when I wondered if I could contract some sort of flesh-eating disease from stepping in the mud. Then I was fine.

I spent a day at a local orphanage in order to complete the Needs Assessment that I was going to use for my Thesis. The staff were incredibly helpful and the children who volunteered to participate in the assessment were all very sweet and cooperative. I wanted to get to know them better, but their school was a little bit further out, and I had to get back to the Nicholsons before sunset. Thankfully, Director Jared was able to give me a ride, so I didn't have to travel to the school and back alone.

At the beginning of my second week there, The Nicholsons asked if I would like to accompany a social worker on a home visit, and I jumped at this opportunity. I had shared with Chris and Sarah that I was a Caseworker back home, before I started graduate school, and they thought that it might be interesting for me to see how a home visit goes in a place like Kisumu.

Evans was a social worker with Ringroad's medical clinic, and part of his job was to visit bed-ridden patients at their homes, to check on their progress. I was eager to shadow Evans and to get a taste of what Social Work was like in Kisumu, but I was also very aware that this would be my furthest step outside my comfort zone yet; solo travel to Africa aside. First of all, I was venturing off to another part of town with someone that I didn't know. I had been assured that Evans was a wonderful and trustworthy guy, and I believed this, but let's be honest here: he was a male stranger who would be bringing me to a place I had never been, in a country that was thousands of miles away from home.

I was also nervous because I hadn't been told anything about the condition of the patient before we arrived at her home. Like you, I tend to struggle when I'm not given the opportunity to mentally prepare myself for something. It's another one of those common threads between us, that I've learned how to manage, but it remains, nevertheless.

I asked Evans about this patient as we were preparing to leave from Ringroad, but he told me almost nothing. I knew that she was an adult female, who was HIV positive, but I didn't know what that meant in terms of her actual physical condition. As we left the compound and began walking down the muddy path towards the main road, I had an uneasy feeling that this visit might prove to be too much for me, but I didn't want to bail. I wanted to experience things that pushed the limits I had once set for myself, especially if it meant that I would be able to help someone. I didn't want to give myself the option of backing out, or I probably would have taken it.

The trip to our patient's home was a long one. We used multiple modes of transportation, and it seemed I was attracting more attention with each step of the journey. Some people shouted at me because I am white, some shouted at me because I am female, and some shouted because I am a white female. I flashed back to one of our group processing sessions, when Dr. Ribeiro had asked us how we felt about hearing the word, "mzungu" shouted at us. Mzungu means "white person," and every time we were in Nyalenda, the word was shouted from all directions; by children and by adults. At the time we were asked, I told Dr. Ribeiro and the group that it didn't bother me. I hadn't even given it a second thought, and a lot of my peers shared that they felt the same way.

It wasn't until I was the only white person around that I began to feel uncomfortable with the word mzungu. This was when I realized that it wasn't just a word being used to identify the color of my skin, but it was a word that was loaded with all sorts of preconceived notions. The word was associated with "wealth" and "privilege," and the more I heard it, the more it made me feel stripped of everything that made me who I am, outside of where I come from. It actually made me feel pretty vulnerable when it was being shouted in my face, and I did my best to ignore it.

We were no longer in Nyalenda, but the slum that our patient lived in looked very similar. Most of the homes were built out of mud, stones, and sticks, with rusted tin roofs and cracked pieces of wood being used as doors.

"Hodi!" Evans announced our arrival, and a woman came to the doorway. The actual door was already pushed wide open, but there was a tiny curtain hanging in the doorway, preventing anyone from seeing inside. The woman pushed the curtain aside and told us to come in.

I followed Evans inside of the tiny house and the woman reached out to shake my hand. Then she motioned for us to sit down and I took my place on the old, worn out sofa that was propped up against one of the mud walls. There were no windows, so the only natural light that this house received was the little bit that crept around the edges of the curtain hanging in the doorway. It was so dark in there, but I could see well enough and was relieved by the sight of this woman. Maybe she was sick, but she sure didn't look it.

She introduced herself as Margaret, and I told her my name. Evans asked her a question in Swahili, and I heard him mention the name of another person.

"Is Margaret our patient?" I asked out loud.

"No," Evans replied. "Margaret is the sister to our patient."

Margaret pulled back the mosquito net that was hanging over the home's only bed, revealing a mattress that was covered in clothing and some other, miscellaneous items. She bent down over the mattress and began shaking the pile of clothes.

"Caro!" She shouted. "Caro! There are visitors!"

I could feel my body shifting into panic mode. I knew that once I saw this patient, I'd never be able to unsee her; and the fact that her frail body couldn't even be detected underneath the bed covers, wasn't a great sign in terms of her physical condition.

I'm about to see the sickest person I've ever seen in my life, I thought to myself.

All of the sudden, you rose within me, with an unparalleled force. You were screaming at me, begging me not to do this. If I saw this level of suffering up close, I would never recover from it.

I thought, *why would I do this to myself?*

And then, there was a switch.

This isn't about me. You aren't the one suffering, this other human being is. You have an opportunity to help her, don't get tangled in your own mess.

You backed down and away from me, so I let you go. I had grabbed on to your baggage and kept it as my own, one too many times, and if I kept doing that, I'd never be able to truly help anyone. I thought that my going to Kenya was the ultimate stand that separated me from you, but my emotional breakdown over meeting Joanie proved that you were still very much alive within me. Kenya just happened to become the biggest motivation I had to let you go.

Don't you dare run away from this moment, from this woman, I thought. *She needs you.*

It was scary. I'm not going to lie and tell you that my decision to ignore you gave me instant peace, because it didn't. I was very nervous as I sat on the couch and waited for this patient to emerge from the bed. The fact that I couldn't make out the shape of a body under the blankets, scared the hell out of me. But no part of this situation was about me, and I wasn't about to make it that way by acting in fear.

Finally, after what felt like an unbearably long time, there was movement in the bed. Margaret stepped back, and revealed a tiny head poking out from underneath the blanket. The woman, whom I heard Margaret call "Caro," blinked her eyes open and locked them with mine.

I smiled at her and she continued to stare; the look of utter pain in her eyes piercing through my body, but not deterring me. I knew I was exactly where I needed to be.

Evans introduced Caro and I to one another and then he conversed with her a little bit, stopping every once in a while, to translate for me. Caro was HIV positive, and she had contracted an illness on top of that. They were not sure what it was, exactly, but she had been put on antibiotics. After conversing for another minute or two, Evans asked Caro to sit up. She winced at the thought of it, and I asked Evans why he wanted her to do that when she felt so weak.

"Because she needs to find a way to stay strong," he said. "If she can sit up then she will be much stronger than if she just stays laying like that."

Caro slowly began to sit herself up, and I looked down at the ground so I wouldn't have to watch. Not only was she incredibly weak, but she was clearly in a lot of pain and I couldn't help but wonder why neither Margaret nor Evans were helping her.

I looked up as Caro finished hanging her legs down over the side of the bed. Our bodies were now facing each other, and even though I could see every single bone in that tiny body, her skin stretched so tightly over them that it was almost clear, I chose to focus on her eyes. They were beautiful, big brown eyes, which told a story of brokenness and despair.

I didn't need to know a single thing about Caro's life to know that she was suffering; her exposed bones and her winces of pain solidified that she was a suffering human being. It wouldn't matter which side of the world someone is coming from, there is not a person on this planet who would look at Caro and not see that she was in trouble. This was something that she could not hide, even if she had the energy to muster up a smile. Her body was fighting, and there was no hiding that from anyone who would cross her path.

Caro had lived a whole life before she reached this point. I'm sure she had faced many struggles that I couldn't even fathom, but I'm also sure that when she was healthier, she could have chosen to go out in the world and hide what she didn't want others to know. Now, here she sat, in this place while her life was, quite literally, disappearing along with her body. This horrible illness, which she was once probably able to conceal quite well, had completely stripped her of her right to exist as the person that she truly was on the inside. She was a living symbol, a statistic; a daily reminder to all those around her, of just how deeply the levels of human suffering can go. The weight of that reality, hit me really hard.

Evans told me that Caro stopped going outside because she was embarrassed by the way she looked. She never left her bed anymore, not even to go to the bathroom. My heart broke for her, and I wished so badly that there was something I could do to take the pain away. Then it occurred to me that even if I couldn't take her pain, I might be able to distract her from it. Or, at the very least, let her know that I see her as a person, not as an illness.

I asked Evans if it was okay for me to take a turn speaking with Caro, and he said I was welcomed to.

"Do you understand English?" I asked her, slowly.

She looked me square in the eye and gave a small nod.

"Is it okay that I am here visiting you?"

She nodded again.

I noticed the polish on her fingernails and then held up my hand. "We are wearing the same color nail polish! You have nice taste in colors!"

Caro held out her hand, like she was noticing her own nails for the first time.

Evans tapped me on the shoulder. "Hey, Jen, do you think you can convince her to walk around?"

45

I turned to him, surprised by his request. "What do you mean? You really want her to walk around in her condition?"

"Yes, because she needs to see that she is strong and that she will keep getting stronger."

My brain could not compute this. Of all of the ways that I saw this woman needed to be taken care of, forcing her to get up and walk around sure as hell was not one of them.

"But she is so tired and in so much pain," I asserted, as gently as I could. "Please don't make her do that."

Evans agreed. He turned back towards Caro and started talking to her about something in Swahili. A fresh wave of sadness lowered over her face.

"I'm telling her that she needs to eat," Evans explained to me. "Margaret has told me that Caro doesn't eat anymore, but I am telling her that she must eat or she can't survive."

"She's not eating because she doesn't want to, or because she doesn't feel good?" I asked.

Evans turned back to Caro and asked her, then answered me. "She says that when she eats, she vomits, and she doesn't like to vomit because it is painful.

Man, did I know how that goes. Our circumstances may have been worlds different, and Caro may have been suffering in a way that I could never understand, but learning the necessary tricks of force-feeding yourself was something that I definitely understood.

I wanted to encourage her to try eating, but Caro was clearly upset, and I didn't want to push her.   As she continued to whimper, Evan's voice softened. "Caro," he whispered.

Caro didn't respond. She was looking down at her hands, lightly touching her nail polish.

"Caro?" Evan's tried again, still speaking softly.

Nothing.

"Caroline!" Still gentle, but firm, Evans asked for her attention once again, and she finally looked him in the eye.

"Wait a second!" I shouted, probably a little bit too enthusiastically. "Your real name is Caroline?"

Caroline nodded.

"That is one of my favorite names in the whole world!" I said to her. And I meant it.

"Did you know that the name Caroline means 'beautiful woman?'"

Of course, I figured she didn't know that, as most people wouldn't. I did, though, because I had recently entered a phase of life where my friends were starting to have babies; and part of my friendship duty was to help them look up potential names, whether they had asked me to or not. I had researched tons of names, and Caroline was one of my favorites.

Caroline looked down again, and a tear rolled down her cheek.

"That name sounds like you," I told her. You really are a beautiful woman."

I asked if I could go and sit next to her on the bed, and when she agreed, I did. I held her hand in mine, and we spent a few moments in silence. Then I offered up my advice on how to make yourself eat when you feel like you can't keep anything down.

We talked about eating small quantities, as slowly as she needed to.

"It doesn't matter how fast or slow you eat the food, the important thing is that it gets in your body," I reassured her.

Caroline listened, and was able to take a few sips of porridge before Evans and I left her home. We said good bye, and then began our journey back to the other side of town. As we traveled, I actively had to stop my brain from wondering how long a human being can survive in a situation like Caroline's. The thought of her living the rest of her days in such physical and emotional pain, pressed heavily on my heart. Evans made a couple of comments about how Caroline seemed to feel comfortable around me, and that this was the first time he had seen her even attempt to smile. Sarah's advice from months earlier, rang in the back of my mind: *Focus on the joy you can bring in present moments.* I was slowly learning to follow that advice, but on this day, it didn't feel like enough.

Back at Chris and Sarah's house, it was almost time for dinner. Sarah was busy cooking pasta, as Chris and their ten-year-old son, Iddy, set the table. Their baby girl, Ruth-Michael, who had recently learned to walk and was constantly on the move, was doing her best to wander around the house in search of things that she could get herself into. So, while the rest of the family prepared for dinner, I designated myself to follow Ruth-Michael around. After a long, emotionally exhausting day, there was nothing better to come home to than a perfectly sweet and innocent baby, who had the freedom of discovering the simplest new things, without having been jaded by the world yet.

In the short time that I had been there, The Nicholson Household already felt like a familiar and comfortable place to me, and after the day

I had with Caroline, the safety that I found in their home was the only thing holding me together. It seemed that no matter what the chaos of a day brought, Chris and Sarah were very intentional about keeping their home a peaceful and happy place. I couldn't quite figure out how they managed to do it, but it was something that I noticed and appreciated.

When it was time to eat, I picked up Ruth-Michael and brought her to the table. Before I plopped her down into her highchair, I planted a kiss on that soft, chubby cheek of hers, and silently thanked her for helping me to feel better after such a hard day.

That week, I wasn't the only one staying at the Nicholsons. A couple of nights before this one, they welcomed a young boy from Ringroad School, named Brighton, to come and stay in one of the empty rooms on their compound. Brighton was a "total orphan," and had been staying in Nyalenda with relatives who were abusive. He was beaten, and often found himself without food. So, while Chris and Sarah worked on finding a safe, more permanent solution for Brighton, they allowed him to come and stay on their compound.

Brighton was very shy, and hardly said much at all. He almost never smiled, but of course none of us could blame him for that. This child had gone through a certain type of hell that we would never be able to relate to, and each time I looked into his eyes I wondered how he found the strength to wake up in the morning.

I commended Chris and Sarah for doing such a beautiful thing by helping Brighton and showing him that they cared, but I more so admired their ability to hold themselves together in the process. Between Joanie's situation, and now knowing Brighton and Caroline, it was getting harder for me to compartmentalize. It was strange, though, because the harder it felt for me, the more convicted I felt to learn how to do it. I wanted to help; I didn't want to walk away.

After dinner that night, when all of the kids were asleep, I sat down with Chris and Sarah to talk to them about how I was feeling. Having lived in Kenya for nearly two years at this point, I knew that they would be able to offer a different perspective for me than my peers at Lipscomb had. On my first trip to Kenya, it was incredibly helpful for me to experience it with others who were there for the first time, as well. Were we noticing the same things as one another? Which parts were more challenging than we anticipated? Which parts were easier? Do you see God here? Because I don't.

Much to my surprise, the second trip to Kenya became more about learning how to emotionally survive in all of it, rather than losing myself in the nostalgia. It wasn't just about visiting people that I had come to love, and having fun with the kids; or basking in this new-found adventurous side that I found within myself. This was bigger and more meaningful than all of that, and I wanted Chris and Sarah to teach me how to lean into it without breaking.

"How do you stay positive here when you see so much suffering?" I asked.

"Well…" Sarah began, giving herself a moment to think. "For us, it's God. We have faith in God and know that this is where He needs us right now. But you're right, it can be really challenging sometimes."

I thought about this for a second. I didn't know God, nor did I ever ask Him what He wanted for my life. I didn't know that was an actual thing that people did.

"Okay, but even if you believe this is what you're meant to do, do you ever feel like you aren't strong enough to do it?"

"Oh yeah," Sarah answered. "All the time. But knowing that we can bring joy and hope and love and faith to people who aren't being given those things on a regular basis, that's what keeps us in it. We want to be able to give them those things, because they deserve to have that in their lives. And the things that I know I can't help them with, I remind myself to leave them in God's hands."

Chris and Sarah Nicholson are faithful people; this is something that I was coming to realize in spending more time with them. They had Bible verses on display in their home, and said a prayer over our dinner each night before we ate it. They stretched themselves in all directions to help the children of Ringroad, and never complained about being tired or missing The United States. I mean, I'm sure they had their moments, but they never led with that. They led with love, always, and I was intrigued by the notion that this love stemmed from a foundation of faith.

You, Sweet Girl, you love so hard. You love your family and your friends and you always want what's best for others. You never want to see people sad or scared or lonely, and when you do see someone who is struggling, you don't know what to do with yourself. You have all of this pent-up love and empathy, but you can't figure out where to lay it down; how to put it to use. So, it gets to feel too heavy and it knocks you down, rather than propels you forward to a place where you can use it to help people. You're feeling stuck where you are, I know. But you're going to find your way out of it.

"Do you think it's possible to do this type of work if you don't believe in God?"

I asked this question, knowing that it might be an uncomfortable one for Sarah to answer, but I needed to know. Could I harness my emotions well enough to do this if I didn't know who God was or what role He plays in all of it?

...*If* He plays a role in all of it?

"You know, I don't know," Sarah responded gently. "I've never had that perspective before so I'm not sure. I know that my faith in God is what keeps me going, but I know there are lots of other ways that people are able to keep perspective in challenging times. So, yeah, I think it's possible."

"So, Jen, do you not believe in God at all?" Chris asked me. There was no judgement in his voice, just simple curiosity.

I told them that I didn't believe in God, and that I wasn't even sure if I could. Just like you, I didn't really know what it meant to believe; nor did I have any real interest in figuring that out. Not then, anyway.

After I finished talking with Chris and Sarah, I went to my room and emailed my Peers. Even though our class together was over, we remained on a group email chain, and they had encouraged me to write to them while I was away. I wrote about Caroline, and how difficult the day felt for me. I told them how much I missed them.

A couple of hours later, before I fell asleep, I checked to see if anyone responded to my email. I was excited to see that I had a couple of messages, and opened them right away. The first one was from a classmate that I grew close with on the trip, and had kept in consistent contact with since. I read her response to me with a smile on my face and tears in my eyes, as I imagined her speaking the words to me.

... "I'm amazed to hear about all that God is doing through you while you're in Kenya..."

And then there was that line. I couldn't make sense of it; I didn't understand how she could read all about the day I had, and think for a second that God was anywhere around this. My day was filled with sadness, the suffering that I witnessed was unimaginable, and she wanted to talk about God doing something about it?

I had a lot of respect for her, and a lot of respect for Chris and Sarah, but I couldn't see what any of them were seeing. All it takes is one look at someone like Caroline, and any chance there was for someone like me to start believing in any type of God, flew right out the window.

50

Chapter Five

I've had a tummy ache all day.

It's Tuesday, and that means I have dance class after school. I love to dance and my teacher is nice, but I don't have any friends in that class. I usually feel too shy to talk to anyone.

Mom picks me up from kindergarten on dance days. She always brings me a snack for the car, but most of the time, I don't eat it because of the butterflies in my stomach. When I see my dance bag on the seat next to me, it gives me even more butterflies, and I want to ask Mom if I can miss the class today. I know she won't let me, though.

When we get to the dance place, Mom grabs my hand and we walk inside together. Like always, she helps me change into my leotard and tights in the bathroom and put on my ballet slippers. Usually after that, she kisses me goodbye and leaves until class is over. First, we do Ballet, then we switch to Tap, and then it's time to go home. I like Ballet better than Tap because the Tap shoes are slippery and I fell a lot when I was first learning. I'm better at it now.

Mom and I walk down the hallway to my classroom. We see my dance teacher, Ms. Lisa, and she greets me with a big smile on her face. She's always smiling.

"Ok, girls!" Ms. Lisa shouts. She is standing outside the classroom door, like we aren't allowed to go in it or something.

"They're doing some repairs in our regular class room, so we are going to use the room next door for today. Everyone, follow me!"

Mom bends down to kiss me goodbye, but I don't want her to go. I already had butterflies in my stomach, but now we have to be in a different classroom, and that makes me feel worse. I don't know that classroom, and what if everything feels different in there?

"I don't want to go today." I cry to Mom. "Please. I don't want to be in a new room."

Mom bends down even more and looks at me in my eyes. "Well, Sweetie, it's your same class and the same teacher, it's just a different room today, that's all. And, Ms. Lisa said it's only for today! That's great news!"

When Mom tries to cheer me up, she always uses her happy voice. Sometimes it works and sometimes it doesn't. Today I don't know if it can work very well. I wish I knew before we got to the dance place that the room was going to be different today. Then I could have thought about it a little and I wouldn't be surprised when it happened.

"Hey, how about I walk you in to the classroom before I go, okay?" Mom says.

"But I don't want you to go at all. Can you stay here today?"

Mom grabs my hand and walks with me into the new classroom.

"Oh, look, Jen! This classroom looks just like your other one! This is perfect!"

I'm too upset to care about what the classroom looks like. I still know this isn't the same room, and that makes me not want to be in it.

Mom bends down again to give me a kiss and tell me she will be back, and I cry harder. Then, suddenly I feel a hand on my shoulder. I open my eyes and see Ms. Lisa's face smiling down at me.

"Come on, Jennifer, let's join the rest of the class! Mommy will be back in just a little while."

I keep crying and beg Mom not to go. Mom says she has to go, but if I agree to calm down and stay in my class, she will come back a few minutes early. I follow Ms. Lisa to the middle of the classroom, but I'm crying too hard to stop. I'm crying so hard that I might even throw up.

I don't know how long I sit on Ms. Lisa's lap, trying to calm down. I gag a few times, and if I had any food in my tummy, I would have thrown it up by now. All of the other girls are sitting in a circle around us, watching me cry. I know they probably think I'm weird or stupid for acting like a baby, but I can't stop myself from getting so upset.

Ms. Lisa holds me on her lap a little bit longer and then says it's time to start the class. She tells me to try doing the first few exercises, and if I'm still feeling sad, I can sit and watch. That feels okay to me because I know that I'll have a choice to sit out, in just a few minutes. I like when someone gives me a choice.

Ms. Lisa puts on the music, and I stand at the ballet barre with the other girls. We always start every class with the same exercises, and I like that because I know them. Doing something that I know always makes me feel better, so I start to feel happy again once the music comes on. The room doesn't feel too different anymore, because everything in it feels the same. I think I'll be okay to dance until Mom comes back to get me.

~ ~ ~

Dear Sweet Girl,

At this point in the story, it would be safe for you to assume that Kenya wasn't going away for me any time soon. There was something about it that resonated with my soul, and I believe that Kenya holds the same space in my soul that you do. Kenya breeds people of the strength and bravery that your heart has always needed to bear witness to, in order to understand certain things about the world. You've struggled to understand that people can carry their pain differently from one another; that those who hurt the most are also the ones capable of tapping into the most profound levels of overcoming. The part of my soul that connected to Kenya, is the same part of my soul that holds your hunger to witness resilience.

Shortly after I returned from my second trip, I found out that the Psychology Department at Lipscomb was planning to go back to Kenya. It would be a different class, with mostly different students, but Dr. Ribeiro would be the one leading again. Since I would be able to apply the trip to a different course credit, one that I still needed to graduate, I was able to sign up for it without paying any extra money. It was a year, literally to the day, since I had made the decision to give Kenya a try; that I found myself there for the third time.

Within our group, Dr. Ribeiro, his wife, myself and two other students, were the only ones who had been to Kenya before. But, among those of us returning, I was the one who had been the most. In my mind, this meant that I knew everything one would need to know. I designated myself to be the student leader, even though Dr. Ribeiro never officially asked for one.

Did you know that you're a leader, Sweet Girl? You may not ever jump at an opportunity outside of the house to be one, but you've got it in you. When you play School and you are the Teacher, or when you play House and you are the Mom; or even when you plan shows for you and Jake to perform at family gatherings…you are acting as a leader. It doesn't matter if they're dolls, stuffed animals or your pesky little brother; you do know how to take on a leadership role. And you are wonderful at it.

Now, back over in Kenya, I was ready to hit the ground running. I couldn't wait to see the children at Ringroad and all of the staff there, and to be reunited with The Nicholsons. Dr. Ribeiro even told us that we would have the opportunity to go out and visit patients in the community and, because of my experience with Caroline, I knew all about how those visits work.

Landing at the Kisumu International Airport had begun to feel quite normal. Even though I never could have imagined that I'd be touching down there for the third time in nine months, there was a very real, almost palpable sense that this journey wasn't going to end here. It may have been my last chance to travel with Lipscomb, but my connection to Kenya was only growing stronger. Before our plane even landed, I knew that this wouldn't be my last time; just like the previous trips hadn't been, either.

When we reached the front entrance hall of the airport, we found Chris and Sarah waiting for us, with a small group of students from Ringroad. Emotions ran high, as some of us reunited with familiar faces, and others experienced the joy of meeting this incredibly special people for the first time. First-timers or not, exhaustion was no match for the abundance of gratitude we felt to be in that moment.

Each student grabbed one of our luggage trollies, and we all headed toward the parking lot. One of the older boys, named Job, pushed my luggage as we walked side-by-side and chatted about how he's been since the last time I saw him.

"You know, we wanted to bring Joan to the airport for you, since you are her sponsor." Job told me, as the sliding doors opened into the scalding hot sun.

"Oh! That's so sweet!" I replied. "I would have been so happy to see her at the airport!"

"Yeah, but, she sick. She actually hasn't been to school for a while."

My heart dropped. "What do you mean, she's sick? Sick with what?"

We stopped at the Nicholsons car and turned to wait for the others.

"I don't know the problem. I just know she hasn't come to school in a while, and we were told it's because she's sick."

This wasn't an uncommon occurrence, at Ringroad or at any other school in the area. Children fell sick often, or sometimes that had to stay home to care for a sick parent. I knew this, but I needed to know more details about Joanie's conditions immediately.

I found Sarah in the middle of our large group, that was still making their way through the parking lot with the rest of the luggage.

"Hey, Sarah? Job told me that Joan is sick and has been absent from school for a bit. Do you know what's wrong with her?"

"I know, we found that out today when we picked the kids up from school to bring them to the airport. We were going to surprise you by bringing her."

Then she turned to Chris. "Hey, Chris, did they tell you today what Joan has been sick with?"

"No, she wasn't at school today, but we can definitely find out how she's doing for you."

I told them that I would really appreciate it, and then I climbed into one of the vans that came to bring us to St. Anne's guest house. There wasn't a tuk tuk option this time, and I was okay with that. I was too distracted by worry over Joanie to join in the excitement of riding in a tuk tuk. I suddenly felt like I wouldn't be able to join in any of the excitement in general, until I knew that Joanie was okay.

That afternoon, once we had settled into our rooms and eaten lunch, I opted to stay behind while the rest of the group went to Ringroad. I was thankful to have Brittany as my roommate, as she was on the first Lipscomb trip with me, and she and I had grown pretty close. I felt safe enough to tell her why I wanted to stay behind. She knew how much Joanie meant to me, and understood why I would be anxious about not knowing whether or not she was okay.

"I'll stay back with you if you want," Brittany offered.

I appreciated her gesture, and would have been open to it if I didn't know how excited she was to get back to Ringroad and reunite with the children as soon as possible. I told her she needed to go.

"Are you going to be okay, though? I mean, you're my other half here, so if you want me to stay, I'll stay with you."

"I'll be okay," I told her. "I wasn't expecting things to start out like this, so I just need to quiet my head a little bit."

Reluctantly, Brittany went to join the rest of our group. As soon as she left the room, I cried into my pillow and begged whatever Higher Power there was out in the universe, to keep Joanie safe and heathy. I cried as hard as I did on the day that I met her, all of those month ago.

How can I keep doing this? I thought to myself. Each of my previous trips had exposed me to various levels of heartbreak, but we weren't even two hours in to this one and I already found myself grappling with the harsh realities of this world that I had come to love so much. I knew that the rest of my classmates, especially the ones who hadn't been to Kenya before, were walking around Ringroad with smiles on their faces and kids hanging off of their arms, while I was sitting alone in my room, contemplating whether or not I was truly strong enough to do this.

You are going to witness suffering here, Jen. All of the time. My mind was racing. *Do you love them enough to fight for them?*

I thought I did, and I really wanted to. But I couldn't be so sure. So, instead of trying to figure it out, I laid in bed and cried, until the rest of my group came back from Ringroad. When it was time for dinner at the guest house, I sat at the table, but I didn't eat.

The next day, Chris, Vanessa, and a couple of other people, went to visit Joanie at her home. They had asked if I wanted to come, but I was too afraid of finding Joanie in really bad condition. In Kenya, children are often sick with worse than a common cold. And, since I knew that Joanie was HIV positive, there was no telling what this sickness was doing to her immune system. So, I decided to stay behind and wait for a report from the others.

I had been hoping that I would wake up that day feeling stronger; that I'd swallow whatever fears or reservations I had, and rise to the occasion, like I'd been able to do in the past. Unfortunately, though, I woke up feeling worse. I was so thrown by my sadness that it sort of just fed into itself, and I couldn't seem to get out of my own way.

For what it's worth, I received an encouraging report about Joanie that afternoon. Vanessa let me know that she was home, recovering from Malaria, and that she would be back at school in a couple of days. I was relieved and overjoyed by this news, and couldn't wait to see that precious girl when she returned. But I was starting to realize that I had a new, underlying issue, that I needed to address.

Those first few days back in Kisumu drew me pretty close to you. I didn't want you there, nor did I want to retreat back to your world, but I found myself doing the bare minimum to interact with the children, and waiting for the time of day where we got to retreat to our rooms. I didn't have a desire to go back home, but I wasn't quite sure how strong my desire was to be there, either.

Less than a week in, our group gathered in our usual conference room for our nightly Processing Session. On this night, Dr. Ribeiro posed the question: What have you learned about yourself since this experience began?

Ha! What perfect timing, right?

One of my peers answered that he was doing better without the comforts of home than he thought he would. Another person shared that she didn't have much experience interacting with children before this trip, and was surprised by how comfortable she felt around the Ringroad students. I always enjoyed listening to my peers answer these processing questions. I love learning about other people, and hearing different perspectives of a shared experience. I'm not going to lie, though; it was pretty hard to focus on this night.

When it was my turn to share, I took a deep breath. I knew that my answer was going to be emotionally loaded, and I didn't know if I had the stamina to work through it in front of fifteen other people.

"Well, first of all, I realized that I don't know who I am without this place anymore. I feel like I have a purpose here that's going to be bigger than these sporadic ten-day trips." My voice began to shake.

"So, before we got here, I had made the decision to come back for an extended period of time, once I graduate this summer. I finish with this Master's program in August, and I'd like to come from September through the end of the year."

"Wow, Jen, that's really awesome!" someone in the group exclaimed.

"How cool!" said another.

But I wasn't done.

"I know I've shared with you all that I don't believe in God. I've never been entirely sure that he exists, and I've never felt the need to and figure it out."

I took another deep breath, as my classmates remained silent.

"I hear people talk about God in this place, and I can't see it. I don't understand where he is, or why the children are being taught that God loves them, when most of their most basic needs aren't even being met."

Another deep breath.

"But over the past few days, while letting my worry over Joanie get the best of me, I realized that I can't continue to come here if I don't open myself up to the possibility of knowing God. I can't keep watching people suffer, or hearing about their suffering, without finding a way to have some sort of faith. So, I guess what I learned about myself, is that I'm ready to bring God into my life."

It felt like everyone broke their silence at once. People were smiling and nodding at me, patting me on the shoulders and telling me how proud and excited they were for my journey to begin. Who knew that making the decision to know God was considered to be such a big deal, right?

I mean, I didn't know that; and I know that you didn't, either. Did you ever even hear about God outside of Sunday School or Synagogue? I don't think you did. So, just as a head's up to you, people who believe get really excited when they hear that someone new wants to learn what all the fuss is about!

"I do have a request, though," I continued. "I respect all of you and your beliefs, but I do ask that you don't push them on me. Someday, I may be ready to hear about your faith journey, or listen to whatever verses speak to you most in the Bible. But, for now, I want to see if I can figure this out on my own, in a way that feels genuine and specific to me."

Everyone nodded in agreement.

"Of course."

"We can respect that."

"Feel free to let me know if you have any questions."

When our session was over, we all walked back to our rooms for the night.

"I'm proud of you," Brittany whispered, as she hung her arm around my neck."

"Ha. Thanks," I replied.

I felt lighter than I had in a while, as I prepared for bed that night. I didn't know what was supposed to happen next, but I knew that if God was out there, it was up to Him to show me.

Alright, God, I thought as I drifted off to sleep. *This is between me and you. Let's see what you've got.*

Chapter Six

This is one of my favorite days of the whole school year.

Ever since I was in pre-school, Dad has been coming into my class once a year to play his guitar and sing for us. Mom always comes with him to video tape it, and everyone gets so excited. We dance while he sings, and he even lets some of the kids stand up and sing with him.

When I was younger, Mom and Dad gave me a choice to stay until the end of the school day, or to leave with them when Dad was finished. They said that I couldn't make a habit of wanting to leave early, but the days when Dad came were special days, and so I was given that choice. Most of the time, I chose to leave with them, but one time in pre-school, I didn't. As soon as they left, I cried, and knew that I'd never make that decision again.

Now that I'm older, though, I'm not given the choice to leave with them on Dad's Music Day. I'm in third grade, and my parents say that it's important that I stay and don't miss the rest of the lessons. Usually, he comes to play in the morning, so if I left with them, I'd miss an entire day of school. I guess the school days are more important when you start growing up.

Just like every other time, my class this year loves Dad's singing. They jump around and laugh and shout, and I am jumping and shouting with them. All of the kids are smiling because of my dad, and that makes me feel special and happy. He always sings for us at home, but sometimes it's more fun to dance around with lots of other people.

When Dad does play the guitar and sing at home, I sing with him. He tells me I have a great voice, and sometimes he even gives me a real microphone to sing into. I'm shy a lot, but not really when I'm just at home with my family. I love to sing with Dad, and I think that maybe I want to become a real singer one day. I might be too shy, though.

After singing a few songs on his own, Dad says it's time for a volunteer to come up and sing the next song with him. He asks if anyone knows the song, "If You're Happy and You Know it," and all the kids in my class raise their hands. He tells them that he will give a few kids a chance to help him lead the song, and that the rest of the class can help out by singing along and doing the motions.

The kids in my class who are usually the loudest and the bravest, are the ones who volunteer to lead the song with Dad. Even before they raised their hands, I could probably have guessed who those kids were going to be. When the song is over, Dad says he is going to play one more song, and then he asks if I want to come up and sing it with him. I really want to, but I'm feeling way too shy.

"Aw, come on Jen, we sing this one all the time at home! Come on up and sing with me!"

I shake my head and tell him that I'll dance with everyone, but I don't want to sing in front of them.

"Not even if you've got me singing with you?" Dad asks.

I shake my head again.

"Alllllllright, maybe next time!" Then Dad taps on this guitar to start the song. "One, two, one two, three four!"

Everyone starts dancing like crazy. Even my teacher is dancing, and Mom is walking around telling all the kids to wave at the camera. I keep dancing like everyone else, and I really don't want it to be over. I want Dad to stay and play for us all day, and I want to feel this happy forever.

When Dad finishes, my teacher tells everyone to say thank you to him

"THANK YOU, MR. RADLER!" Everyone shouts at the same time.

Dad puts his guitar away, and Mom puts away the video camera. Then they come say goodbye to me, and I can feel tears in my eyes.

"We'll see you when you get home, okay honey?" Dad says.

"Have a great rest of your day!" Says Mom.

I nod and give them kisses; then I watch them walk out the door.

My teacher tells everyone to go back to their desks, and I'm trying really hard not to cry. This time, I'm not just upset that they left me, but I'm upset that I told Dad I didn't want to sing with him. I really did want to sing with him, I was just feeling shy. But I know now I will spend the rest of the day hoping that I didn't hurt his feelings.

~ ~ ~

Dear Sweet Girl,

As you know, I'm no stranger to a therapist's office. Your love of therapy stuck with me, kid, and that is probably a huge reason why I

60

decided to go into the field of Psychology, myself. Well, actually, it might be the only reason.

I remember you falling in love with the process of therapy. You studied the way your therapists spoke to you, and sometimes you even tried to figure out what questions they were going to ask, before they asked them. Oftentimes, you understood why they were asking you the questions that they were, and when you didn't, you always wanted to try and figure it out. You knew there's purpose in everything they said to you, and trying to understand that purpose, was actually helping you understand yourself.

I first started seeing Kathy when I got back from my second Lipscomb trip to Kenya. I decided that my first step in my new spiritual journey, should be to find a therapist who works from a spiritual perspective. You see, in all of the therapists that we have seen, collectively, neither you or I ever spoke to a therapist whose approach centered around faith.

I'm actually really thankful that this is true, because I don't know how you would have received spiritual counseling as a child, but I definitely was not open to receiving it as an adult, until this moment that I'm about to dive into with you now.

As I mentioned before, Lipscomb University is a Christian school. Like most other colleges and universities, they have a counseling center on campus, where counseling services are offered to their students for free. As a Christian school, all of their therapists on staff have some sort of a spiritual background, and I felt that this was exactly what I needed.

Now, let me just take a moment to say, that we've been pretty lucky when it comes to finding therapists. Some have taken longer to warm up to, but in the end, you and I have benefited from every single therapist that we've ever worked with. So, just you wait until you meet Kathy, because she is very gently, and patiently, going to rock your world.

I returned from that third trip to Kenya in March of 2014, and I started seeing Kathy in April. She looked to be in her early fifties, had straight, shoulder-length brown hair, and glasses that accented her big brown eyes. Her smile was warm, her temperament was warm, and I knew from the moment I met her that we would get along just fine.

"So, Jen, why don't you tell me a little bit about what brings you in here today."

As concisely as I could, I explained to Kathy what led me to her office. I talked briefly about my history with anxiety, (You may have been

61

sitting on a chair next to me, you felt so tangible in that moment), and then I talked to her about Kenya. I expressed my desire to discover some sort of faith in God, and my concern that if I couldn't find God, I wouldn't be able to keep Kenya in my life.

"So, for you, Kenya feels like it's supposed to play a bigger role in your life than just going on a few mission trips. You don't think this was meant to be an experience that you learn from, collect memories from, and then move away from it."

"Right. I know it's supposed to play a bigger role in my life, but I don't know what that role is, or how I'd be able to sustain it without believing in something...bigger."

Kathy nodded and wrote down a few notes.

"'Bigger' meaning God."

"Yes."

"Now, I'm assuming there are many things in your life that you have loved, but also found to be quite challenging, right? Especially given your history with anxiety."

(Ha! You want to answer that question for me, Little One?).

"Yes, absolutely."

"Can you give me some examples?"

I didn't have to think very hard. "Well, when I left for college. Undergrad, I mean. I ended up loving it, but I was miserable the day my parents dropped me off because I was so nervous. Also, when I moved from Connecticut to Tennessee, I was really anxious about that, too. You know, because I was going somewhere that I didn't know."

Kathy wrote down a couple more notes. "Mmhmm, so in the beginning of those life events, when you were feeling anxious and hesitant about them, what made you push through them?"

"Well, with college, I didn't have a choice. My parents made me go. And with moving to Tennessee...my friends were excited about it, and I had already proven to myself that I could live away from home by going to college, so I figured I would just give it a try. Plus, I knew I could always go home if I wanted."

Kathy smiled. "And in either of these scenarios, did you ever think to call on God to help you work through your anxieties?"

"No. I didn't even know that was a thing. I mean, I knew some people believed in God, and that they prayed, but I didn't know how to do that. My family doesn't do that."

"Does your family practice a specific religion at home?"

"Well, we're Jewish. But really only by tradition, not by faith."

Kathy jotted more notes on her pad.

Like, I had a Bat Mitzvah when I was thirteen. And we follow certain holiday traditions. But I think we only do that to keep the traditions alive. None of us really know where those traditions come from, I don't think."

Kathy seemed respectfully intrigued by this, like she had never met a Jewish person before. And I hate to admit it, but I probably wasn't the best Jew to meet if she had never met one before. I was able to offer very little insight into the details of our religion. I could have read to her in Hebrew, though, thanks to that Bat Mitzvah!

Anyway, I knew where Kathy was going with all of these questions, and I liked that. Just like you, I love understanding the path that a therapist is taking me on, and trying to figure it out before she takes me there. In this conversation with Kathy, I knew that she was going to ask what tools I've used in the past to cope with my anxiety, and how is it different this time? If I've conquered difficult situations in the past, using tools that were not based on any sort of faith, why was this the time to bring God into the mix?

Of course, I was exactly right. Kathy asked me those very questions, and my answer to her was pretty simple:

"Because I no longer feel strong enough to do this without having faith in something. It's either find God, or lose Kenya; and I am not willing to lose Kenya."

Chapter Seven

I can't believe that I was chosen.

Out of the whole entire second grade, only five students were picked to read their letters at the Anti-Smoking Rally; and I am one of them. We get to go to our State Capital building and read what we wrote, on camera, and in front of so many people. I'm going to be on TV!

Today is a snow day, so no one is going to school. At first, we didn't know if the rally would be canceled, too, because it was still snowing a lot this morning. But one of the other moms just called my mom and said that the rally is still on. We are going to meet in the school parking lot and then one of the parents and one of the teachers are driving us to the Capital building.

I know the other students who will be with me, but I'm not friends with them. We are all in the second grade together, but they have different teachers than me, so we only see each other at lunch and recess. I usually don't like going somewhere that I don't know, with people I don't know, but today feels different. I know this is an important thing that we are doing, and that it is very special for us. There's like over a hundred kids in the second grade, and we were the only ones who were picked.

Mom helps me put on one of my favorite winter dresses and then she does my hair in my favorite way. I love when she uses her blow dryer and her special brush to make my hair straight, because it makes me feel like a grown up. Then she ties it back in a half-pony tail, and tells me I can put on a tiny bit of her lipstick. I've never felt more like a grown up in my entire life!

Dad is the one who brings me to meet up with the other kids, and he tells me how proud of me he is.

"This is a big deal, Jennifer," he says. "There are going to be a lot of important people there and they're all going to be listening to hear what my little daughter has to say. My little Squirt."

I've been to downtown Hartford with Dad lots of times. His job does something with insurance and a lot of the buildings that he visits for his business are down here. He always tells me that Hartford was once known as the "Insurance Capital of the World." I don't really know what that means, but it sounds important. I know it's important to Dad, anyway.

I feel some butterflies in my stomach when we get to the school parking lot. Some of the other kids are here already and I wonder if they're feeling nervous about speaking in front of so many people. I'm a little nervous, I think, but it's not the bad kind of nervous.

We've been learning about why it's bad to smoke cigarettes, and our assignment in class was to write a letter that would convince someone not to smoke. It was easy for me to write the letter because my Grandma and Grandpa smoke, and I imagined myself writing my letter to them. I've wanted them to stop smoking, ever since I learned that it's a bad thing. I knew that even before we started learning about it in class, because my Grandma always tells me not to start smoking like she did.

I don't really know what a rally is or why they would want to hear from kids there, but my teacher says it's because we're the voices of the future. She says that even though we're small, we can make a big difference, and I like that idea. I always thought that we couldn't make a difference in anything until we're old.

There's a lot of people at this rally. In the middle of all the people, there's a stage with a bunch of microphones. I know that's where we are going to be reading our letters, but the microphones look too tall for us to reach. Hopefully someone remembers that they'll have to help us.

Our teacher and the mom chaperone, line us up and tell us to read our letters silently to ourselves, for practice. I read mine a million times this morning already, but I'm happy to read it a few more times. I want to have it completely in my memory, so that if I lose my place when I'm on the stage, I'll already have the words in my head. Also, I'm proud of what I wrote and am happy reading it over and over.

I feel like I do at my dance recitals. I always get butterflies when I'm waiting backstage, but it's not like the anxiety I get that makes me not want to do things. If someone ever walked up to me at my dance recital and told me I didn't have to go on stage, and that my butterflies would stop if I walked away, I still would choose to go out there. I never have an appetite on recital days, but I don't get anxious enough to throw up or anything. It's exciting when we get to dress in our costumes and show our families what we've been practicing for a long time. I think maybe because I've practiced reading this letter, like I always practice my dances, I feel okay about being in front of all these people. I don't like the waiting, though. The longer we have to wait, the stronger the butterflies get.

The teacher puts me third in line to speak, which means I'm right in the middle. When the first student, Megan, goes up to the microphone, that's when I start getting more nervous. I can't even pay attention to what she's saying because I'm only thinking about how it's almost my turn. I do notice that they put a milk crate on the ground for her to stand on, and that makes me feel a little bit better. It would be embarrassing to go on the state and have no way of reaching the microphone.

When Megan finishes reading her letter, everyone claps and whistles. Some people made signs that they're holding in the air, and they're waving them while other people are clapping. It seems like a lot of people already know that cigarettes are bad for them.

When the kid before me goes up to the stage, my butterflies grow again. I can't concentrate on anything that he's saying; I'm even getting too nervous to look at my own speech again. Reading it one more time won't help me now anyway, so I just hold the paper in one hand and start tearing off tiny pieces of it along the sides. My hands are so sweaty that it's making the paper feel wet.

When everyone starts clapping again, I know that it's only a few seconds before my turn. The person who's in charge of helping us, puts her hand on my shoulder, like she's telling me to wait just a second before I walk on the stage. When it's time, she pats me on the back and whispers, "Go ahead, sweetie."

I walk onto the stage and step up onto the milk crate. Then the grown up who's standing here with me, brings the microphone down a little bit more, so that it reaches my face. I'm glad someone is here with me because it makes me feel a little more relaxed, I think.

The words start coming out of my mouth. I know them so well, that it's like they're coming out without me thinking about them. I can hear the sound of my own voice, and it sounds different on a microphone. It echoes a little, and reminds me of when I sing with Dad at home. In the car this morning, our teacher told us that sometimes when people get nervous, they talk too fast. She reminded us to read our letters slowly, so that everyone can understand us and the message that we're trying to present. I think I'm speaking slowly enough, but I can feel my voice shaking a little.

Even though it's cold out, we were allowed to take our jackets off when it was our turn to speak. I don't even really feel cold, because I'm concentrating on reading my words. I can see cameras and bright colored posters from the corners of my eyes. I want to read what the posters say, but I have to concentrate. It feels good to read my words out loud, instead of quietly to myself. I think people are listening, and I hope this will help someone to quit smoking. Maybe the smoking laws will even change; I think that's part of the reason why we're here. I'm not so sure, though.

I read my very last sentence and I feel so relieved. People start clapping and cheering for me, and I look at one of the cameras. I smile, I wave, and then I jump off the stage.

"Great job!" says one of the ladies who's working here. She points to where our teacher is standing, and I walk over. There are still a couple more kids who have to speak, but the ones who went before me, give me a high-five. I'm so proud of all of us because we did something really special.

After the rally is over, we shake hands with some government people and have our pictures taken. We heard we might get to take a tour of the Capital building, but then someone decided that the day was too busy and there were too many people there.

"We'll get to come back here and tour the building with your entire grade," our teacher said. "But only you guys will have this extra special experience to remember forever."

It's almost lunch time and I'm starting to feel hungry. Now that the hard part of the day is over, my appetite is completely back, and I am ready to eat something. We all get into the car and our chaperone says that we get to go to McDonald's for a special treat. Our parents will pick us up there, instead of back at school.

We get to McDonald's, and I order my cheeseburger, fries and vanilla milk shake. It's one of my favorite meals in the whole world, and I only ever get to have it for a special treat. I'm excited to eat it, but I'm also excited for my parents to come and pick me up. My brain feels tired from doing something so big today, and I'm ready to be in my own house again.

The other students ask if we can eat in the play area. I don't love the play area because sometimes I feel trapped in there, and I also don't always have the energy to play. But all the other kids want to go in there, so our teacher and chaperone say it's okay. They all race to finish their lunch so that they can get a few minutes on the playscape before their parents come to take them home.

"Jennifer, you don't want to play?" The chaperone asks.

"Not today," I tell her.

I haven't even finished my meal yet, and I'm too tired to play. I think if someone asked me, I'd tell them it was more fun speaking in front of lots of people, than playing on a playscape will ever be. I was nervous while I was waiting to speak, but I really liked doing it, and I hope I get to do it again someday. But if I never play on another playscape, ever again for the rest of my life, I'm okay with that. Playscapes feel more scary to me.

~ ~ ~

Dear Sweet Girl,

In case you were wondering; Mom and Dad aren't the ones who paid for me to go back to Kenya. I know you might assume that they would have, but the agreement was that I'd have to find a way to pay for my own travels.

Since I had moved in with Mom and Paul when I started graduate school, I had saved a substantial amount of money. Traveling to the other side of the world can be pretty expensive, though, and I didn't want to use all of my savings for it.

In order to raise money for my next trip, I wrote a little children's book, and printed it with pictures that I had taken on my previous trips to Kenya. I was able to cover the cost of my ticket on my own, but it was important for me to raise enough money to cover three months-worth of living expenses.

The books were selling well among my family and friends, but my ultimate goal was to hold a proper fund-raising event. I wanted a chance to speak to a group of people about my experiences in Kenya, and hoped that they would feel moved enough by my stories to donate toward my future work there.

I was willing to speak to anyone who would listen; which is why I gleefully accepted the invite to speak at our local senior center, where Grandma played Bridge a couple times a week. I thought long and hard about what I would say, but I didn't feel the need to write any of it down. I had told my stories from Kenya a million times, and telling them at the senior center would feel no different.

My presentation took place in the senior center's dining room during lunch time. I was offered a meal, but I declined because of the butterflies in my stomach. I enjoy public speaking, but the anticipation of it always makes me a little bit nervous. I had my spiel ready to go and I wanted to get started before I had time to second guess myself.

Finally, when it looked like no one else would be coming, and everyone that did show up had taken their plates of food, the "Special Events Coordinator" walked up to the front of the room to introduce me. I took a sip of water and looked out into the crowd of about fourteen; five of whom were my own family members, and one who was the professional Videographer that Mom hired to capture what was sure to be an inspirational event.

... "And now she is here to share a bit about her experience with us. Please welcome, Joan's beautiful granddaughter, Jenny Radler!"

I took my place behind the music stand that doubled as a podium. The Events Coordinator had set it up there for me as a place to hold my note cards, but I didn't have any notes. The stories I wanted to tell were permanently etched into my heart, so I didn't need to write them anywhere else.

"Hello, everyone!" I began, my voice shakier than I expected it to be. "My name is Jenny and I am so thankful to be here today."

I spent the next eighteen minutes and thirty-four seconds sharing my experiences from Kisumu, Kenya. I talked about the children who had nothing to eat at home, but who came to school ready to learn, anyway. I showed photos of myself with them, and other people whom I had come to know and love there.

At the end of my speech, I talked about my plan to go back to Kenya and help as much as I could. Kenya had stolen my heart, and I wanted others to feel as inspired to help, as I did.

The audience clapped at the end of my presentation, and I asked if there were any questions. I was more than willing to answer whatever people wanted to ask, as I felt this meant they were taking an interest in contributing to my mission.

A man sitting at the front table, raised his hand first.

"You said that you plan on being there for three months this time, is that right?"

I smiled and nodded. "Yes, that's right."

"So, my question is, what do you actually plan on doing for those three months that would make a significant impact?"

I was thrown by his question. I felt I had done a pretty good job of explaining why I wanted to go back to Kenya, and what I would be doing once I got there. Had I not been clear enough?

"Well, the school that I've been visiting there, doesn't have a Counselor and that is what my background is in," I answered, sensing that this wouldn't be a good enough answer for him. The man didn't say a word, as he sat with his eyes locked on mine and his arms crossed over his chest. I suddenly felt very defensive.

"And, of course, I'm willing to do anything else that I can to help while I'm there; whether that be serving the students their food, helping tutor outside of the classroom, taking the sick children to the clinic, helping them write their sponsor letters. Really, I'll do anything, as long as I can help."

The man stayed quiet for another second before giving the slightest nod, signaling to me that he was done with his question. I still got the sense that he wasn't satisfied with my answer, but I was flustered and ready to move on.

The questions that followed were a bit easier. People asked about what the food is like in Kenya and what the children learn in school. I got a question on how I was able to ensure my own personal safety while staying in a developing country, and I was okay answering that one, too. Lots of people had asked me questions like these before, and I understood them. I understood why people who had never been to Kenya, would ask about what it was like there for myself and for the children that I was working with.

It was that first question- the one that seemed to challenge my compassion- that I was uncomfortable with. And, lucky for me, the "challenger" tested me once more before my time was up.

"I'm sorry, dear," the man interjected, this time beginning to speak without raising his hand and waiting for me to acknowledge him.

"What I am still having trouble understanding is what your actual purpose will be there, other than to do things for them that they can do for themselves."

My heart was pounding, my hands began to sweat. Whether it was from nerves or frustration, I didn't know. It was probably a combination of the two, but I just wanted this man to stop questioning me and my purpose.

"Yes, they can do those things by themselves."

I paused for a moment, acutely aware of the Videographer that Mom had hired, who was hunched over in the corner, capturing this uncomfortable dialogue.

"But these people work incredibly hard and the suffering in their lives is so constant, that if I can do anything to help make their lives easier, I am going to do it. I love them and I want to help them. It really is that simple."

With that being my final answer, I thanked everyone for coming, and let them know that I had set up a table outside of the dining room, where I would be collecting donations for my trip. My crowd of fourteen clapped, and then the five who were family members rushed over to give me hugs and tell me what a fantastic job I had done.

"Oh my God!" Mom exclaimed with more enthusiasm than I had given at any point during my talk. "I have no words! That was just beyond amazing!"

I fought back tears as I looked up at her, Paul, Jake, Grandma and Grandpa.

"I thought these people were going to be gentle and sweet, but that man seemed to really want to challenge me."

Jake draped his arm over my shoulder. "Yeah, that guy was kind of tough," he said. "But don't worry, Jenny, you did great. And all of us believe in you."

I slowly made my way to the table outside of the dining room, where we had placed a shoe box to collect donations. As the crowd filtered out, each person stopped to wish me luck, and some of them put a contribution in the box. After twenty minutes of sitting at the table, when it was just me and my family left, I counted the money. I raised 140 dollars that day.

I share this reigning success story with you, because it opened the door to a much bigger issue.

Shortly after my talk at the senior center, Aunt Mindy came to visit. Grandma and Grandpa were living with us in Tennessee at the time, and Aunt Min traveled from New York to Tennessee often, so that she could visit and help Mom take care of them.

You know how Aunt Min always brings you souvenirs when she travels around the world for work? Well, it's because of her love and appreciation for travel that I assumed she would be the most supportive of my endeavor. Aunt Min thrives off of experiencing new parts of the world and learning about different cultures, so obviously she would be ecstatic that I was starting to do the same thing. Much to my dismay, however, that was not the response that I got from her.

"Well, honey, what's your long-term goal there?" She asked me.

We were standing at the kitchen counter, chopping vegetables for dinner. I had just finished telling her about the children at Ringroad, how special and beautiful they are, and why I wanted to get back to them as soon as possible. I felt so convicted by my own desires that I couldn't bear to answer that same question all over again, especially now that it was coming from someone close to me.

"I don't have a long-term goal right now," I replied. "But I feel like I need to go back to Kenya and continue helping. I can't know what the future holds yet, because I haven't stayed in Kenya long enough to know."

Aunt Min continued to push.

"I know you want to help, honey, but don't you think that it would be more worth your efforts and money, and more impactful for the children, if you took your time and figured out a way that you could help make a lasting difference, rather than a temporary one?"

I didn't answer, letting her sense my discouragement. But she pressed on.

"You've got a good heart, Jen. And if you love Kenya so much, you can find an existing project to become involved with there; one that is designed and equipped to make a long-term impact."

"I do make a difference when I go there. The children are so happy and thankful when I'm around, and they have such little joy in their lives."

"Of course, you want to make them happy, and that is such a beautiful thing!"

I felt like I was going to explode.

"Then why are you trying to talk me out of it?"

Aunt Min stopped chopping her vegetables and put her arm over my shoulder.

"Oh honey, I'm not trying to talk you out of helping those children. But I do want you to consider that there are more productive ways to do it."

I didn't want to think about what she was saying anymore, but I had a feeling that I probably should. Both she and the stranger at the senior center felt that I may be going about this all wrong, and I needed to figure out what that meant.

Chapter Eight

I knew Mom and Dad would get divorced.

They fight a lot, and Dad's moved out of the house, and then back in, a couple of times. Whenever he moves back in, they get along for a while, and then they start fighting again. I never know what they're fighting about, even though they yell pretty loud. I try not to listen to their words because then I'd have to decide who I think is right and who is wrong, and I don't want to choose. All I know is that they really don't like each other sometimes.

When Jake and I ran into their bedroom last night, I knew something was wrong. They had been yelling at each other a lot again, and they both looked so sad and tired when we walked in there. As soon as they told us to sit down on the bed, I asked,

"Are you guys getting a divorce?"

Dad was crying when he answered, "Yes."

I don't remember very much after that; there was just a lot of crying, and then some hugs and kisses. This morning, Mom and Dad told us that we could stay home from school if we wanted to, but I decided to go anyway. I actually really like the fifth grade, and think I'd rather be with my friends, than at home watching Mom and Dad figure out whatever is supposed to happen next. They had to start telling people, and make other decisions that I knew I didn't want to hear about. I remember asking last night whether or not we would have to move out of our house, and Mom said they hadn't made any decisions yet. That's the decision I am dreading the most.

I walk on to the school bus and my friend, Hillary, stands up in the very back row. She reaches out her arms and says, "Oh my God, I am so, so sorry."

I guess Mom called Hillary's mom already.

I tell her that I am okay, and that I don't want to talk about it. There are tears in Hillary's eyes, and I know she's feeling so sad for me, but I don't have any tears left. I cried all of my out last night.

Even though I like school this year, I didn't think I'd ever pass up an opportunity to skip a day, if Mom and Dad were going to let me. But I don't know, I just don't feel like being at home today. I know everything is going to feel weird and sad there, and I don't want to be around it. I always feel best in places that feel most familiar to me, and right now, I think my classroom will feel more normal than my house.

I'm not sure if Mom has called my teacher yet, so I don't say anything to her. There are times in the day where I'm distracted by what we're learning, and then some times when I start to cry because I feel like I can't stop myself. I guess there are always tears left to cry, after all.

I wish that Hillary was in my class, but she's in the one next door. I also wish that Sas was with me, but she goes to a different school now. I still see her almost every day though, and I really hope she can still come over later. I want someone around that makes me feel normal.

When I get back home, the first person that I see is Dad's secretary, Barb. Dad's business runs from our house, so Barb is here every day. She's getting one of her sodas from the fridge when I walk in the back door, from the bus stop.

"Hi, honey," Barb says.

Then she comes over and gives me a hug. My eyes fill with tears again, and I remember why I decided to go to school today. I don't want to be around all of these sad people. I'm afraid to think about how everything is going to be different now, and how we might have to move and stuff. Even though I haven't heard my parents fight since they made their announcement last night, and they promised they will make the house feel as normal as possible, I can still feel the sadness.

Jake seems fine. He chose to stay home from school today, but I know it's because he thought playing with his toys would be more fun than sitting in his class. He was sad last night, but he doesn't look sad now. He's only seven years old, so I don't think he really even understands what's happening yet. I kind of wish that I was the younger one, so that I could play with my toys without thinking of all the ways life is going to be different now.

Actually, though, I still would have felt this sad at seven, I think. That's just how I am. So, I guess what I wish is that I wasn't so sensitive to everything all of the time. And, while I'm wishing for things...I really wish Mom and Dad weren't getting a divorce.

I haven't seen Rachel in a while. I stopped going to therapy with her like, months ago, because my anxiety wasn't as bad. I've been doing well in school and I love that dance studio that I go to now. It's in my town, so I get to dance with some of my best friends, instead of girls from other schools that I don't know. Everything is easier for me when I'm around people that I know.

Mom and Dad had agreed that it would be okay for me to stop going to therapy for a while, since I felt better. I always liked talking to Rachel, but I was happy because if I wasn't going anymore, that meant I didn't need her. If I didn't need therapy, then maybe I could live the rest of my life feeling normal.

The only reason that I'm back in Rachel's office right now is because of my parents' divorce. Mom said that since we're going through a lot of hard changes, it might be good for me to talk to someone about them. She and Dad even made Jake start seeing a therapist, but he sees a boy. I asked if I could go back to Rachel because she knows me.

Rachel's eyes look different when I see her today. She has that same sad look on her face that everyone else has when they find out that my parents are getting a divorce. Everyone feels sorry for me, and I can see it in their faces. I actually really hate it.

"When your mom called to schedule your appointment, she did tell me what's been going on," Rachel said.

I already knew that.

"Tell me how you've been since all of this happened."

I don't want to hurt Rachel's feelings, but I'm not in the mood to talk about this today. I talk about it with my friends sometimes, and it's the only thing I can think about when I'm in our house. Even when Mom and Dad aren't saying anything about it, I still know it's happening. Dad's sleeping in the guest room and people who sell houses are coming over to tell us how our house should look before they start taking pictures of it. I want to have some time where I don't have to think about this at all.

"I'm okay, I guess. I'm not really surprised that this is happening."

"Why do you say that?"

"Because, Mom and Dad fight a lot, and they've been separated before. I asked if they're getting a divorce before they even had a chance to say it. I just knew."

Rachel doesn't say anything right away, and I know she's trying to be gentle.

"Do you think since your dad has moved out in the past, and then moved back in, there's a part of you that thinks maybe that's what this is?"

I never even thought about that.

"No, I know they're getting a divorce this time. They never used that word before this, or talked about selling the house or anything."

"How are you feeling about them selling the house?"

"I don't want to leave our house because it's the only place that'll ever feel like home to me. We've lived in it since I was a baby, and no other family has ever lived in it. My parents had it built specially for us."

I actually remember moving into our house. Mom says I only think I remember because we have home movies of it, but I remember watching the movers when I was in my playpen. We don't have any home movies from inside of my playpen.

Watching Rachel's face, I can tell that she feels sad for me. I understand why she feels sad; divorce is a sad thing, and she knows I don't do well with sad things. But it isn't like I've never felt this way before. There's always been a part of my brain that feels like something sad is happening. The only difference now, is that everyone else around me feels sad about the same thing that I do. This time, if Rachel asks me what I'm feeling sad about, I could tell her. I have a real live thing to point to and tell her, "This is why I feel sad."

It's not just Rachel, either. Everyone around me keeps saying how sad this is, and asking me how I'm doing. I'm glad that I have people who care about me, but they're acting like I've never felt bad about anything before. This may be the first truly bad thing to happen to us, but the feelings I have aren't new ones. I've known what anxiety and sadness feel like, for a long time now.

~ ~ ~

Dear Sweet Girl,

Do you know how discouraging it is to find a calling in your life, and then be told that you're "doing it wrong?" Well, you will cross that bridge someday, and I'm so sorry about the strain that is puts on your heart. It's one of the greatest lessons you'll ever learn, though, so I'm happy to report that you stuck it out.

After Aunt Mindy, and the man at the senior center, questioned whether or not spending three more months in Kenya was the right thing for me to be doing, I decided to talk to Kathy about it. Not all of our conversations revolved around God, and I figured I might be able to get her opinion on what they each said to me.

"Why do you think it upset you so much, what they said to you?"

"Because it felt like they were challenging my compassion. Like me wanting to help people that I love, isn't a good enough reason to go and do it."

Kathy nodded. "Mmhmm, that makes sense..."

78

Kathy's voice trailed off a little bit, and I could tell that she wanted me to look at the situation from a different angle.

"You're holding back an opinion, aren't you?"

Kathy smiled. "Well, no. But I would like to encourage you to try and see where they might be coming from."

"Okay, so you agree with them?"

"Not necessarily. But let's try to understand their point of view."

"Okay."

"You felt as if your Aunt and the fund-raiser guest were trying to discourage you, but have you considered the possibility that they were actually trying to *encourage* you?"

To be honest, I had been considering this possibility. I replayed their words in my mind over and over, wondering if my idea of what helping looked like at Ringroad, wasn't the most productive or essential way. Perhaps there was a better way that I could spend my time helping; a way that could make a bigger impact in the future. But how could I possibly know that if I didn't go back and see for myself?

I conveyed this thought to Kathy, and she asked if this was leading me to second-guessing my trip.

"No, I'm absolutely not canceling my trip. But I'm afraid that if I think about it long enough, I'll feel like I should. Do you think I should cancel my trip?"

"You know I can't tell you what decision to make," Kathy answered. "But I do think that once you're able to build a relationship with God, He can help you find that answer."

I agreed.

"Have you considered that God might be the one who is actually placing this calling on your heart, in the first place?" Kathy asked.

"I know that's what other people would say about it, but I don't feel it. I guess I'm just not there yet."

I continued to see Kathy once a week. As I finished up my work for graduate school, and prepared to spend three whole months in Kenya, I sat with Kathy week after week and attempted to sort out my feelings.

Just like I had done with my classmates, I shared with Kathy my desire to find God on my own. I told her that if we are all meant to have a relationship with God, and that He is capable of reaching all of us who desire, then He will know exactly how to find me. All I had to do was sit back and wait, without any input or influence from others.

Kathy agreed strongly that my faith journey should be my own, and she was respectful of my wishes. However, she did stress the importance of keeping an open heart. She was concerned that my desire to challenge

God, might interfere with my willingness to hear Him. As badly as I wanted confirmation that He is present and working in my life, I continued to be very quick to push away the idea that anything coming into my life was an act of God, rather than luck or coincidence.

"Why do you think that is?" Kathy asked me one day. "Why do you think your first instinct continues to be finding an answer that excludes God, rather than one that includes Him?"

It was a good question, and I had been working hard over the past few months to figure out the answer to this, myself. I was about a month away from my return to Kenya at this point, and I wanted to be as enlightened as I could be by the time I was set to leave. Trying to understand my resistance to God, was a huge part of that process.

"In therapy, in the past, I've been given different tools to cope with my anxiety; Mindfulness exercises, breathing techniques, topics for journaling. I know that those things help me, that they're concrete tools that I can literally envision pulling out of a tool box."

Kathy kept her eyes on me, intrigued by where I was going with this.

"To be somewhere like Kenya, though, I'll need stronger tools. It can't be just about keeping myself calm and grounded for my own sake, but for the sake of others, who are suffering in ways that are painful beyond my scope of understanding. The tools that I have- my coping mechanisms- aren't enough to help me sustain the perspective that I'll need in order to help them, without consistently hurting myself. I get caught up in other people's pain very easily, and I know that I need a higher power to help me make sense of what's happening around me."

Kathy continued to listen.

"But if I am going to rely as heavily on God as I do my other coping skills, I need to know that He is just as concrete as the rest of them; if not more so. I want to feel Him in my life, without a shadow of a doubt, so that I won't wake up one day and think that He was just an illusion that I no longer feel connected to. And as long as I'm able to look at what's happening in my life, and credit something other than God, I know that I am still at a place where He is nothing more than a hopeful illusion to me. Does that make sense?"

Kathy nodded and wrote down a few notes.

"It does make sense. And I believe that is part of the process, because it'll make your confirmation from God that much stronger and sweeter."

"But what if that moment never comes? What if I never truly feel the presence of God?"

Kathy smiled as widely as I'd seen her smile since we started working together.

"I know I'm not supposed to influence you with my input, but I truly believe that that it will. The moment that you are searching for, will come.

While I was in graduate school, I worked part-time at a daycare. I loved working there because I've always loved working with children; not to mention my schedule was flexible and I made some great friends.

When I told them that I would be leaving my job to live in Kenya for three months, my co-workers, bosses, and all of the parents, were very loving and supportive of my decision. We celebrated together, and they helped to raise money for my mission. They donated bags of clothing, as well, and I couldn't have been more thankful.

I picked up as many shifts as I could before my last day. Since we spent so much of our time together, I was starting to feel sad about leaving my co-workers, and the kids, and wanted to soak up as much of them as I could. As ready as I was to leave, it was hard preparing to close such a significant chapter in my life.

Each day, my co-workers would ask me where I was in the planning process. They asked about my packing, how I was feeling, and if there was anything else that I needed. Not only did I feel incredibly loved, but I was as happy as I had ever been. Until everything came to a screeching halt.

About two weeks before my departure date, I received an email from Sarah Nicholson. She informed me that there was some turmoil in Kisumu that might jeopardize their ability to continue working there. Then she said that it would be best if I didn't come, because they weren't sure if their family would be able to stay there, and they didn't want to put me in a compromising position.

Well, Sweet Girl, talk about the world falling apart. I couldn't even finish the email. My mind went blank and I was thrown into a type of grief that I had never experienced before. I laid on my bed and cried for hours. I thought about the Nicholsons and Ringroad and all of those precious children. I was heartbroken over the turmoil that they were experiencing, and heartbroken that I couldn't be with them during such a difficult time.

In an instant, all of the planning, and the fund raising, and the dreaming of returning to my happy place, was over. I had finished school and quit my job. My bags were packed. Now I had to unpack them and figure out what I was going to do next. Of course, I had options, but I already knew that I didn't want to explore any of them. All I wanted, was Kenya.

Not knowing how else to share the news, I decided to send out a mass email to all of my family, friends and co-workers. Some people wrote back, some called or texted, but I didn't want to talk to anyone.

At work the next day, as soon as one of my co-workers gave me a hug, I fell apart. Just twenty-four hours ago, that same co-worker and I were standing in the very same spot, talking about how my packing was coming along. How could any of this be happening and what the hell was I going to do now?

I asked Mom to cancel my flights, as I was too much of a mess to take care of those logistics myself. Mom canceled the entire itinerary for me, which included two international flights through the same carrier. They could not refund my money, so they put it in an account for me to use when I was ready to go on another trip. Mom wrote down all of the cancelation information, and then it was over. My three-month trip to Kenya no longer existed.

Four two whole days, I was in mourning. I cried, I went to work, I came home, I cried some more, and went to bed. Per usual, Mom sprang into action and set herself on "Jen's In Crisis" mode- asking me how she could help and trying to draw out my appetite by offering up some of my favorite foods. She and Paul have a time share on the beach, and they offered to let me use it for a couple of weeks, so that I could clear my head and maybe even start working on the book that I always wanted to write. Anything to clear my head...

I decided to take them up on the timeshare thing, because I needed to get away from Tennessee. It was the first time in my life that I was seeking comfort *away* from home, rather than in it. I just couldn't bear the thought of my travel date coming and going, and leaving me behind. If I couldn't go to Kenya, then a beach in California it was.

On the third day after I received the news, I was still heartbroken, but I was moving forward. I reached out to Sarah and asked that they would please keep me updated on the situation in Kisumu. I told her that I loved them and that I wished I could be there. She responded and told me that they were working towards a resolution of the conflict, and that she would keep me posted.

A resolution? I thought. *There's hope!*

I tried praying. I prayed to God for a resolution; for safety and wisdom for all involved. I prayed that I would get to spend my three months in Kenya, after all.

And then, I received a phone call.

"Hey, Jen, you didn't cancel your flight yet, did you?" It was Chris Nicholson.

My heart leapt.

"I did. But if you give me the green light, I will re-book it right now," I told him.

"I'm giving you the green light. We worked everything out, and it looks like we'll be able to stay in Kisumu, so we would love to have you."

I dropped to my knees and cried. Mom immediately got online to re-book my trip.

"You know if we try to book you back on your original flights, those are going to cost a fortune by now," my mom said. "That itinerary is like ten days away, and last-minute tickets are extremely expensive."

I understood, and agreed, but I didn't want to waste any time. I couldn't risk leaving time for something else to happen, and my trip being canceled all over again.

"Please try to book something as close to my original dates as possible," I told her. "I just want to get there, and I don't care about the cost."

"Well you should," Mom replied. "You don't have endless amounts of money."

She got on the phone with the airline, and told them that I wanted to use the credit from a previous booking to make a new one. She gave them the confirmation number to my cancelation, and then she fell silent. There was of confusion on her face.

Oh, Lord have mercy, I thought. *What now?*

"Yes, she has a credit of almost two-thousand dollars, and that is the confirmation number. I have it written right here."

"Oh my God mom, they lost my money? Oh my God!"

Mom shook her head and waved her arms at me, signaling for me to be quiet. I felt like I was going to pass out, so I sat down on the floor and waited.

"Yes, that's correct. Those were her flights. Yes...okay but I don't understand...hang on let me get out those confirmation numbers right now."

I couldn't stand it.

"What is happening?" I yelled at her.

She held up her pointer finger, and my heart fell from my chest to the floor. I desperately needed to know what was going on.

"Yes, I'll hold."

Mom put her hand over the mouth piece of her phone.

83

"They said the refunded money isn't there anymore because your flights are re-booked already."

"What do you mean, my flights are re-booked? You didn't give them any information to book anything yet."

"I know that, Jen. They didn't book you *new* flights. Somehow your original flights have been re-booked already."

She perked up at the sound of someone's voice coming back onto the phone.

"Yes, I'm ready. Okay...yes those are the same confirmation numbers I have...but I don't understand...the flights were never canceled in the first place?...Oh, so they were canceled but then you re-booked them?...Yup...okay...I see...but then who re-booked them if you didn't?"

My heart was racing.

"Okay you know what, it doesn't matter. The bottom line is that they are booked now, is that correct? Yes? Okay, thank you so much, take care."

Mom hung up the phone and looked at me, still confused, but with a smile on her face.

"They had a record of your canceled flights; same confirmation number and everything. But yesterday, those flights were booked again, and they don't have a record of a person re-booking them."

"So...the flights re-booked themselves?"

"It appears that way. Unless...do you think the Nicholsons could have done it?"

"They didn't know what my itinerary was. And they also didn't tell me that I could come until today. You just said that my flights were re-booked yesterday."

Mom thought about this for a second.

"Oh yeah, that's right."

"So yesterday, while I was crying my eyes out about my canceled trip, my flights were already booked again?"

I could not believe that any of this was happening.

Mom nodded. "Yup."

"Wait, but were the prices the same?"

Mom's smile grew even wider. "You don't owe a penny more, and your seat assignments are exactly the same."

I screamed, I cried, and then I began telling every person that I knew. I was ecstatic, and in complete shock. I racked my brain as I tried to understand how this was possible, while every single person that I told, tried to convince me that this was an act of Divine Intervention.

By the time I had my next therapy appointment, I had a lot to catch Kathy up on. She didn't even know that I had to cancel in the first place, because all of this happened in between our appointments. As I told her the story, tears welled up in her eyes.

"People keep telling me that this was an act of God," I told her. "Like this was his confirmation to me that I belong in Kenya."

"Well, what do *you* think?"

I had been thinking about this for days. All I had wanted over these past six months, was a clear sign from God, a miracle; and according to everyone that I told this story to, I finally got one. But I wasn't convinced.

"Um, I don't really know. I want to believe that was Him, but it could have just as easily been a coincidence."

Kathy could not help but to let out a little laugh. "Wow, you are pretty stubborn when it comes to this, aren't you?"

"Yes, I am," I admitted. "Maybe that was an act of God, but I'm going to need another one to be sure that this wasn't a coincidence."

Chapter Nine

I don't know why Dad loves football so much.

I didn't know it was possible for something to seem boring and so confusing at the same time, but that's what football feels like to me. It's like nothing is happening and too much is happening, all at once.

Every Sunday, my Uncle Gary comes over and he and Dad watch football together. They cheer really loud when something good happens, and they don't like it when you accidentally walk in front of the TV. I know that because I've done it a bunch of times.

Dad's tried to explain this game to me, but I still don't get it. He says if I focus, then I can understand, but I guess I just don't care to. All I know, is that people who play football can get hurt pretty badly sometimes, and I don't want to see that.

I didn't mean to see it today; the player dropping down on the field. I was just walking through the living room, trying to find one of my toys, when I heard the whistles and looked over at the TV. The player was on the ground, and there was a crowd of people around him. Nothing looked wrong with his body, but you could tell he was hurt badly because he couldn't get up by himself. Emergency people had to come on the field and get him.

I wonder if he was scared. I bet his family was scared when they saw that happen. Maybe he has little kids, and they were so upset to learn that their dad was hurt. I know I'd be scared if that were my dad.

Ever since I saw that fall happen this afternoon, I can't get the sadness out of my brain. I can't stop wondering how he's feeling, or how his family is feeling. It's almost dinner time, but thinking about him is making me lose my appetite.

I really hope that he isn't in pain, and that he isn't scared.

I hope his family isn't scared.

I hope he can play football again someday...although I don't know why he'd want to.

~ ~ ~

Dear Sweet Girl,

There aren't words to describe how relieved I felt when I landed back in Kenya. It was September of 2014, and I was set to live in Kisumu for three whole months. I had raised enough money to support myself, and to give towards community needs, as I saw fit. It was hard saying goodbye to Mom, especially since we hadn't spent more than ten days apart in quite some time. But she knew I had to go.

After getting a brief glimpse of what life would feel like if Kenya wasn't a part of my future, I knew beyond a shadow of a doubt that I made the right decision by going back. Sure, I still had a lot to figure out, but I felt very strongly that Kenya was the place to do that. There was something there for me, and I needed to figure out what it was.

Going into these three months, I knew that there would be some challenges. Although Kenya had become my "Happy Place," I wasn't disillusioned enough to think that living there would feel the same as visiting. It was time to learn how to be independent and create a life for myself, in a country and a culture that weren't my own. This would sound like an absolute nightmare to you, I know, but I was very much up for the challenge. There was nowhere in the world I wanted to be more than Kisumu, Kenya.

Prior to my arrival, Chris and Sarah let me know that I would be able to stay in their home for the majority of my time there. They had some other visitors, and a few prior commitments scheduled for the month of September, so we agreed that I would stay at St. Anne's Guest House during that time. I would then move in with them in October, and stay until I left Kenya, right before Christmas.

Since I was familiar with St. Anne's, and it was walking distance from the Nicholsons, I felt comfortable with this arrangement. My room was tiny, and I definitely had moments where I felt lonely, but I knew that it was important for me to learn how to live on my own. I went grocery shopping for myself, and the staff at St. Anne's let me use their kitchen to prepare my own meals. I hand-washed my clothes, and hung them across a make-shift clothing line that I put up across the center of my room.

Sarah taught me how to properly sanitize my fruits and vegetables, and showed me which brands of food were most reminiscent of what we have in the States. Chris introduced me to the tuk-tuk drivers that they used and trusted most, and I made arrangements with them to drive me around on a daily basis. When I had been with a group, I enjoyed walking to Ringroad, but it felt different doing it alone. I was shouted and whistled at a lot more aggressively when I was alone, and found that receiving that kind of attention was one of the hardest things to adjust to. I really just wanted to blend in.

September was all about finding my bearings in town, and carving out a place for myself at Ringroad. It was important for me to figure out where I could be most helpful, and then put together a schedule of what my days and weeks would look like. Of course, there was always the possibility that something would come up and flip our entire day upside down, but Chris and Sarah encouraged me to have a general idea of what my weekly routine at Ringroad would consist of. This way, I wouldn't have to start each day by wandering around looking for something to do, and getting suckered into doing trivial tasks that didn't necessarily require outside help.

It was in trying to establish this routine, that I began to see what Aunt Mindy and the man from the senior center had been talking about. While I found joy in helping the students and teachers in any capacity that I could, it was clear to me- almost immediately- that my purpose for spending three months with them needed to be bigger and more impactful than grading papers and serving porridge. I loved doing those things, and still volunteered to do them every once in a while, because they brought me great joy; but they were also things that would be done each day, whether I was there or not. What could I offer this community that they would benefit from, and weren't already receiving?

One thing that Sarah mentioned to me, was the need and desire for Ringroad School to have a Guidance Counselor. Each student was facing his or her own challenges, some of which were severe enough to leave them debilitated on a daily basis. They would come to school each day bearing the burden of a sick, dying or abusive parent or guardian; hunger homelessness, or an untreated medical condition. They carried these burdens with them, and were expected to perform well in school in spite of them. Some students were able to strike a balance that helped them manage, while many, not surprisingly, could not.

Myself, the Nicholsons, and Director Jared, agreed that the best use of my time would be in working with the school's most vulnerable students. In a western culture like ours, every single one of Ringroad's students would be considered vulnerable. They were all impoverished, and most of them had endured the death of at least one parent. Many were exposed to various types of abuse. However, the deeper you dive into a community of vulnerable people, the more clearly you see the different levels of vulnerability that exist.

Given that I wasn't familiar enough with the background of each student, or how they were performing in school, we decided that the teachers and the administrators would bring me the students that they felt needed the most help. I was confident in my newly designated counseling role, and was ready to use the tools that I had acquired through graduate school and years of therapy, to help these kids process through their own obstacles.

We'll call my fist student, Liliane.

I was introduced to Liliane by her class teacher, who told me that she was sleeping in class, wasn't completing her assignments, and that her home life was extraordinarily difficult. According to her school records, Liliane lived with her mother and her two younger siblings, but her mother frequently left them in order to find ways to make money. This meant that Liliane often found herself in charge at home, at the ripe old age of eleven.

"It is also believed that she's been raped many times," her teacher told me.

I didn't want to believe this.

"How do you know that?"

"Because people around here know her family and where they used to stay. They know what's been done to her."

I felt sick.

"Do You know if that's still happening to her?"

"I don't know. But maybe you can find out."

When I think about you, Little One, the first thing I think about is your need to feel safe and secure. All children have this need, but not all of them live in an environment that nurtures it. You see, one of the greatest gifts you've been given in this life, is the assurance by Mom and Dad that you are loved and cared for, every single day. You may live in fear of your world coming undone, but you've never questioned whether someone would be there to catch you if it did.

You've been wrapped in a blanket of unconditional love from the day you were born, and you developed the ability to recognize that at a very young age. You lean into this love, and rely on it when you feel like you need to be held together. And, because you rely so heavily on the promise that Mom and Dad's love will always be there, you will grow up with a fire in your heart for those who don't have the same thing. Liliane is one of those people.

In trying to prepare for my meeting with Liliane, I remembered something that was discussed in my Multi-cultural Counseling class. In a western culture, it is often encouraged for victims of trauma to process that trauma through various forms of counseling. In order for a client to do that, a therapist must ensure that the client feels safe enough, and that they have a physically and emotionally safe place return to, after their session is over. To encourage someone to dive into their deepest and darkest emotions, and then knowingly send them home to a situation that isn't considered to be safe, is viewed as unethical, because it may cause further emotional distress.

In the slums of developing countries, where safety at home is often in question, and there aren't always community resources to turn to in times when safety is threatened, encouraging a person to process their trauma may not be the best option. If they aren't in a position where they can move away from the source of the trauma, it may be best to encourage them in other ways.

The day that I met Liliane, I gave her a small notebook and asked her to draw pictures of things that made her happy. She drew flowers, hearts, pictures of her friends, and food.

"It looks like you have a lot of things in your life that make you feel happy," I affirmed. "That's great!"

Liliane didn't say anything, but she gave the tiniest, faintest hint of a smile.

On the next page, I asked her to write what she loved most about herself. That's where she got stuck.

"Hmmm, let's see…are you kind to your friends?"

Liliane nodded and wrote that down.

"Are you respectful of your teachers?"

Again, Liliane nodded and wrote.

"Those are great qualities to have. Now try to think of another one. What is another thing that you love about yourself?"

Liliane sat quietly and stared down at her notebook, her pencil hovered over the page as she tried to think of something. Finally, without looking up at me, she said,

"I try my best in school."

Her answer made my heart hurt. There she was, sitting with me because her teacher felt she stopped caring about school, while she felt she was trying her best. It may not have looked like it, but for sweet Liliane, simply showing up was trying her best.

That afternoon, when I returned to St. Anne's, I cried for what felt like hours. Over the time that I had spent in Kenya so far, it seemed like I was constantly learning of a new level of vulnerability, and struggling to wrap my mind around them all. There was Joanie, and Brighton, and Caroline; and now there was Liliane.

These were the people and the stories that awakened my desire to know God, and I was so discouraged that I hadn't found Him yet. It had been my hope that I'd have some understanding of who God is; or, at least be at a place where I could acknowledge His existence, before I started my three months in Kenya. That way, when I came across heartbreak like Liliane's, I'd be able to use Him as a compass, like I had seen other people do.

As Kathy and I had discussed, when it came to finding God, I was open, but skeptical. After meeting Liliane, I was also becoming impatient.

I'd like to share another story with you; one that to this day brings me back to remembering why you fear the world so much. To know that such tragedies and injustices exist, and to still feel that you want to go out and explore the world anyway, is something that doesn't feel like a possibility to you. If I'm being honest, it doesn't always feel like a possibility to me, either. I'm still working on it.

Anyway, it was a Sunday afternoon, and I was tired. I had gone to church at Ringroad that morning, and then spent some time with Sarah and Ruth-Michael. I was still living at St. Anne's, and Sarah would bring Ruth-Michael over to visit me there, almost every day.

After they left on this day, I decided to take a nap. I'm not sure how long I had been sleeping, when I started to hear screams just outside of my window. I was used to hearing screams, as the house directly behind St. Anne's, had children living there. Each day I would hear them play, and they always ended up fighting with one another. But this sound was different. It was louder and more frantic.

Still in a slight daze from my nap, I rolled over and thought: *It sounds like someone's leg is being chopped off.*

I listened for another moment, trying to decipher if it actually sounded like someone was being hurt, or if the noises were being exaggerated in my head. I could have sat up and looked out my window, but I didn't. My gut told me that those weren't playful screams, and I was afraid to see what was causing them.

I knew that the emergency response system in Kenya is different from what we have in the U.S., so I wasn't sure what I should do. Suddenly, the screaming stopped, but I wanted to make sure that everything was okay. I headed down to the front desk to ask if they had heard the screaming, too, and if we should report it to someone.

When I reached the lobby, I found the staff hovering around Reception. All of them were quiet, and their heads were hanging down.

"Hey, did you all hear the screaming from outside?"

"Yes," replied one of the housekeepers.

"The man in that house has just stabbed his wife to death with a knife."

My brain couldn't make sense of this.

"Wait. Someone was *murdered* back there just now?"

"Yes."

My legs were numb.

"How do you know that for sure?"

"Someone who saw the murder just came in and told us."

I ran back upstairs, before my legs had a chance to give out. As soon as I opened the door, I fell to my knees and threw up in the washing basin, because I couldn't make it to the toilet.

With shaking hands, I called Sarah's phone, and asked that she or Chris come and pick me up. The sun was setting and I didn't want to sit in a small hotel room, alone with my thoughts.

The Nicholsons were just about to eat dinner when I called. Chris picked me up and brought me back to their house, where I took a seat at the dinner table but didn't attempt to eat a single bite of food. I felt sick to my stomach. I replayed the woman's screams over and over again in my head.

"She was murdered in front of her children," I cried to Chris and Sarah after dinner.

"She had children, and they were there. I heard them playing before my nap. They watched their father murder their mother."

My words were heavy, but my mouth felt numb as I spoke them. I couldn't believe such a cruel, senseless, heartbreaking act occurred right outside of my window. I wished I could have stopped it; that I could have reacted sooner. I expressed this to Chris and Sarah.

"I promise, even if you had reacted quicker, you couldn't have done anything to stop it," Chris said.

"Even if you asked to call somebody, no one would have come in time. Emergency responders don't work here like that."

"I'm so sorry, Jen." Sarah sat down next to me and put her arm around my shoulders.

"I know it just feels like too much sometimes."

I continued to cry, because I wasn't able to stop myself.

"Yeah, it feels like too much. Especially when you're living here. The whole experience feels different, now that it's not just a visit."

Both Sarah and Chris nodded.

"You know, we see that a lot." Chris shared.

"We have people who come to visit and they fall so in love that they want to come back. So, they come back expecting to feel that same magic; but what they realize is that it actually gets harder, because they end up seeing more."

I thought about how magical everything felt when I arrived in Kenya for the first time. It seemed like so long ago, but it was just over a year earlier that my first group from Lipscomb made their trip.

"The people who struggle with the magic wearing off, are the ones who tend not to want to come back."

That made sense to me, and I would've thought for sure that I'd be one of those people. Why continue to put yourself in a place that surrounds you with heartbreak, when you have a choice to walk away?

"Well, I can tell you for sure that the magic has worn off," I whispered. My throat was tired and sore, my eyes burning and swollen. "But this is my fourth time here in just over a year. I jumped from ten-day visits to a three month stay. So…what does that say about me?"

We all started to giggle a little bit, my swollen eyes struggling to stay open.

Sarah got up to grab her glass of water from the dining table, as she gave me her answer.

"Well, I think it says that God's showing you your place here."

Chapter Ten

I love Grandma and Grandpa, but I don't like visiting them without Mom.

They do fun things with us, like take us to the toy store and let us put on shows for them, but then at night I get scared that something bad is going to happen. Grandparents are old, and my grandparents even smoke cigarettes; which are bad for you. I get scared that they're going to die in their sleep, and that I won't know what to do.

Would I run to a neighbor's house and ring the doorbell?

Do I even know how to call 911?

I'd have to call Mom, too, and I don't know how to dial her number. I know what her number is, but I don't know how to use that phone in Grandma and Grandpa's kitchen.

Sometimes, I want to tell Mom or Grandma that I'm afraid of this, but I don't want to hurt Grandma's feelings or make anyone feel sad. So, I always decide not to say anything.

We had a fun night tonight. We ate dinner at my favorite restaurant in Grandma and Grandpa's town, and I got to order baked ziti. Grandpa taught me all about baked ziti, the first time that they ever took me to eat at that restaurant. I was really little then, but now that I'm six, I can even read the menu and find where the baked ziti is, by myself.

Z-I-T-I. That's what I look for on the menu.

After we got home from the restaurant, Grandma gave Jake and I a bath, and then she let us watch a movie. I was so happy laying in Grandma and Grandpa's bed watching the movie on their TV, but I knew that I would start to feel sad and scared once it was over. That meant it was time for bed, so Jake and I would have to move to the guest room down the hall. I like that I get to share a room with my brother, but I still feel scared when we're there in the dark, and we don't know if something is going to happen to them in the middle of the night.

It took Jake a while to fall asleep, and that made me happy because I didn't have to stay awake alone. He's younger than me, but he has lots of energy, and he likes to be silly and move around a lot before he falls asleep.

Now that it's just me who's awake, I lay still and listen for Grandma and Grandpa. They always watch TV in bed, and fall asleep without turning it off. Grandpa snores really loud, though, so I listen for that sound to let me know that he is okay.

I listen and listen, until I can't keep my eyes open anymore.

~ ~ ~

Dear Sweet Girl,

As you would probably imagine, I had some things to process from my three months in Kenya. There were moments of joy that I wanted to celebrate, and a whole lot of pain that I needed to come to terms with. Needless to say, booking an appointment with Kathy was one of the first things I did upon returning to the United States.

My first session back with Kathy was in January of 2015. I had been in Kenya up until Christmas time, and Kathy was out of her office for winter break. As soon as she returned to her office in January, so did I; saddled with stories, questions and personal revelations.

Of course, the biggest event that I needed to work through, was the murder of my backyard neighbor. After she died, I wanted to find a way to honor her memory, so I asked the staff at St. Anne's if I could plant a small garden on their property. What I really wanted to do, was check and make sure that her children were okay, but I didn't have the option to do that. We received word at St. Anne's that the children were taken to stay with relatives, and that they were going to try and sell the house. The husband had attempted suicide immediately after he committed the murder, but he lived, and was taken away to jail.

The garden was a small gesture, but I wanted to create a peaceful space where my friends at St. Anne's could go throughout the day to pray, or just relax. They all took such good care of me whenever I stayed there, and I knew that they had been shaken by our neighbor's murder, just like I was.

When I first introduced the idea of a memorial garden to them, they thought my intention was to create a space for the woman's body to be buried.

"Oh no, Jen, it is not possible to do that," one of the receptionists had said. "In our culture, it is a must that people are to be buried at their family's homestead. We cannot just have the body brought here."

I was half humored, and half mortified, that they believed I would take it upon myself to decide where a stranger's body should be buried. I didn't even know the sweet woman's name. I tried asking around, but no one knew.

After clarifying myself and my intentions for the garden, I could tell the staff at St. Anne's were still a bit confused. They liked the idea of a garden, and designated a sunny little spot on the compound for me to use, but they couldn't quite understand why I would want to create something in memory of a person that I didn't know.

"Did you find that planting the garden was therapeutic to you in any way?" Kathy asked me, after I told her the story.

"Kind of. I mean, since she died in such a horrific way, I wanted to attach her memory to something peaceful, you know? I wanted to create a space where my friends at St. Anne's could go and pray or cry, or just have some quiet time to reflect."

"Mmm. And you?"

"What about me?"

"How were you hoping to use the garden?"

Kathy's voice was soft, and I knew what she was getting at.

"I couldn't help her, or save her," my voice cracked. Ten minutes back in therapy and I was already breaking down into tears.

"So, I thought creating something beautiful, that could help bring others peace, would be a nice way to honor her."

"And were you, yourself, hoping to find peace there, too?"

I let out a tiny sob and reached for the box of tissues that was sitting on the book shelf next to me.

"Yes. A woman was murdered, while I was laying in my comfy bed and listening to her scream. I didn't know that's what was happening at the time, and I know that I couldn't have done anything to stop it; no one stopped it."

"That's right," Kathy asserted, as forcefully as I'd ever heard her assert anything.

"You could not have done anything to stop it."

I nodded in agreement and blew my nose into the tissue.

"I Keep thinking about her pain, though. Like, the pain she was in during her final moments on earth. I can't get past it."

"I can imagine that must be a hard thing to process. Have you been able to acknowledge that she is at peace now? That she is no longer suffering?"

"I tell myself that a lot, but I find I'm focused more on her last moments of pain, than I am her peace. I think that's part of why I started the garden. I'm trying to erase her pain with peace."

Per usual, Kathy jotted some things down on her notepad.

"Where do you see God in this story? Do you see Him in her peace?"

I thought about God a lot during my three months in Kenya. It was my first time being back there since I felt fully ready to see Him, to feel Him and to hear Him.

My desire was strong, but I was never able to connect the dots I felt I needed to. I regurgitated words to the children at Ringroad, about how God is with them, and that He loves them, because that's what they were being taught. And, to be honest, it seemed like those words did bring a certain level of comfort to the children. However, I'd be lying if I told myself, or Kathy, that I believed any of it.

"I really, really want to tell you that I could place God in that situation. But I keep replaying her pain, and that stops me."

Kathy and I spent the rest of my session mulling over the same dilemma I'd been facing for months. I wanted to build a foundation of faith but I didn't know how, nor did I want anyone to show me. I wanted God to reveal Himself in a way that made sense to me; that I wouldn't question or deny. Up to this point, I was continuing to question everything.

Finally, at the end of my session, Kathy asked me the question that she had been skating around since the beginning.

"What do you think you need God to reveal to you, that you won't be able to deny any longer?"

"What do you mean?"

I thought I knew what she meant, but I wanted her to explain it anyway.

"There have been moments in your life, and in the lives of those around you, that others would consider to be 'God moments.' The rebooking of your plane tickets is a big one that comes to mind."

"Yeah, that was pretty crazy."

Kathy smiled. "It seems that you are waiting for a very specific moment from God, and up to this point, you've not defined what that is because you've not been able to."

"Right."

"What I'm asking is, now that you've spent time searching for understanding, do you have a more defined idea of how you'd like to see God reach you?"

I was slightly taken aback by the timing of Kathy's question. After three months in Kenya and a desired faith that still seemed to be missing, I found myself asking this question every single day.

What am I looking for? What would be the "thing" that God could do to let me see Him once and for all?

"I actually have been thinking about this a lot, and I hadn't figured it out until just now."

Kathy was delighted by this.

"Oh good! Would you like to share your thoughts on that with me?"

I took a deep breath.

"Yes. I think I need to watch somebody die."

"Oh. Okay. Can you explain that a bit further for me?"

The evident surprise on Kathy's face made me smile. I knew that my answer would catch her off guard, and it sort of caught me off guard, too. It was an unexpected answer, to say the least.

For as long as you've been alive, Sweet Girl, you've feared death. You've feared your own death, the death of a loved one; and you passed that fear on to me. Losing someone that I love is my biggest fear in the world. It is the ultimate way that the world could turn on us. In all of the ways that life fails to make sense to you, and subsequently, me, death is biggest.

In processing the death of my backyard neighbor, I started to notice how often I pictured someone coming to pick her up. I would replay her screams in my head, and then I would imagine a presence coming down and wrapping itself around her. Eventually, her screaming stopped, and she was at peace.

Up until this moment in Kathy's office, the peace that covered my neighbor, didn't have a name. I would acknowledge it, and then immediately switch back to focusing on her pain, because that's what spoke louder to me at the time.

"I've heard people say that we are closest to God, as physical beings, when we are born and when we die. Those are the times in our physical lives when God's presence is closest to us. So, maybe if I'm with a person when they die, I'll feel God come to that person. Does that make sense?"

"It does make sense. Although, I have to tell you, I've never heard this one before."

This didn't surprise me.

"I know it's weird, and kind of dark. But I think if I watch what happens when God takes someone, I'll feel Him."

It was a heavy answer to a somewhat-loaded question. As soon as I said it, though, it felt like a weight had been lifted.

And, like always, Kathy listened without judgement.

When I walked into the house that afternoon, I was greeted by Grandpa Teppy. He and Grandma moved in with Mom and Paul shortly before I did, because they were getting older and Mom wanted them close by. They lived in a separate part of the house, but I always entered through their side, so that I could say hello.

"Oh, you're back!" Grandpa Teppy said with as much enthusiasm as he could muster up at his age.

"How ya doin', Hun?"

I walked over to the chair that he sat in during most of his waking hours, and gave Grandpa a kiss on the forehead.

"Hi, Tep. I'm good, how are you doing?"

"Eh, you know, same as I was doing yesterday and the day before. Nothing exciting to report here."

I rubbed Tep's shoulder and told him that I would be down later for dinner. Grandma loved to cook for us, and nothing made her happier than the nights that I would join them for dinner.

That night, Grandpa didn't eat very much. Grandma kept trying to force-feed him, as she did with anyone who had the audacity to sit at her table and not eat the food that she prepared, but Grandpa wouldn't budge. Instead, he excused himself early, and went back to the living room to sit in his chair.

"You feeling okay, Tep?" I asked him.

"I don't know, Hun. I feel a little bit cold and my bones ache a bit. But I'll be fine."

Mom was working, so I called Paul down to the apartment, and then took Grandpa's temperature. He had a fever, and his shaking seemed to be intensifying. Due to his age, and a couple of pre-existing medical conditions, Paul and I decided it was best to take him to the walk-in clinic.

Grandpa, being the stubborn man that he was, didn't want to go to the clinic. It was a cold January night, and he didn't feel like going out in that weather. That's what he told us; that he didn't feel like going out in the cold. Can you not hear him saying that? That's so Grandpa Tep, isn't it?

Paul and I knew that he also didn't want us to worry, which is why he told us that he would drive himself to the doctor if he still didn't feel well in the morning. We refused this suggestion, and ultimately convinced Grandpa to put on his warmest clothing, and get in the car.

100

Thankfully there was no wait at the clinic, so he was seen right away. After being examined by the nurse and briefly speaking to the doctor, it was recommended that we take Grandpa to the emergency room. Being in his mid-eighties, with congested lungs in the middle of Flu season, was a cause for concern.

Even with a doctor's opinion, Grandpa didn't want to go to the emergency room. He thought it was silly, and tried suggesting again that we wait until morning.

He was too tired and weak to argue for long, so he eventually laid his head back and fell asleep in the passenger seat. Paul drove, and I called Mom.

Before we reached the hospital, when I had a moment to think in the car, I thought about you. To me, the epicenter of your brain, sort of resembles an emergency room. There is chaos and distress and urgency in emergency rooms. People are suffering, some are dying, and even though there are glimpses of hope in the miracles that they witness, those aren't necessarily the first thing we think about in association with that place. After all, it's literally called an "Emergency" Room, and they are always preparing for the worst.

I was afraid to go back there with Grandpa, because I was afraid of what else I would see. I pictured all of those medical shows on TV, that made emergency rooms look exactly like what I just described, with all of the chaos and the suffering. I knew that if you were to ever see those things in real life, you'd probably never recover. So, did that mean that I would never recover, either?

No, I knew better than that. My loved one needed me, and I was going to be there for him. They wheeled Grandpa back, and Paul and I followed. The lights were bright, and it smelled like latex gloves and sanitizer. I was surprised by how quiet it was, even though it was clearly a busy space. The doctors, nurses, and administrators whirred around in completely organized chaos.

Oh My God, I thought. *This is it. God is showing me something here.*

It wasn't even six hours earlier that I had been sitting in Kathy's office, telling her that I felt God would reach me through witnessing a death. Suddenly, I found myself in an emergency room, surrounded by people who were clinging to their lives, and I was overcome by a presence that was telling me to pay attention.

I watched a nurse write down information on a huge white board that hung in the middle of the emergency room triage. Another nurse lifted her hand beneath the automatic hand sanitizing pump outside of a patient's room, then opened the door with the same ease that I walk into my own home with. They all knew exactly what they were doing; and if there was any fear in them, you couldn't even see a glimpse of it.

Mom, Paul, Grandma and I waited in the hallway, as they wheeled Grandpa down for a chest x-ray.

"You know, sweetie, you don't have to wait here if this feels like too much for you," Mom said to me. "This could be a while, and we've got both cars here, so you may as well take one home."

I told Mom that I didn't want to leave, that I felt like I needed to stay. Then I continued to stand in the hallway outside Grandpa's room, and watch the flurry of activity around me.

As I watched, I found myself wondering where our ability and desire to care for others comes from. I thought about the impossible number of steps that the human race needed to conquer- the endless trials, errors and new discoveries- to get to where we were in that moment. Not only had those doctors and nurses been equipped with the knowledge and wisdom necessary to save another human life, but they had the compassion and desire to do so. We value life so much, that these people were going to great lengths to save human beings that they didn't even know.

Why do we fight so hard for our lives and the lives of others?

Where does compassion come from?

Where does our ability to love come from?

Where does our ability to grieve come from?

I stood in the middle of the emergency room, asking myself each of these questions, and knowing that God was showing up for me. He was guiding me, by allowing me to see Him in each of the people who were working so hard to save the lives of others.

Grandpa Tep was diagnosed with Pneumonia. They admitted him, since Pneumonia is very dangerous for an elderly person, who already has a pre-existing Pulmonary disease. We went to visit him every day, and while we knew there was a chance that he wouldn't make it out of the hospital, I felt very strongly that we would get to bring him home. Therefore, when he was discharged less than a week later, I was overwhelmed with gratitude, but I wasn't surprised.

Aunt Mindy flew down to help us care for Grandpa at home. His Pneumonia was gone, but he was still weak and in need of constant care. I told Mom that I thought this was the beginning of Grandpa's journey toward his final phase in life, and that he would likely continue to decline. I didn't want to scare her, nor did I feel ready to come to terms with this myself, but I wanted us to be prepared. I was terrified, but I let God know that I was open to see what He had in store for us during this time.

The next four months were filled with some of the most beautiful moments of my life. I had planned on going back to Kenya for the second half of the year, and using the first half to work and raise money for that trip. Because of this, I was able to pick up some shifts at the daycare again, and spend the time that I wasn't working, at home with the family. I was able to see my friends, too, but they were unbelievably gracious in working around the schedule I had with Grandpa. Being available to take care of him was a priority for me.

He had moments where he seemed to be improving, and moments that scared us enough to bring him back to the emergency room. He slowly began to lose his faculties, and even on his "good days," I could tell that his body was tired.

Grandpa Teppy was a proud man, and, as I mentioned before, a stubborn one. He never wanted to admit when he needed help, so getting him to accept it was often a big challenge. Thanks to his insurance, we were able to get him enrolled in home-health care, and a nurse would come by to check his vitals every once in a while. If his condition worsened, they would come to us. No more doctor's offices, no more emergency rooms.

Eventually, the transition was made from basic home-health care, to hospice care. Grandpa Tep remained at home, but the primary goal of his treatment shifted from treating his symptoms to just keeping him comfortable. He was still able to walk with assistance, so we would get him out of bed each morning and move him to his chair in the living room, so that he could watch TV. Towards the end, there were days that he would just sit in his chair for hours without turning the TV on.

"Do you think he forgot how to use the remote?" Mom asked the visiting hospice nurse one day.

"No, he didn't forget," she answered.

Mom, Paul and I were sitting on the couch together in our living room. It was separate from my grandparents' space, and we always had meetings with the visiting nurse, before she would go check on Grandpa. It was our time to ask questions and receive guidance, as caring for a dying loved one is not something that the average person does on a regular basis.

"Well then why isn't he turning on the TV?" My mom continued.

"Oftentimes, when a person is approaching the end of their life, they turn inward and start to reflect a lot more," the nurse responded.

She removed some brochures from her bag and passed them out to us as she spoke.

"This could mean a number of things: maybe that he is rectifying his mistakes and regrets with God, or maybe he is reliving past events from the course of his life…we can't really know unless we ask him."

"Wait a second, we can't ask him that, can we?" There was an uneasiness in Mom's voice. She was afraid.

"Are we supposed to sit him down and tell him that he is dying and then ask him what he is thinking about?"

All of the nurses from the agency had been kind to us, but this one was particularly gentle and patient.

"Well, he does know that he is dying. His soul is preparing to transition, and that is something that your father is sensing. As far as asking him what he is thinking about, that is completely up to you."

I sat next to Mom and listened to the nurse's words. I was so afraid of losing Grandpa Tep, but I had sensed that this was coming for months now. It wasn't something that I was running from, it was something that I was embracing, because God was guiding me to. This I knew for certain.

After we finished asking our questions, my mom brought the nurse down to see how Tep was doing. I sat and read the information that she had given us, because I wanted to know the signs that we were supposed to look for, as Tep walked through the "Phases of Dying." The first thing I learned: that there are phases of dying.

One responsibility that I took on, was helping Tep get to bed each night. This was a multi-step process, the details of which I will keep private out of respect for our grandfather's dignity, but it was a routine that I began to cherish.

That was our time, when Tep was vulnerable enough to let me take care of him, but still strong enough to talk to me as my grandfather. It was a time that that just the two of us shared, and I never skipped out on it. Even when I would make plans to have dinner or drinks with friends, I would set those plans for after I tucked Grandpa Tep into.

Eventually, when Tep started getting weaker and was spending less time awake, the hospice team ordered him a fully-functioning, electronic hospital bed, and set it up in their living room. They brought in an oxygen machine, and a box full of medications that were to be used to keep Tep comfortable. Myself, Mom and Paul were taught how to use the bed and the oxygen, and how to administer the medication. We were told, based on the way that he was presenting, that Tep likely had less than a week.

"I would say it is time to call your family now," the nurse told us.

Mom alerted Aunt Min, Aunt Jill, and other extended relatives. Jake had come to see Tep a couple of weeks prior, and that had been his "goodbye." Some relatives called, but were not able to make the trip down to Tennessee.

As soon as Aunt Min, Aunt Jill, and cousin Jacqueline booked their flights to come and be with us, Mom let Tep know that they were coming, as per the advice of one of our nurses.

"But won't that freak him out if he knows all of these people are coming to see him?" Mom had asked her.

The nurse then gently reminded Mom that Tep knows he is dying.

"I just don't want him to be scared," Mom expressed through her tears.

"Trust me," she had said, "This is a lot scarier for you than it is for him. Your father isn't scared at all."

Aunt Jill arrived first. After days of sleeping almost constantly, Tep perked up upon the arrival of his youngest child. He was talking, more so than he had in days, and he actually wanted to do things.

"Maybe this isn't really it?" My mom wondered aloud to us.

But I had read the brochures. I knew that Grandpa Tep was rallying. This was his "last hurrah," and although it was scary to think about what was likely coming next, all of us wanted to enjoy that time while we had it.

Tep asked for music, a cigar and a good shave. He always shaved for important events, so when he asked for one before he died, I thought to myself that he wanted to look handsome when he reached Heaven.

The next time we got a visit from one of the nurses, Mom told her about Tep's sudden burst of energy. This did not surprise the nurse one bit, but she was delighted to learn that we had that wonderful day together, and that Tep got his wishes.

"How long will he be up like this?" mom asked.

"Are there any other family members who are coming to see him, that he knows about?"

"Yes," Mom answered.

"My niece, Jacqueline, is arriving tomorrow."

"So, if your dad knows that one more loved one is coming, he will wait for her. Once he sees her, that is probably when he will go to sleep."

"Go to sleep like…*die,* you mean?"

"Well, he won't necessarily pass right away, but once he enters that state of sleep, it will only be a matter of time."

I was intrigued by the nurse's ability to be gentle, but direct. It was scary to think about the days ahead, and none of us really knew how to prepare, but being guided through the process was a huge help to all of us.

I also found it fascinating that the mind, body and spirit go through such a defined process when preparing to cross over from the physical world. This was a journey that so many had been on, and that so many had the opportunity to bear witness to, that people like us were able to read about those experiences and use them to guide us through that journey of our own loved ones. I just knew there had to be more to that than simple coincidence.

Like clockwork, Tep stayed awake long enough to greet Jacqueline when she arrived. They had a full conversation, and he was so happy to see her. That night, it took Mom, Paul and I to move him from his chair to the hospital bed, which was less than two feet away. He had no strength left, but just as the nurse predicted, he stayed awake long enough for his last visitor to arrive. We tucked him in, said goodnight, and then he went to sleep.

The next day, we took turns checking on him. His eyes remained closed but he could sometimes nod in response, if we asked him a question. He still responded to his name.

We all happened to be gathered at his bedside, when Mom called us up for dinner. Each one of us gave him a kiss, and we told him that we would be back down to check on him after we ate.

Everyone stood to go upstairs, when Tep suddenly held his hand up and pointed in my direction.

"Jenny…." he whispered.

I sat back down at his side and held his hand in mine.

"Yeah, Tep? I'm here"

"Jenny…stay" he whispered again.

"You want me to stay down here with you?"

He barely breathed a "Yes," but it was clear enough for me.

"Just me?"

"Yes."

The rest of the family went upstairs for supper and I stayed by Grandpa's side. We didn't speak, but I knew that he was trying to show me something. It was almost as if God had spoken to him and told him what I needed. Tep seemed to know exactly what I had been searching for, and that God was using him to show me. I knew that Tep was not dying for me or because of me; but in his inevitable passing, he was giving me a gift. And he knew it.

Eventually, I got up and joined the rest of my family. We ate, we talked, we laughed some and cried some, and then we went back down to say goodnight to Grandpa. We told him that it was okay, he could go, and that we would take good care of Grandma.

In the middle of the night, while no one was watching, Grandpa Tep passed away. The nurse had predicted that he would pass while he was alone, once we all had a chance to tell him that it was okay to go. She had said that he likely wouldn't want to "burden" us, and that he would feel free to make that final transition on his own. And that's exactly what he did.

When the funeral home came to take Tep's body away, I went down to see him one last time. I kissed his forehead, told him I loved him, and vowed over his body that I would never deny God's presence, ever again.

In Loving Memory of Grandpa Tep and Grandma Joan

Chapter Eleven

I'm not afraid of the doctor's office.

I know a lot of kids don't like the doctor, but he's the one who knows how to make us feel better, so I don't mind it. I like that he can tell what's wrong by looking at me. When I'm with my therapist, I have to explain what's bothering me, because she can't see. But when I go to my regular doctor, he can figure out what's wrong, and how to fix it, just from looking at my body.

The only time I don't really like the doctor is when I have to go for a physical. Every year we have to go see him, even if we don't feel sick, so that he can make sure we are growing and developing properly. At least, that's what Mom says; and I guess it makes sense. I'm just always afraid that he's going to find something wrong with me, that we didn't know about before. I know that happens to some kids.

Today is a Physical Day. I've mostly been feeling fine and healthy, besides the days that I don't have an appetite, and I know that Dr. Leonard is going to ask me about that. I think he's the one who suggested those disgusting drinks that Mom and Dad are giving me.

Before I go in to see Dr. Leonard, the lady at the front desk gives me a cup to pee in. Then when I'm done, she has me stand in a doorway, put my hand over one eye at a time, and read letters off of a chart. Some of the letters are big, some are small, and I can see all of them.

"Perfect eye sight!" She tells me, and I feel proud.

After my eye test is done, she brings me and Mom into the room where Dr. Leonard will see me. I climb onto the exam table, and the paper that covers it makes a crinkling sound. I don't know why, but I really hate that sound.

We only have to wait a few minutes before Dr. Leonard comes in. He shakes Mom's hand, and asks her how everything is going, then he turns and starts asking me questions.

"Have you been eating all of your meals?"

See. I knew he'd ask.

"Sometimes," I answer him, honestly.

If Mom wasn't in the room, I'd probably lie to him so that he doesn't ask me anymore questions, but I know Mom always tells my doctor everything; just like she tells my therapist.

"She has days where she eats all three meals, and some days where she skips a meal or has one of her protein drinks instead. She does well with those, when she needs them."

Dr. Leonard examines me, and reassures me after each thing that he does.

Strong and steady heartbeat.

Clear chest.

No pain or sensitivity in my abdomen.

Responsive reflexes.

No fluid or inflammation in my ears, nose or throat.

Then he opens a plastic box that has a bunch of things in it, and pulls out one of those little prickly tests. It isn't a shot, but it's four tiny needles, that I know he's going to poke into my arm. When he's done, he gives Mom a piece of paper that has pictures of different bumps on it. If you touch the pictures, they actually feel like real bumps.

"What is that for?" I ask.

"That little prick I just gave you is called a 'TB Test,' and your mom is going to watch and see if those prick marks turn into bumps."

I'm about to ask him what it means if I get bumps on my arm, but Dr. Leonard starts talking again, before I have the chance.

"You don't have to worry, most people don't develop the bumps, okay? It's a disease that isn't very common here, at all."

A disease? That sounds scary, so I turn to Mom.

"Mom, What's TB disease?"

"You don't have to worry about that, sweetie," she answers.

Then she rubs my shoulders, then squeezes my hand.

"Tuberculosis is a disease that is very rare where we live. We don't even have it, really."

She looks over at Doctor Leonard. "Isn't that right, Doctor?"

Mom knows me really well, and she knows I need him to reassure me again.

"Yeah, you don't have TB," he says. "I've been a doctor for a long time, and I've never come across a child here who has it."

I think about this, gently touching the prick marks on my arm.

"Then why do we need the test?"

"TB is mostly found in developing countries, like those in Africa. This test is just to make sure that you haven't been exposed to it by someone who has recently visited one of those places."

I turn to my mom again. "Do we know anyone who has?"

"Nope! This is just a precaution, sweetie, not to worry. You'll see in a few days, there won't be a single bump on that beautiful arm, okay?"

110

She smiles and gave me one last bit of reassurance.

"You heard what the doctor said; TB is a disease found mostly in developing countries. You don't have to worry, okay? TB isn't something that you ever have to worry about."

~ ~ ~

Dear Sweet Girl,

I can't tell you that Tep's death wasn't painful.

As beautiful as his journey to Heaven was, grieving the physical loss of him introduced the most profound pain that I had ever experienced. I began crying as soon as they removed his body from our home, and I thought I would never stop. I spent days looking for him, imagining that I would walk down to Grandma and Grandpa's apartment and find him sitting in his chair. Each hour of the day- once filled with a routine of medications, feedings, physical therapy and the simplest, sweetest conversations- suddenly felt empty.

I don't know how to explain it, but it almost felt like a part of me went with him. My existence, or, our existence, is an extension of Grandpa's existence. We live because he did, and it took me some time to understand that I could exist without him here. There is a piece of our being that is solely attached to his, and I tried to hang on to everything I could that reminded me of his physical presence. I wanted his shoes, his sweatshirts, the comb that he insisted on using for the three hairs that he had on his head. Anything that I could get my hands on, that held even the slightest reminder of his physical existence, I wanted.

At the same time, I felt very aware of Tep's spirit. When you watch someone cross over to Heaven, you realize that Heaven isn't actually very far. In his final days, even when he couldn't speak, Tep had moments where he would look past us and fixate his eyes on something that we couldn't see. The nurses described this sensation as his soul connecting to the "other side." He was physically still with us, but his spirit was being called back to where it came from. His energy was shifting, but it wasn't disappearing.

You'd think this would be a scary thing to watch, but it was actually quite peaceful. Watching God's presence pour over Grandpa Tep and guide him Home, so to speak, was the gift that I had been waiting for.

111

God had finally revealed Himself to me, and He used our grandfather to do it. He could have taken him in the hospital, or while I was away in Kenya, but He didn't. There's no doubt in my mind that this was intentional.

During the last four months of Grandpa Tep's life, I did my best to keep my weekly sessions with Kathy. Her office was one of the few places that I didn't mind leaving the house for, and I was thankful that I had her to process my emotions with. Like me, she was in awe of God's timing; but she wasn't the least bit surprised by it. We had been working together for over a year, and it felt wonderful to have finally found what I was searching for, all of that time.

Now, don't get me wrong here. It wasn't like Grandpa died and I suddenly had all of my answers. I had a lot of questions for God, and a lot that I knew I still needed to make sense of. What Grandpa's death did, was open up the door for me to ask those questions, and not feel like I was asking them in vain. Someone was in control- protecting us and hearing us- and that was all I needed to know in order to start building some sort of faith. I didn't know exactly what my faith would end up looking like, but I finally felt like I could build the foundation.

There was just over a month between Tep's passing and my next trip to Kenya. Even before he passed, my flight was booked for June, and I had prayed that I'd get to see Tep's journey through before I left. Sarah Nicholson was in the States visiting family with Ruth-Michael, and their newest addition, five-month-old Abby-Jones, and our plan was to fly back to Kenya together, so that I could help Sarah travel with the girls. I was so thankful that I had been able to stay with Tep until the end, and also honor my commitment to Sarah. Again, God's timing.

I spent the month in between, preparing for my trip, and searching for ways that I could connect to God. I decided to turn towards nature, because that made the most sense to me. It was Spring time, and I allowed myself to truly appreciate the blooming of new life that I was surrounded by. The trees, the flowers, the little chipmunks and birds...all of them were so beautifully created.

I watched documentaries about the intricacies of life on our planet, and home videos that people posted online of their babies being born. I researched the process between conception and birth, and marveled over how each step of the process exists with such perfect intention. Our bodies know exactly what to do, from the time we're just a couple of cells. How crazy is that? When people say that childbirth is a miracle, they sure aren't joking.

I found that the more I observed the foundation of life itself, the more connected to God I felt. One day, I literally looked at a tree outside of my bedroom window, and listed all of the ways that trees give to other forms of life. They provide food, shelter, shade, oxygen. All of our most basic needs can be met with a tree, which, to me, that felt like a pure reflection of God's love and wisdom. It's amazing how something so tangible and concrete, can make you feel connected to a presence that is so abstract.

While I continued to explore this world with a new set of eyes, I thought a lot about how my blossoming faith would translate over in Kenya. It was starting to feel easy to detect God's presence in the "beautiful," but I didn't know how that would carry over into the "broken." Was I feeling comfortable enough in God's sovereignty to hang onto it in the midst of pain and suffering? I wasn't sure. All I knew was that I needed to go and find out.

My plan was to stay in Kenya from June through the end of the year. By then, I intended to make a decision as to whether or not I would commit to living in Kenya as a missionary, or come back to the United States and look for a full-time job. Giving up Kenya completely, never felt like an option to me, but I knew that I couldn't sustain a life where I traveled back and forth all of the time. Finding a job in the States would offer me more financial stability, but I'd have a lot less freedom to travel.

As I prepared for the upcoming six months, I didn't know which direction I was leaning towards, but my heart was in a new place altogether. Having seen God show up in such a profound way through Tep's passing, I knew that He was the one who would lead my heart to making a decision about Kenya. It felt sort of strange to lay such a trust in the hands of someone whose existence I adamantly denied, only months before, but I also felt a sense of freedom. For the first time, I was about to walk into an experience with the conscious acceptance that God was going to lead me, one way or the other.

Upon my return to Kisumu, one thing that I felt very convicted about, was finding a way to honor Grandpa Tep. I wanted to take what I had learned from his experience, and use it to help people who had the same needs as he did, but no access to the same resources. Not every dying person has an adjustable bed, a team of nurses, and a constant supply of adequate pain medication. I thought about patients like Caroline, and felt that those were the types of patients that God was leading me towards in this new season.

To be honest, I didn't know if I was strong enough to bear witness to that type of suffering again. I was thankful to have met Caroline when I did, but I also remember it being a significant emotional struggle, that I didn't wish to conquer again. It was almost as if I had identified a threshold in my mind, of what my limitations were, and God was using Tep to break that threshold down. He placed this calling on my heart, and I promised that I would see it through, when the timing felt right.

My role at Ringroad was beginning to expand a bit. On top of counseling the students, both individually and in groups, I started helping Chris and Sarah manage some of the physical health needs that individual students had. Sometimes the need was as simple as a pair of glasses, and other times it was life-saving medical treatment, but I took each opportunity to learn about the resources that were available within the community, and how we could work together to facilitate our children's needs. Each time a medical need was met, the stronger I felt God's desire to lead me deeper into the community.

After about a month of being back in Kenya, I finally felt ready. I found Evans at Ringroad's clinic, and asked if he had any bed-ridden patients that we could visit together.

"I want to visit a patient whose condition is similar to what Caroline's was. Are you working with anyone like that?"

"Yes," Evans replied. "There's a woman who is new to the clinic. I've met her here, but I haven't been to her home yet. I am to visit her soon, per the recommendation of our doctor."

"Can I go with you?"

"Yes, she needs a lot of help."

Any trepidation that I had left, suddenly disappeared. A new patient, who needed a lot of help, joined the clinic at the same time that I was preparing my heart to work with someone just like her. I knew for certain that there was no coincidence in that.

"Do you know anything about her condition?"

"She's very sick," Evans answered. "Her weight is reducing and her family says that she has been down for a long time."

"Is she positive?" I asked, referring to her HIV status.

"I don't think that she is."

"Has she been diagnosed with anything yet?"

"They haven't found the problem. But we are suspecting that it's TB. Do you know TB?"

"Yes," I answered. "Tuberculosis."

I met Caren on a Friday.

114

Evans and I walked through Nyalenda, for what seemed like an unreasonably long time. The deeper in we went, the less familiar I became with my surroundings.

"I have no idea how you guys find your way around here."

Evans laughed as we dodged a barbed wire fence and slid through its narrow wooden frame.

"We are just used to it. When you grow up here, you must know your way around."

I enjoyed seeing other parts of Nyalenda, as long as I wasn't by myself. For the most part, my awareness of the second-largest slum in the entire country, consisted of what I saw on my short commute to Ringroad. There was so much life there, and I wanted to explore all of it, but the attention that I attracted made it difficult. Man, woman or child, it didn't matter; every human that I passed always singled me out because of the color of my skin.

"Mzungu! Mzungu! How are you?"

I hadn't quite figured out how to deal with that yet, and on this particular Friday morning, I tried my best to tune everyone out. I wanted to focus on reaching this patient's house, and pouring all of the love and energy I had, into helping her.

We walked for a little while longer, until we reached an area that was significantly less crowded than the landscape that we were emerging from. Set back from the main road, across a patch of emptiness, sat rows of long, mud and stone structures, with doorways hallowed out every couple of feet. Each doorway led to one room, and each room was a family's home. One of those homes was Caren's.

We were led inside by a neighbor. The single-room house couldn't have been more than ten feet by ten feet, and it was very dark inside. The sun baked on the mud walls, giving the air a heaviness to it that made me feel claustrophobic.

There was no real floor, only smoothed over mud that still had its fair share of bumps and rocks in it, and there were no windows. I had been around long enough to know that of all of the housing options Nyalenda had to offer, this sort of setup was the poorest.

Pushed up against the back-right corner of the room, there was a bed. A sheet had been hung across a clothing line, to separate the bed from the dilapidated couch and two plastic chairs that constituted as a sitting room. It reminded me a lot of Caroline's house.

The neighbor pulled back the hanging sheet, revealing a bed frame with a well-worn mattress on top. The sheets where torn and only covered the mattress half-way; piles of clothes and other miscellaneous items taking up most of the surface.

Caren was wrapped in a blue blanket, covered up to her neck. Even with her body covered, I could sense how severely thin she was, because I couldn't tell where the rest of her body laid, relative to the folds in the blanket. She was sound asleep and her breathing was shallow. The neighbor bent down to rattle her awake.

"Caren!" she called out, followed by a phrase in Swahili that I didn't understand.

Caren slowly began moving her body, but she didn't open her eyes. I walked over to the bed and smiled at the neighbor.

"It's okay." I put my hand on the neighbor's shoulder and then sat down on the edge of Caren's bed.

"If she is feeling too tired to wake up right now, then it is okay."

I gently placed my hand on Caren's back and began rubbing in circles. She was damp with sweat and I could feel her spine protruding through her skin.

"Hi, Caren, my name is Jen," I whispered softly.

"I'm so sorry that you are not feeling well. Evans and I are here to help you."

Slowly, Caren rolled over and opened her eyes. I wasn't sure if she heard me the first time, so I repeated myself.

"Hi, Caren, my name is Jen."

I hesitated for a second, and then added, "Do you speak English?"

Caren nodded. "Yes. I can speak English."

Her voice sort of caught me off guard, in the most pleasant way. I smiled, and I'd like to believe that Caren smiled back at me, although I don't remember. What I do remember, is her grabbing my hand from her back, rolling over, and placing my hand on her rib cage.

"You can rub here," she said. "This is where I'm hurting."

"Okay. Then let me rub there."

For the next hour or so, I sat on Caren's bed and talked to her while I gently rubbed her rib cage. She told me that she had three children, and that she owned a hair salon before she became sick. She showed me a photo of herself in salon school, and I didn't even recognize her. She looked so happy and healthy.

"How old are you?" I asked her.

"I was born in 1985."

I felt a sharp pain in my chest. At thirty years old, Caren was only three years older than me.

"Where are your kids?" I asked her.

116

"The boy is away at school. He received a scholarship from the bank that will take him through university."

I knew what a huge deal this must have been for Caren and her son. In Kenya, there is no free education for high school students, and children are often denied their education due to lack of funds. For someone as sick as Caren was, working to pay for school fees simply wasn't possible.

"That's wonderful! And the others?"

"One of them goes to school in Nairobi, and one stays with me. She takes care of me."

I had been wondering if someone, other than her neighbor, was helping to take care of her, so I was glad when she told me this.

"I'd like to meet your daughter some time, if that's okay. The one who lives here with you."

Caren rolled onto her side so that I could switch to rubbing her back.

"She has traveled to our rural village, but she will be back. I want for you to meet her when she comes."

I rubbed my hand back over Caren's spine, as gently as I could, and promised that I would come back to meet the daughter.

Chapter Twelve

I don't always like field trips.

Sometimes they're fun, but sometimes they make me feel anxious. Like this one time when my class went to the children's science museum in West Hartford. I panicked really badly when they showed us a stuffed tiger that was actually alive once. It was a real tiger, that died, and then it was preserved somehow. We weren't allowed to touch it, but our Museum Guide told us that we could walk up to the ropes that were around it, and look as much as we wanted.

Everyone in my class was so excited. They kept saying that they were up close to a real-live tiger, even though it wasn't alive anymore. I wanted to be excited, too, but all I could think about was what would happen if the tiger came back to life. Tigers are dangerous animals, and I imagined what it would do to us if it suddenly became a living creature again. How could anyone be sure that it was dead forever?

I was only six years old back then, and now that I'm nine, I know how stupid it was to be afraid of something like that. Usually, when I'm done feeling anxious about something, I can see that there was no point in feeling that way. I wish that stopped me from feeling anxious in the first place, but it never does.

Anyway, I'm a little nervous about today's field trip. We're going to another school, to meet kids who are the same age as us. My classmates say that it's going to be boring, but that's not my problem with it. I barely feel comfortable enough in my own school, with teachers and kids that I know. I don't think I'm going to like being at a new school, that I know nothing about, even if it's just for one day.

Our bus driver brings us to a town that seems to be poorer than ours. The houses look like they're falling apart, and a lot of the cars aren't very nice, either. I feel really lucky to live in Farmington, and I know that people in this town probably have a lot more to be worried or scared about than I do. That makes me feel really sad.

When we first get to the school, I'm still a little bit unsure. The principal brings us down to the gym, and the other students are already in there. Our teachers shake hands with each other, and then all of us kids have to stand up and say our names. This feels okay to me, but I don't know how I'll feel once we have to start doing activities together.

I also don't really know why we're here in the first place. We're not going to be able to change anything about these other students' lives.

When they go home today, they're still going to, what adults call, "underprivileged" neighborhoods. Are we here because we think it's supposed to change something, or because we feel sorry for them?

The first activity that we do is a craft. We are all given big sheets of paper, and we're told to draw a picture of ourselves, and what we love. After I draw myself, I draw my family, some flowers, a rainbow, and a pair of ballet slippers. Then I write my name in the bubble letters that I just learned how to do. Nobody calls me "Jennifer," but I want to write the longest version of my name so that I have more bubble letters to draw.

Our teachers split us into groups. Each group has kids from my class, and kids from the other class. We take turns showing each other our pictures, and talking about the things that we love. One of the girls in my group says that she likes dance, too.

By lunch time, I feel happy to be here. Now that I know what the school looks like and who the other kids are, it doesn't feel like such a big deal to be away from our school for the day. We're told that after lunch, it'll be reading time, and then we'll get to play games out on the field. I don't really like those kinds of games, because I don't think I'm very good at them, but I'm not worried about it. I'm sure there are other people here who won't want to play, either, and maybe I can hang out with them.

I finish my peanut butter and jelly sandwich, and feel proud of myself for eating it all. I don't always eat when I'm in a new place, because new places make me nervous, but I'm comfortable now. I like it here.

Since it's a nice day out, the teachers say that we can have our reading time outside. We find a spot in the shade, and they each take a turn reading us a book. A bunch of us lay on our stomachs, and rest our heads in our hands, as we listen to the stories. Some kids fall asleep, and everyone laughs while other kids keep trying to shake them awake. It feels like we've all been in the same class for days.

Even game time isn't so bad. We play a game that's kind of like tag, and the time goes by pretty fast. Before it's time for us to go back to Farmington, the teachers tell us that we have one last activity to do. They take out the pictures that we drew earlier today, and pass them back out to us. Then, they tell us that when they call our names, we are to trade our pictures with one another. Each person will trade with someone from the other class.

This is very exciting to me. I want to have something that will help me remember this day, and the new friends that we made. Maybe we'll even get to see them again, some time. I sit quietly, with my legs folded in the grass, and wait for my name to be called.

"Jen!"

As soon as I hear it, I stand up and raise my hand. The teacher from the other class, looks at her list of students, to find which name is paired with mine.

"Joceyln!"

A girl with dark skin and long black hair stands up with her picture. I remember she was one of the first people that I noticed when we got here, because I wished my hair was long and straight, like hers. We walk over to each other, smile, and hand each other our pictures. Her drawing has flowers on it, just like mine, and I can't wait to bring it home.

Nothing about today, had anything to do with us trying to change or fix anything. No one pointed out who were the privileged kids, or who were the underprivileged. No one seemed to be feeling worried or sad. All we did, was meet new kids and play together. Maybe that was the point.

~ ~ ~

Dear Sweet Girl,

Not a single one of us, knows how our lives are going to turn out. I know you see that as a scary thing, but it can also be sort of exciting. We can make our own plans, and dream about what we hope our futures will look like, but we don't always know what we'll end up wanting or needing. Sometimes our definition of what makes sense, is challenged or disrupted, but in a beautifully unexpected way. That's how you know it's a "God Thing."

What if I told you, that as you're growing up, there's another little girl who's growing up with her family. She's three years older than you, she lives eight-thousand miles away, and she is going to change the entire course of your life.

Would you believe me?

Would that scare you?

I thank God every single day that ultimately, it didn't…

A couple of days after our first visit with Caren, Evans and I brought her to see a private doctor. We arrived at her house with a tuk-tuk, and our driver, William, pulled up as close to Caren's door as he could. We didn't want her to have far to walk.

121

When we went inside to get her, we found Caren sitting on the edge of her bed, dressed and almost ready to go. She had on a red button-up blouse, a green skirt, and all she had left to do was put on her sandals. The air smelled of lotion and soap, and the full basin that she used to bathe with was still sitting in the corner.

When I'm sick, I don't get out of my pajamas for anyone, including the doctor. Seeing Caren dressed like she was going to a social gathering, deepened the ache in my heart for her. I imagined the physical and emotional energy it must have taken for her to make such an effort; the exposed bones in her tiny body a reminder of how sick she was, in spite of how beautiful she looked, all dressed up.

Her neighbor was there to help her get ready, which I was thankful for. I was hoping that her daughter would be back by then, so that I could meet her, but Caren told us that she wasn't around. As she continued the painstaking process of putting her sandals on, I debated whether or not I should ask if she needed help. I then realized that there was a reason why no one else was offering to help her, and I decided that I wouldn't offer, either. This was probably one of the only things that Caren could still physically do for herself, and no one wanted to take that away from her.

Once it was time to leave for the doctor, Evans helped Caren to stand up off the bed. She took a couple of steps on her own, and then stopped in the doorway to catch her breath. Evans called over to William, and asked for his help. While the two of them carried Caren's tired body out of the house, I walked ahead and climbed into the tuk-tuk. I wanted to be in it before her, so that the guys could gently place her in my arms, rather than have her struggle to prop herself up.

The roads in Kisumu aren't very smooth, especially in the slum. I told Caren to lay across my lap, and had Evans sit up in the driver's seat with William. I asked William to drive as slowly as he could, in an effort to keep Caren comfortable. William agreed, and dodged the bumps as best as he could, but even the main roads had stretches where the bumps were unavoidable. Caren winced in pain, and I did my best to soothe her.

"You're doing a great job," I whispered as I gently rubbed her back. "We're almost there, you're doing great."

William dropped us off at the front of the doctor's office, where Evans went in first and found Caren a wheelchair. There were a lot of patients in the waiting room, but based off of appearance alone, Caren seemed to be the sickest. Out of fear that people would stare at her, or that she wasn't feeling strong enough to sit upright while we waited to see the doctor, I asked the receptionist if there was another place for us to wait.

The receptionist was very kind and led us to an empty examination room, where Caren would be able to lie down.

It was about an hour before we saw the doctor. A nurse came in to ask us a couple of questions and take Caren's vitals, but we spent the better part of the hour just waiting, in that tiny examination room. Caren's older sister, Judy, came from another part of Kisumu to meet us for the appointment. Since Caren's daughter couldn't be there, we felt it was important for another member of her family to receive first-hand information from the doctor. Judy spoke English, so we were able to converse a bit while we waited.

Caren slept on and off. She would feel hot one minute, and cold the next, so we used the pink shawl that she brought with her as a blanket to cover her tiny body. I rubbed her back and encouraged her when she needed it. Another missionary in town, who had met Caren before, stopped by the office to pray over her.

When the doctor finally came in for his initial examination, he poked around at Caren's body, without saying much. Then, after telling her that she could lay back down, he turned to us and declared,

"This is a very sick woman."

He wasn't wrong, but I felt irritated by his bluntness. As if Caren needed someone else to remind her of how sick she was. The least he could have done was approach her with some bedside manner.

Hours later, we left the doctor's office with a handful of ultrasounds, and blood work results. We were still waiting for the results of her sputum test, and it was recommended that we take her for x-rays in the meantime. Like us, the doctor suspected that Caren was suffering from Tuberculosis. The sputum test would give him a definitive answer, but he still wanted to see what her lungs looked like.

Evans volunteered to bring Caren for her x-rays, and Judy went with them. I felt I had reached my emotional capacity for the day, so I traveled back to St. Anne's, and spent a good thirty minutes crying on my bed. As I cried, I found myself wondering if Caren ever felt free or safe enough to allow herself to break down. Did she ever truly have a chance to grieve what was happening to her body?

I wasn't sure if that would be an appropriate thing to ask; so instead, I grieved on her behalf.

Evans came and found me in Chris and Sarah's office. It was less than a week since we had taken Caren to the doctor, and he wanted to let me know that her results came back positive for Tuberculosis. Although I was heartbroken, I knew that TB is treatable with antibiotics, and that gave me hope.

"When does she start on the medicine?" I asked Evans, trying to maintain focus on the sponsorship letters that I was organizing. Some days, it was nice to sit in the office and do administrative work that required little to no emotional energy.

"She can start tomorrow. The doctor said she is below the weight that they recommend for this drug, but it is her best option for now."

This scared me a little bit, her body already being so weak.

"Does that mean her body won't handle it well? Since she's under weight?"

Evans sat down on the couch and picked up one of the sponsorship letters, amused by the child's drawing of what he perceived his sponsor to look like.

"No, he thinks it's okay, because her weight is close enough."

He put down the letter and stood up to leave the office.

"Well, anyways, Caren's daughter is over at the clinic. She was sent so that she could meet you."

"Oh!" I pushed my pile of letters to the side and followed Evans out the door.

"I've been waiting to meet her! I want to tell her how brave she is, and let her know that we are here to help."

"Yes. It will be good for you to finally meet each other."

Evans and I walked across the compound and into the clinic. He led me up the narrow stairway, towards one of the tiny consultation rooms that the doctors and community health workers typically used to meet with their HIV and AIDS patients. He pushed open the door, and there she sat; Caren's fifteen-year-old daughter, Anyango.

Evans introduced us to one another, but Anyango barely took her eyes off of the floor. She was thin, but not as thin as Caren, and her hair was pulled back in tiny, worn out, orange braids. She had on denim board shorts and a navy-blue polo, that was slightly ripped at the collar. I wanted to give her a hug, but I didn't want to startle her or make her uncomfortable.

"It's so nice to finally meet you, Anyango. Your mom told me that you've been helping her a lot."

Anyango looked up at me, but she didn't say anything. There was an emptiness in her eyes, that pained me to look at. I knew she must have been so scared, watching her own mother's health decline the way that it had. I found myself wondering when the last time was that she smiled.

Evans explained to Anyango and I that Caren's new medication needed to be taken at the same exact time each day, to avoid the possibility of her body building up a resistance to it. He then suggested that he and I go to their house every day for the rest of the week, to be sure that there were no complications. He asked Anyango if this was okay, and she nodded, but still didn't say a word.

"Hey, Anyango?"

She looked up at me in response, but quickly averted her eyes back to the floor. I walked over and knelt down in front of her, and gently placed my hand on her knee.

"I know this is a scary time, but we're really going to try to help your mom get better, okay?"

Anyango nodded, and a single tear rolled down her cheek.

"Is there anything that you want to talk to us about?"

She shook her head.

"Okay, I understand. I know this is a really hard thing to talk about, isn't it?"

This time, Anyango didn't answer, even with a nod.

I looked over at Evans, with an expression of sadness and loss.

I wish I could do something to help her feel better, I thought; and as if Evans were reading my mind, he made a suggestion.

"Anyango, maybe let Jen give you her phone number, so that way you can call if you or your mom need something. Is that okay?"

Anyango was responsive to this, and took out her phone to record my number. It was an old, small talk-text phone, that was being held together by a rubber band. After she took my number, I told her to call me, so that I would have her number in my phone, as well. Then we said good-bye, and I promised that I would see her in the morning.

Evans and I both cleared our schedules, to ensure that we could reach Caren's house by 7:30am, and spend some time there, the following day. Caren was to take her first round of medication at 8am, and we wanted to be there with plenty of time to spare. Since it was her first day of treatment, it wouldn't have mattered if she took her pill a bit later than we had planned, but Evans and I both agreed that we wanted to instill a strict starting time, from the beginning.

Each time I went into her home, it took me a moment to adjust to the dark. Even when the door was open, it yielded little light and virtually no ventilation. This was a concern for me, as TB spreads through air droplets. I was afraid that if there wasn't enough ventilation in the house, Anyango would catch it.

We found Caren sound asleep, while Anyango was preparing porridge in a small pot on the ground. We both greeted her, and then sat quietly on the plastic chairs next to Caren's bed. Evans encouraged Anyango to wake Caren, as soon as she was done making the porridge. It was important for Caren to eat before she took her medicine, and we had twenty-two minutes before it was time for her first dose.

Anyango stood up and walked over to the bed. She gently nudged Caren's shoulder, until she began to stir. As soon as Caren opened her eyes, she spotted me in the chair. She shook her head, then pointed to the empty corner on her mattress.

"Come here," she said, very simply.

"You want me to sit with you?"

"Mmhmm," Caren responded.

For the next twenty minutes, Evans and I talked to Caren about how she was feeling, and reminded her about what her treatment would entail over the next few months. She had antibiotics, and vitamin supplements to take. Every week, she would go for a check-up at the government hospital's TB clinic, as they offered all TB treatment for free. Evans promised that he would go with her to each appointment, because Ringroad was going to continue providing his community health services to her.

As we chatted, Anyango kept her distance. She silently washed dishes and mixed porridge, in the darkest corner of the room. She came back over to us when it was time to offer Caren her cup of porridge. We wanted her to try and take a few sips, before she took her first pill. Caren whimpered at the thought of it, and refused.

"Okay, but when you take the medicine, you must wash it down with the porridge," Evans gently advised her.

Caren whimpered again, and closed her eyes.

Minutes later, when the alarms simultaneously went off on all of our phones, Evans removed the first red pill from its package and handed it to Caren. He summoned Anyango to bring the cup of porridge back over, and I moved out of the way so that she could help prop Caren up against her pillow.

Caren let out a small, sharp cry as she was forced to sit up. She took a moment to catch her breath, and then popped the pill into her mouth. Anyango handed her the cup of porridge, which Caren swallowed half a sip of, before she put it down and covered her mouth, as if she was going to vomit.

Instinctively, I crawled back onto the bed, and began rubbing her back.

126

"It's okay," I whispered. "Just take a deep breath and relax your body. The porridge and the medicine will stay down; just take some nice deep breaths."

Caren attempted to take a deep breath, but she coughed and winced in pain, instead. I remembered that she was suffering from a lung disease, that made deep breaths challenging, if not impossible, and I felt horribly stupid for suggesting such a thing.

Eventually, Caren's breathing evened out. I encouraged her to imagine the medication making its way through her body, beginning the healing process and offering reprieve to her lungs. Once she was confident that she wasn't going to regurgitate the porridge or the pill, Caren rested her head on my chest, and I continued to rub her back. In minutes, she was sleeping again, and Evans and I felt it was okay to leave.

The next couple of days went similarly. Caren never had an appetite for the porridge, and almost always fought the urge to throw it back up. Even though she was still feeling weak, her body was handling the medication well enough, and the doctor at the TB clinic told Evans that was the best we could hope for, at the moment. We were all feeling cautiously optimistic.

The weekend came and went. On Monday morning, Evans went back down to the TB clinic to pick up Caren's next pack of medication. Initially, she was only given enough for a week, to ensure that her body could tolerate it. Evans was instructed to pick up the rest, once she made it through her first couple of days. Before he went to Caren's house to drop the medication off, he stopped by the Ringroad office, to see if I wanted to go with him.

I hadn't seen Caren and Anyango all weekend, so I was tempted to go. I was also in the middle of helping Joanie, who was suffering through one of her chronic ear infections, and I had designated that morning to try and figure out whether she needed to be seen by a specialist. Joanie suffered from ear infections at least once a month, and antibiotics were proving only to be a temporary solution. The doctor at Ringroad felt that her infections were a result of poor hygiene, and suggested that she visit a place that could properly clean out her ears. Joanie was in pain, and I didn't want to put this on the back burner.

"Just tell Caren I'll come by later," I told Evans. "And tell her I love her."

Evans agreed, and left for Caren's house. I turned my attention back to Joanie, who was waiting for her class teacher to contact her mother. I offered to take Joanie to the specialist myself, but it was encouraged for parents or guardians to try and manage their children's medical needs, before one of us intervened. This made sense to me, but I couldn't stand to see Joanie so uncomfortable.

I sat with her and waited for her mother to arrive. She was a girl of few words, but Joanie loved to be goofy and play with any gismo or gadget that looked remotely interesting. I didn't have anything fun for her to play with on that day, so we both picked up sticks and drew designs in the dirt. As long as she was stimulated by something, Joanie was happy.

Moments later, while she and I were still sitting outside, I saw Evans walk back through the gate. He came right over to me and asked if we could have a moment to talk in the office.

"I'm waiting with Joanie right now, so can we talk about it here? How's Caren?"

Evans turned his head away from me. "I think we should talk privately in the office."

I looked down, and noticed that he was still holding Caren's medication in his hand.

"Why do you still have her meds?" I heard myself ask, even though I already knew the answer.

Evans was silent.

"Why didn't you leave Caren her meds?"

"Please, can I tell you about it in the office?"

There was a lump in my throat, and I could feel my heartbeat in my ears. I stood up from Joanie, and our designs in the dirt, and followed Evans to the office.

Once we reached the doorway, Evans took a deep breath.

"I'm sorry, but I have been informed that Caren died yesterday."

I don't remember what I said in response to him, but I remember chaotic thoughts screaming in my head.

How could this happen?

She was supposed to get better.

Please, God, don't do this to Anyango.

What's going to happen to Anyango now?

How could this happen?

Why did this happen?

Could I have stopped it?

How could this happen?

How the fuck could this happen?

I crumbled to the floor. Chris and Sarah were working from home that day, so I called Sarah and told her what happened. They experienced the loss of multiple loved ones throughout the course of their ministry-loved ones whom they had tried to help- so I knew that Sarah would understand the complexities of my heartache.

She told me how sorry she was, and suggested that I focus on what would help me feel safe enough to grieve in that moment. I'd need to process what happened, so that I didn't let it paralyze me; and it was okay for me to step back and do that, without feeling guilty.

Talk about guilt. The news of Caren's passing brought forth an unrelenting surge of guilt, that I had previously been able to hold just beneath the surface of my consciousness. Every day, I looked into the faces of people who were living "without." Food, clean water, adequate medical care, loving families...I was surrounded by people who were lacking all of the things that I've always had, and I still felt like I didn't have enough to give. Even with the fierce desire to give all of myself, whatever I had to offer them, never felt like enough.

This often resulted in my feeling guilty. I hadn't done anything wrong, but I also never did anything to deserve the privilege that I have. I found myself fighting the urge to apologize, wanting them to know that I see the injustices, and that I wish I could do something to fix or erase them. But instead, I buried the guilt, because I was afraid that I would get stuck in it. I knew I couldn't help anyone if I got stuck.

When I learned that Caren had passed away, I lost my ability to bury the guilt. I felt very attached to her, and all I could think to do was torture myself over how this could have played out differently. What if I had enough money to admit her to a private hospital? What if she were diagnosed sooner? What if she were born in a country where Tuberculosis is uncommon, but they test you for it just as a precaution? Why did I have that privilege, and she didn't?

Ringroad was the last place that I wanted to be. I sat on the floor of the office and listened vaguely, as one of the younger classes shouted out answers to math questions.

"TWO-PLUS-ONE-EQUALS-THREE! SEVEN-MINUS-FIVE-EQUALS-TWO!"

Their voices were loud, bright, and perfectly in unison. I knew they were so proud of themselves for learning how to add and subtract, but all I could think about was the probability that a handful of them would end up just like Caren. So many of those sweet little souls, rattling off math problems at the top of their lungs, would grow up only to succumb to the injustices of their environment.

I couldn't listen to their voices anymore. I called one of my tuk-tuk drivers, and asked him to come and get me. As soon as I heard the tuk-

129

tuk approach the gate, I pulled myself off the ground and walked out of the office. I didn't say goodbye to anyone; I just left.

Back at St. Anne's, I allowed myself to fully unravel. I cried for the physical pain that Caren endured, and for the immense number of obstacles that Anyango would now be up against.

There was a small part of me that was thankful for Caren's peace, but it was a lot harder for me to feel that with Caren than I had with Grandpa Tep. He lived a long, full life, and died surrounded by every comfort that was available to him. Of course, he deserved that, but so did Caren. I found that it was harder for me to acknowledge her peace, because I was so fixated on how badly she had suffered for it.

If I were back home, sitting in a session with Kathy, she would have asked me if Caren's experience changed my feelings towards God. I would have told her that I didn't know; that it was too soon to tell. But then I would have told her that I turned to Him, anyway. In the midst of my grief, desperate to know why such suffering exists, I asked God to show me, instead of turning away from Him.

Chapter Thirteen

Going back and forth felt weird at first, but now I'm used to it.

On Tuesdays and Thursdays, we get to have dinner with Dad, and then we spend nights with him on some of the weekends. Before he found a new house, he lived at a really cool hotel, where all the rooms are like apartments and there's a swimming pool and a snack room and stuff. I think I would've been fine with him staying at the hotel forever, but he really wanted to find a house. At least the one he chose is nice, and it's only in the next town over, so we don't have to travel far when we see him.

Mom, Jake and I stayed in our normal house for a while, but it started to feel less normal at the end. The people who were helping us sell it, made Mom put up all of these weird decorations that weren't ours. She even had to put a new blanket and pillows on her bed, because the people said it looked nicer for photos and showings. I hated showings the most, because we had to keep everything perfectly clean, and leave the house whenever someone wanted to look at it. Not knowing when we would have to leave the house next, made me feel really anxious all of the time. Even though we were still living there, it felt like the house didn't belong to us anymore.

On our last night, I slept on a mattress in Jake's room. Mom sold my furniture, so my room was completely empty, and I refused to sleep in it. I was going to try, but the emptiness made me nauseous. For almost all eleven years of my life, that was my space, and I couldn't imagine never, ever seeing it again. I kind of wanted to fall asleep so that I wouldn't have to think about how sad I felt, but the other part of me wanted to stretch our last night as long as I could. I knew that once morning came, I'd have to say goodbye.

Since Mom didn't find a new house for us right away, we moved into the same hotel that Dad stayed at. He had already moved out of it by the time we got there, but I think it would have been pretty cool for us to all stay there at the same time. Mom and Dad probably would have hated that, though. The good thing about moving to the hotel, was that I had gotten used to it from visiting Dad there so much. It felt very familiar to me, and that was what I needed. Sometimes, I forgot that we were living there, and imagined that we were just on a really long vacation. Even though we had so many things from our house with us in that hotel room, it still always felt like we were going back home at some point.

Tonight's the night I've been dreading for a long time. Mom found a new house for us, and tonight will be our first time sleeping in it. We've been living at the hotel for five whole months, so it really feels like home to me, and I don't want to leave it. I know this house will never feel as comfortable to me as the hotel, or especially our old house. Nothing will ever feel as comfortable as our old house, which is why I'm going to buy it back someday when I'm older.

Mom moved all of our stuff into the new house while we were on vacation with Dad this past week. He brought us to Florida to see his side of the family, and it was so much fun. At first, I didn't want to go, because we had never been there without Mom before. I got anxious a couple of times, but it ended up being just as fun as it always is. I started to feel sad about the vacation being over, a whole day before we actually left, and knowing that we had to come home to a strange house made me feel even worse. I was excited to see Mom, but I wanted to see her at a place that I knew.

We landed back in Connecticut really late tonight. I knew that by the time we got our suitcases, picked up the car, and Dad drove us to the new house, it would be way past our bed time. I was kind of hoping that Mom would let us miss school tomorrow, so that we could have a day to settle in, but she said that we already missed enough school because of our trip to Florida. Tomorrow is Monday, and she wants us to start the week on our new routine. Man, I really hate new routines. They make me feel sick to my stomach.

This house is in the same town as our old one, but it's on the other side of it. I didn't even know this neighborhood existed until Mom brought us to see the place a few weeks ago. It's nice, I guess, but it's a lot smaller than our old one. It's weird seeing our furniture in it, because the house doesn't feel like ours. I keep asking myself why I see our furniture in a stranger's house.

Mom seems really happy. She's proud of herself for setting everything up while we were away, and she can't wait to show us our new rooms. Before we left for Florida, I got to pick out new furniture for my room, because mine was so old and it didn't look good anymore. The new furniture has flowers painted on it, and it's pretty, but I miss my old furniture. Jake's so lucky that he got to keep his.

Every room smells like new paint. I remember that smell from when Mom and Dad redecorated our other house, and if I close my eyes, I can pretend that I'm there. I can picture everything about our old house so clearly in my mind still, and the smell of the new paint makes it feel even easier to pretend that that's where I am.

132

I take a shower, and it feels weird. I don't recognize these walls, or this shower curtain. Thankfully I'm using the same shampoo and soap that I always do, so at least I have other smells that I know. I wish this was enough to make me feel better, but it isn't. When I pull the curtain back to get my towel, I'm looking at a bathroom that doesn't feel familiar to me, and I hate it. I feel bad that Mom is so excited, when I don't even know how to pretend to be excited in order to make her happy. She says that it won't take long for this place to feel like home, but I can't imagine it ever feeling that way. I don't like it here at all.

When it's time for bed, I crawl under my new sheets. I've never used them before, but they already smell like laundry detergent because Mom washed them for me before she put them on my new bed. She put all of my favorite books and toys on my new shelves, and hung all of my clothes in my new closet. It's weird seeing all of my things in a place that I don't know. I can't decide if having my things here makes me feel better because I know them, or worse because it reminds me that we aren't going back home.

Even though it's late, I don't try to fall asleep. I keep thinking about tomorrow morning, when I have to wake up and get ready for school in this new place. Then, I have to stand at a new bus stop, and get on a new bus. I'm going to the same school, but getting there will feel different. I'm not even sure I know where my school is from here. And what if I can't find anyone to sit with on my new bus?

I don't want the morning to come, so I am going to try to stay awake as long as possible. In the darkness, I face the new door of my new room, and imagine that I'm back home, where everything feels normal. I can't wait for everything to feel normal again.

~ ~ ~

Dear Sweet Girl,

When I think about you, my first instinct is to imagine you frozen in time. Whether I'm recalling a memory from your early childhood years or from high school, you look the same in all of them. Maybe physically you don't, but the way you "feel" to me, on the inside, is the same. Wherever you are, you seem to be stuck there. Eventually, all of those

133

places begin to look the same, so it's no wonder that you do, too. Being stuck, is being stuck.

Fortunately, I also have the privilege of seeing past the things that you can't. I can reflect on the times, upon times, that you felt paralyzed by fear or sadness, and recognize that you are so much bigger than any of it. You are not just the girl who hates change or the unknown; who never wants to step out of her comfort zone, in fear of never finding her way back to it again. You are the girl whose feelings about the world, breed the type of empathy and compassion that will set your heart on fire. You are the girl whose deep desire to care for others will never, ever allow you to stay within your comfort zone.

You are NOT your fear, you are NOT your sadness. And believe it or not, you DO exist without them…

I wanted to lead the way to Caren's house. It was the morning after we found out that she had passed, and Evans and I were going to pay our respects to her family. Though impossible to ever truly know my way around Nyalenda, I'd been to Caren's house enough, and wanted to see if I could get us there without Evans' help. It felt like a good way to distract our minds for ten minutes, and not focus on the reason why we were headed there in the first place.

Evans told me that extended family members would be at the house, packing up Caren's things and starting to make funeral arrangements. I was thankful for the opportunity to pay my respects to her family, but what I really wanted to do was check on Anyango. I couldn't fathom what she must have been going through; grieving the loss of her mother, while trying to figure out what would happen to her next. I imagined her feeling alone and afraid, and I wanted to get to her as soon as possible.

The walk to Caren's house felt different that morning. Everything we passed was exactly the same, but there was a heaviness in the air that tainted everything I looked at. We passed women bent over their laundry basins, and children playing with bottle caps in the dirt, and all I saw when I looked at them, was sadness. Not strength, not perseverance; not creativity or resourcefulness. Not hope, not optimism. The women were playing music as they washed, the children laughed as they played, but all I could see was sadness.

I successfully led us to Caren's without asking for help, and found myself wishing that I could run inside the house and tell her. She knew the ins and outs of Nyalenda just as well as Evans did, and I thought she might get a kick out of my small, navigational accomplishment. A part of me thought that we may walk in and find Caren laying in her bed, right where we left her. I knew it was impossible, but it didn't stop me from hoping for it. My brain did the same thing after Grandpa Tep died.

As we approached the land leading up to Caren's neighborhood, we were bombarded with loud music.

"Is someone honestly having a party right now?" I snapped at Evans. "Don't they know that their neighbor just died?"

"That is why they are playing the music," Evans responded, patiently excusing my ignorance. "It is how people raise money for funerals; they play music and show photos of the deceased, and people come to contribute money for the burial."

This may have been tradition for them, but I struggled to take it in. A family was grieving the loss of a loved one, while a giant speaker and hype-men with microphones blared outside the house like a radio station kiosk in the parking lot of a strip mall. It felt counter-intuitive to everything I thought I knew about the grieving process, but who was I to make such a judgement?

While I was ready to walk right past the men and the music, in order to go find Anyango, Evans told me that we needed to greet the men first. They were the ones leading the charge to raise money for Caren's funeral, so it would have been rude to walk past them and not acknowledge their efforts. I could see that the men had already begun drinking, but I reluctantly followed Evans over to them.

"Aye! My sister!" One of the men stumbled over to me, half-empty liquor bottle in his hand.

"Do you know who I am, my sister?"

The man looked vaguely familiar, from times that I had been there before, but I never would have recognized him outside of the neighborhood.

"Yes, I remember you."

"What is my name, sister? Do you know my name?"

"I'm sorry, I don't know it."

The stench of alcohol was nauseating. It pierced the air around us and gave me goosebumps.

"I am called Samuel, my sister."

He grabbed my hand with one of his, and held up a photograph with the other.

"Today we are crying because of this lady. Do you know this lady?"

The woman in the photo looked healthy and strong. A lump grew in my throat as I looked into her eyes and identified her: the version of Caren that I would never get to meet.

"Yes, I know her."

The rest of the men gathered around us, the smell of alcohol intensifying. I felt suffocated.

"Ah, mzungu! Kuja udance namimi!" One of them shouted out.

I turned to look at Evans.

"He wants you to dance with him," Evans answered, without me having to ask.

I couldn't stand any part of that scene anymore. The blasting music, the rancid alcohol, the shouting in my face, all felt like too much.

"If we don't walk away from them right now, I am going to lose my mind."

Before I waited for Evans' response, I turned toward the alleyway where Caren's door was. Sitting in the dirt beside the doorway, with her knees pulled up to her chest and tears rolling down her cheeks, was Anyango. I walked up and knelt on the dirt in front of her. Then I pulled her towards me and wrapped her in my arms. She began to cry harder, and then she pulled away, stopping herself.

"I am so sorry, Anyango."

I knew that my words were insufficient, but I had no others to offer. There was a deep pain, and a profound numbness that coexisted in her eyes, and I wondered how the hell she was going to survive this.

Anyango stood up and led us inside, where we were greeted by her relatives. Among them was Caren's oldest sister, Janet, who looked exactly like her. She was sitting on Caren's bed, crying quietly, and didn't look me in the eye when I went to shake her hand. Someone brought in additional plastic chairs, so that we would all have a place to sit in the tiny room. I motioned for Anyango to come sit in the chair next to mine.

We spent about an hour there, as Evans helped the family discuss the logistics of Caren's funeral. They had already begun packing her belongings into a torn-up suitcase that she had, and I wanted to ask where all of it was going. I thought about the day that we packed up Grandpa Tep's things, and my visceral desire to hold onto anything that represented his physical existence. As I watched this family dump clothing, jewelry, plates and photographs into the suitcase, I wondered if any of it held significance to them anymore. What could once be identified as Caren's belongings, were now just…things.

Among the things that I saw, was the light pink shawl that Caren brought with her to the doctor. During the hours we spent in the examination room, Caren must have taken that shawl on and off a dozen times. It was the only thing that seemed to give her any physical comfort, as she laid on the table and waited to be seen.

"Are you saving any of her things for yourself?" I asked Anyango.

Anyango shrugged her shoulders and looked at me for a fleeting moment.

"She seemed to really like that pink shawl; it comforted her. Maybe you want to hang on to something like that?"

Anyango stood up and gently pulled the shawl from the pile of clothes in the suitcase. Then, she handed it to me.

"Oh, no, you keep it," I told her. "I think you should have it."

She put the shawl off to the side, and sat back down next to me. I could feel the heaviness of her heart, silently holding the weight of the world, as her relatives continued to speak with Evans in their native tongue. Every once in a while, he would lean over to me and translate what they were saying, but it all seemed to be about the funeral. No one was talking about where Anyango would go.

In my head, I began to cry out to God. I asked Him why He had allowed this to happen, and how He was going to protect Anyango in the aftermath of it. Where was His love? His mercy? His provision? All of God's goodness had been so easy to identify after Grandpa Tep passed away, but I didn't know how I could possibly find it in a situation like this one.

When I looked back over at Anyango, I followed her eyes to a small pouch on Caren's bedside table. The pouch was open, and the unfinished sleeve of red Tuberculosis pills was poking out from the top of it. Evans still had her new pack of medication sitting at Ringroad, because she never even had a chance to finish the ones on her bedside table. The lump in my throat began to rise again, as I spotted a single tear roll down Anyango's cheek. I knew she was thinking the same thing that I was: that medication was supposed to be her mother's saving grace.

I've never felt so desperate for a person's presence, as I silently begging Caren to come back.

Please come back to your daughter.
Please don't leave her alone here.
She needs you to come back.
Please, please come back.

"Anyango," I whispered gently. "Do you know where you will be staying now?"

In the States, it is common for parents to pre-determine who their children's legal guardians would be, should a situation like this arise. As

I was beginning to discover more about the Kenyan culture, I learned that the placement of the children was usually an afterthought. They would go to whichever family member was willing to take them, based on how useful they felt the children would be to them around the house.

Anyango's eyes remained on Caren's medication. She shook her head, and another tear rolled down her cheek.

"Can you stay with one of your aunts?" I asked.

"I don't know."

She choked on her words, and I didn't want to push her any further. I also didn't want her to think that she was going to have to figure all of this out on her own, because I wasn't going to let that happen.

"Anyango, look at me."

She turned her head and looked me in the eye.

"I will make sure that you are taken care of, okay?"

Anyango didn't respond, but she let out a small cry. I embraced her again, held her for a second, and then asked Evans if we could go. I may not have understood God's reasoning for taking Caren when or how He did, but I knew that He wasn't done using me in her story. It was time I found her daughter a safe place to stay.

On our walk back, I expressed to Evans how sad I felt for Anyango.

"You know, I had the same troubles as her," he responded. "I am also an orphan."

This caught me by surprise.

"You are?"

"Yes. I lost my parents when I was young, too."

Evans was only in his early twenties, so I wondered how young he was when his parents died, but I didn't ask.

"How did you get through it?" I asked instead.

"I just did. What other option did I have?"

When I returned to St. Anne's, I went up to my room and allowed myself to cry. A lot.

I had been holding onto those tears all day, and as I finally sprawled across my bed and released them, I wondered what Anyango's grieving process would look like. She was already packing up the house and planning the funeral. As Evans shared with me, she would likely be the one to identify her mother's body at the mortuary. Then, she would have to attend the funeral, and bury her mother in front of her family's homestead in the village. After all of that, she would need to figure out where she was going to stay, and how she was going to survive. Surely, she couldn't do all of that and grieve at the same time.

I continued to weep, until there was a knock at my door.

"Jenny? Are you inside there?"

I knew that voice. It was Mercy, the housekeeper who cleaned my room every day. We had come to know each other a little bit, and would often chat while she was cleaning. I really enjoyed her company, as she had a sweet and spunky spirit. Talking with her helped me to not feel so lonely.

"Yeah, I'm here," I responded. "Hang on."

I wiped my eyes, blew my nose and retied my hair, before I opened the door. It was my hope that she wouldn't notice I had been crying, but my face was red and swollen, so I was kidding myself.

"Ooohhh my, Jenny. Why are you crying my dear?"

Mercy already knew about Caren's passing, because she had been cleaning the guest house the day before, when I spent the entire evening crying over the news.

"I went to visit Caren's daughter today. They're packing up all of her things, and I don't know who is going to take Anyango or what is going to happen to her."

My throat and eyes felt raw.

"She has aunts, but I don't know if any of them will take her."

Another blow into my tissue.

"So then what happens? She'll bounce around from house to house? Or just live on the streets until a man picks her up and gets her pregnant? She'll never get to go back to school? What will happen to her, Mercy?"

Mercy came and sat next to me on the bed.

"No, Jenny. It will be okay. If the family won't take Anyango, then I will take her as my own."

I didn't understand.

"Wait, what? You would just take in a child that you don't know, because she has nowhere else to go?"

Mercy gave the slightest hint of a smile.

"Yes, Jenny. We must take care of our orphans in this community. She is only a child, and she needs to be taken care of."

I thanked Mercy profusely, and after she left my room, I got down on my knees and thanked God. Not wanting to wait until I saw Anyango again to share this good news, I called the cell phone number that she had given me the day I met her at Ringroad. I wasn't sure that she would answer, but when she did, I told her that I had a friend who would be willing to take her in.

"Would you be okay to come and meet her before you leave for your mom's funeral?"

"Okay."

Anyango spoke so infrequently around me, that the sound of her sweet, timid voice caught me off guard each time I heard it. We made arrangements for her to come to the guesthouse the next day, so that she and Mercy could meet, and work out the details of this perspective arrangement.

Once we got off the phone, I contacted a family friend in the States, named Rhonda, who had previously expressed interest in sponsoring a child. I explained Anyango's situation, and asked Rhonda if she would like to help support her living expenses, rather than sign up for traditional school sponsorship. Although Mercy hadn't asked me for money to help her take care of Anyango, I knew that she could not afford to do such a thing without financial assistance.

Rhonda was moved by Anyango's story, and said that she would be honored to help support her. She even offered to reach out to her friend, Kathy, to see if she would also like to support Anayngo, by paying for her education. By bedtime, I had secured a place for Anyango to stay, and a commitment to get her back into school. It felt like there was hope for that sweet girl's future, and God was protecting her after all.

As planned, Anyango came to St. Anne's the next day. While we waited for Mercy to finish cleaning, I offered to buy Anyango a soda from the dining room.

We were sitting and drinking our soda's together when Violet, one of the receptionists, came over to greet Anyango and offer her condolences. She spoke to Anyango in Swahili, and Anyango nodded in response, but she never spoke.

"I'm telling this girl that she must be strong now," Violet said to me.

"Losing parents when you are still a child, is a sad thing that happens, and our only choice is to be strong and move on. That is the only thing that this girl can do now, so that is what I am telling her."

Violet went back to the reception desk and I followed, leaving Anyango to finish her soda alone. Like everyone else at the guest house, Violet had been so patient and nurturing towards me the day that I came home with the news of Caren's passing. Her blunt approach towards Anyango confused me a little bit, and I wanted to ask her about it.

"Why does it seem like everyone expects that poor girl to be strong, when her mother just died? How is she supposed to be able to do that?"

Violet put her hand on my shoulder.

"She doesn't have a choice, Dear. It happens too much here in Kenya, and we don't have a choice but to move forward. We couldn't survive if we didn't know how to be strong."

I turned to face the dining room, where Anyango continued to slowly nurse her soda.

"When my mother and father died, everyone told me that I needed to be strong," Violet continued.

"That really helped me because I had my brother and sister to take care of, and I knew the only way that I could do it, was to be strong. There was no time for sadness."

"Why did you allow me to feel sad the other day, then?"

"Because you don't know any better, Dear. For you, it is a must to have those feelings."

I flashed back to Anyango sitting outside of her house, knees to her chest and tears on her cheeks, with no one making any attempt to soothe her. Having grown up in a world where there was never a shortage of comfort, it was hard to imagine a life where I didn't long for it. But people like Anyango, Violet and Evans, were never given a chance to seek comfort the way that I was. Their unparalleled strength and resilience were rooted in a lack of choice.

Pondering Violet's words, I began to identify God's hand in a place where it felt so hard to find Him. He knows how to equip His people, and there is such beauty to be found in that; even in the midst of such brokenness.

Anyango finished her soda, and we continued to wait for Mercy in the lobby. Rather than try to assess Anyango's grief, I attempted to strike up a conversation about her likes and dislikes. I didn't get much out of her, other than her favorite subject being English, and her love of scary movies. It was the first time I had ever heard her speak in full sentences.

When Mercy finally came down to meet us, she introduced herself to Anyango and immediately began making plans with her. Unlike everyone else, Mercy spoke to Anyango in English so that I could follow along. In all of the cultural processing that I had done over the last couple of days, you have no idea how readily my brain welcomed a conversation that I could listen to, without the use of a translator.

"You will have your own mattress," Mercy told Anyango.

"My kids are sharing a mattress, I have one, and I will get you a new one. Everything will be ready for you when you come back from the burial."

Anyango didn't acknowledge what Mercy was saying, so it was hard for me to know how she felt about any of it. I imagined that it was overwhelming for her to meet the stranger that she would be living with, days after her mother died, but I also understood that my idea of "overwhelming" looked slightly different than hers.

"Is this okay, Anyango? Do you want to live with Mercy, or do you want to see if someone in your family can take you?"

"I want to live with her," Anyango whispered.

As we continued to make plans, I oscillated between disbelief and acceptance that any of this was normal. A child who just lost her only living parent, was about to move in with someone she didn't know, without the rest of her family questioning it. No one else was fighting for her, so Anyango was left to go with the only viable option that she had been presented with.

According to her tribe's burial traditions, Anyango would need to spend an entire week at her family's rural homestead, in order to fulfill all of her obligations as the daughter of the deceased. We agreed that once she returned to Kisumu, she would come back to St. Anne's, so that she could go home with Mercy.

I explained to her that Evans would attend the funeral on our behalf. Having spoken to Chris and Sarah about the nature of Kenyan funerals, I decided that it was best for me to stay behind. There would be huge crowds of people, lots of drinking, and I would be the only white, American girl there. Knowing how much attention I received on a daily basis in Kisumu, I wasn't comfortable going to a place in rural Kenya, that I didn't know, where there would be crowds of people ingesting alcohol.

Anyango told me that she understood, and asked if I had something that she could wear to the funeral. I brought her up to my room, and gave her one of my favorite dresses; a black and purple floor-length dress that I purchased from a market in town. It fit her beautifully, and I was honored that she would be wearing it when she laid Caren to rest.

We hugged goodbye, and I told her to call if she needed anything while she was gone. Anyango agreed, and promised she would come back to St. Anne's, as soon as she returned to town. Dress in hand, she walked out the front gate of the guesthouse. As I watched her go, I could almost see a little bounce in her step; a sign from God that she was going to be okay.

Chapter Fourteen

I'm so excited to go to the Nurse's office.

I go there all of the time, but it's been months since I've gone in with an actual physical illness. Usually I visit her when I'm feeling too anxious to sit in class, and she'll either let me lay down or write me a pass to walk a few laps around the hallways. She used to tell me to go back to class and try to tough it out, but my Guidance Counselor finally had a talk with her. She said that my anxiety has become a big enough problem to start taking it more seriously.

This may be news to them, but not to me. I mean yeah, maybe I went a little while without having such bad anxiety, so no one here at the high school really knew about it, until recently. But they should go back and ask some of my previous teachers what it was like having me as a student. Or, they could probably just talk to my parents.

As someone who always has to explain why I don't feel well because people often don't understand, it feels like a victory to walk into the Nurse's office today with a case of Pink Eye. Not only is it something that the Nurse will be able to see for herself, but it's highly contagious and I'll need to get sent home. I can't believe that I actually get to go home today for a sickness that I don't have to defend.

I walk into the office and point to my eye.

"I think I have to go to the doctor."

She takes one look at my eye and tells me that she will call my mom.

"How was your eye when you left the house this morning?"

"It was a little crusty but it wasn't red, so I just washed it."

"Okay. You'll need to go to the doctor for eye drops and stay home for at least 24 hours, so that you are no longer contagious."

My eye may be burning like hell, but I've never felt more vindicated by an illness in my entire life.

~ ~ ~

Dear Sweet Girl,

It's hard for me to explain what hearing God's voice sounds like, especially since you've never gone searching for it. As I shared earlier, God opened my heart up to Him by revealing Himself through the process of life. Birth, death, the perfect flow of our planet's ecosystems- all helped me to acknowledge God's existence. Figuring out what to do with that, was its own challenge.

The next step for me, was understanding how to identify God's voice in my own life. As the creator of all living things, it only made sense that His creation came with intention. So, what was His intention for me? What gifts and resources did He equip me with, and how was I intended to use them?

In moments of stillness, when I began seeking these answers, was when I learned to recognize what God's voice sounds like.

I was worried that I may never see or hear from Anyango again. She seemed certain that she would come back after the funeral and move in with Mercy, but there was still a possibility that her own family would take her instead.

Of course, it wouldn't have been the worst thing if Anyango's family decided to take her. If there was a chance that she wouldn't have to be separated from every one of her relatives, that would have been the preferred option. My only concern was that I wouldn't be able to check on her as easily, so having her stay with a trusted friend of mine, who knew my values and expectations, gave me a lot more peace of mind. Either way, I would make sure that she was taken care of, and I trusted that God would reveal to me how I was supposed to do that.

In the meantime, my life in Kisumu carried on as usual. I spent most of my days working with the children at Ringroad, and my evenings at St. Anne's or Chris and Sarah's house. I've always been one to value my alone time, but family dinners with the Nicholsons had become a true saving grace in this foreign, often lonely environment. I would typically walk to their house and arrive shortly before dinner time. Iddy would be finishing up his homework, Ruth-Michael and Abby-Jones playing with their toys, as Chris and Sarah prepped food in the kitchen with the music on. Their ability to leave an emotional day at the door and keep their home a joyful and peaceful place, was something to be admired.

144

While they continued to be significant mentors to me, we also developed a very deep and genuine friendship over the two years that I had been traveling back and forth to Kenya. Not only did we share lunches and dinners, but we shared holiday celebrations. We rejoiced together when sick children recovered from life-threatening illness, and mourned the realities of circumstances that we couldn't fix or change.

I met their family members and close friends who visited from the States, and they cheered me on as I learned how to navigate life as a young, single woman in a developing country. They watched me grow in my faith after Grandpa died, and I watched them grow into a family of five when Abby-Jones was born. It's amazing how closely people bond when they are walking through such a unique version of life together.

"I wanted to give you a quick update on where we stand with our ministry," Sarah said to me one night after dinner.

Chris had taken the girls up to bed and Iddy was busy washing the dishes. My heart sank as Sarah and I continued to clear the table, and I braced myself for a conversation that I had been anxiously anticipating. They were just five months away from completing their three-year commitment to Ringroad, and it was time for them to start considering where they would serve next.

"There is a chance that we'll stay in Kisumu, but we've decided to start exploring a couple of other options, as well."

"Ok. But those other options would still be in Kenya?"

"Yes, we will stay in Kenya for a few more years, we just aren't sure where yet."

Sarah wiped the last of the crumbs off the table.

"There's a children's home in Kitale that we are going to see, and we'll probably look at a few other possibilities, as well."

We walked into the living room to finish our conversation; the weight of it sitting heavily on my chest.

"Regardless of what comes next, you're going to finish out this year at Ringroad, right?"

"Yes, that's the plan."

We sat in silence for a moment before Sarah turned to me and said,

"I know you aren't quite sure what your plans will be after this year. Just know that if you do decide to be in Kenya full-time, you're always welcome to work with us, wherever we end up."

I tried to imagine my life in Kisumu without the Nicholsons, and I couldn't. But I also knew that it was important for me to make my decisions based on where I felt God leading me, rather than what felt more desirable. Chris and Sarah would be leaning heavily on God's voice when it came to planning their next steps, and I needed to do the same; even if that meant being apart from them.

Anyango returned to St. Anne's just over a week after Caren's funeral. She called to let me know that she was coming, and I was relieved to hear her sweet voice. I so badly wanted to ask how she was feeling emotionally, but I trusted Violet's wisdom and shifted my focus to moving Anyango forward. The burial was over, it was time to move on.

Before she and Mercy left for home, I brought Anyango up to my room and gave her some of my clothes, along with a soft purple blanket that I brought from the States. I asked if she felt ready to move in with Mercy, and she said yes. She was still relatively shy and distant, but her spirit seemed to be a bit lighter. I was in complete awe of her resilience.

When it was time for them to go, a motorbike met them at the gate. They both climbed onto the back of it, with Anyango's few possessions sandwiched in between them. We agreed that she would take a couple of days to settle in, and then we'd begin the process of enrolling her at the primary school nearest to Mercy's house. I allowed myself to feel hopeful, as they drove away from St. Anne's and I waved goodbye.

Lord, please protect that beautiful girl.
Keep her safe and allow her to heal.
Give her strength, provision and peace,
And grant me the wisdom I'll need to care for her well.

I prayed harder and more often for Anyango than I had for anyone else in my three months of newly found faith. I believed that Caren died knowing I would take care of her daughter in one way or another, and I felt convicted in honoring that. The conviction was the sound of God's voice.

Weeks went by, and Anyango adjusted to her new life. She joined the eight-grade class at Shauri Moyo Primary School, and was easing into a routine at home with Mercy's two young children. I didn't go and visit her there, but I called to check in, and asked Mercy for updates almost every day.

"Oh, Jenny, she is doing very well. She is a good girl."

Relieved by Anyango's progress, I was able to step back and refocus on my work at Ringroad. I still held group counseling sessions, but it seemed that the majority of my time was being used to address the medical needs of our students. I was learning more about the nature of diseases like HIV and Sickle Cell Anemia, and helping to coordinate treatment plans with the resources that were available in town.

With my ever-expanding knowledge of Kisumu's medical community, came many more opportunities to learn the cultural norms that were necessary for me to understand. For example, it is very uncommon for a patient or their caregiver to ask a doctor any questions, whether they understand the diagnosis or not. Sometimes they don't know exactly what to ask, but there is also a fear that the doctor will perceive a question as a challenge to his or her medical degree. Not wanting to insult the doctor, patients simply listen and take the medication that is prescribed to them.

My biggest personal challenge in terms of navigating Kenya's cultural norms, was learning not to coddle people who were in physical or emotional pain. As it turns out, Violet's advice on how to encourage Anyango, applied to more than just a child facing the loss of a parent. In places where means of comfort are often unavailable, the "tough it out" mentality becomes ingrained and passed down from one generation to another.

Therefore, if a child has a high fever due to Malaria, and needs to leave school early, it is okay for them to walk home without assistance. There won't always be someone around to offer them a ride, or to help them carry their books. They may not even have someone at home who can come retrieve them, so they need to know that they are strong enough to get home on their own.

One afternoon, I was walking by the Ringroad clinic and heard a child screaming at the top of his lungs. I walked inside to find out if this was one of our students, and why he was in so much pain. The receptionist let me know that the patient was ours, and gave me permission to go back and check on him.

I walked in to the room and found nine-year-old Ryan, lying face down on the examination table, screaming and shaking.

"Hey, what's going on in here?" I asked, rushing over to Ryan's side.

"This boy is having Malaria and Typhoid. He is very sick, so we must give him some injections."

I ran my hand over Ryan's forehead, which was burning up, and asked if he wanted me to stay with him. Ryan nodded and grabbed onto my leg.

"Jen, I don't want the injections, they are painful!"

I rubbed Ryan's back in an attempt to calm his shaking little body.

"I know they're painful, but that pain will only last for a second. If you don't get the injections, you will be in pain for much longer because you'll still be sick. You don't want to stay sick, do you?"

Ryan let out a tiny whimper and shook his head. The doctor came up behind him, told him to lay still, and pierced him in the bottom with another injection. There was some more screaming, followed by more shaking, and I continued to rub his back until he was able to calm down completely.

"Can you feel the medicine working yet?"

Ryan thought for a second, a faint smirk running across his face.

"Yes, I am starting to feel better now."

"See? I told you injections aren't so bad!"

With a full smile, and slightly cooler skin, Ryan rolled onto his side and fell asleep.

On my way back out, the receptionist asked how our patient was doing.

"He was able to fall asleep, so I think he feels better."

"Mmm, that's good news."

"Yeah. I felt so sad for him when he was screaming like that. I'm thankful that I was here to help calm him down, especially since his mom isn't here."

The receptionist chuckled and very respectfully responded, "Yes, it's good that you were here. But he would have also been okay by himself, He's a strong boy."

It's ironic, I know, but the norm that was hardest for me to process, happens to be the one that I admire most. The strength that Kenyan people display, in every sense of the word, is beyond anything that I can emulate or explain to you. You'll just have to take me at my word, when I tell you that you've never seen anything like it.

By the end of August, I felt that I had hit my stride. I was becoming more familiar with our students' medical challenges, and worked well with Ringroad's Directors and clinical staff, in order to address them. I began to accept that coming from a world full of resources, wasn't an automatic qualifier to having all of the answers. I didn't always know what worked best, and it wasn't always essential that I took the lead. My job was to identify the gaps, and how I could be useful in helping this community bridge them together.

The possibility of Chris and Sarah stepping away from Ringroad, posed an interesting challenge for me. While I hated the idea of being at Ringroad, or in Kisumu, without them, it felt like God was preparing my heart to do just that. On days that they were working off-site, or exploring opportunities that would be a good fit for their family and their ministry, I was comfortable enough to be at Ringroad without them. I didn't want to be, but I couldn't ignore the fact that I was capable of being there on my own.

Before I could make any decisions about my future in Kenya, I needed to spend some time addressing the present. I was two months in to my proposed six-month stay, and while I felt emotionally prepared to honor my commitment, my finances were indicating something else. I was receiving a discount for my stay at St. Anne's, but boarding there was an expense that I couldn't carry for four more months. The Nicholson's house had a constant rotation of visitors, so staying with them would only be possible sporadically. Any other housing option that was safe enough for me, was also one that skirted the very top of my budget.

Every once in a while, someone from back home would make a donation that allowed my work in Kenya to continue. I did a fairly decent job of providing updates on how my mission was progressing, and there were people in my life who felt compelled to support it. I was always thankful, but not being able to guarantee any sort of consistency in funding, meant I also couldn't guarantee a true timeline for my stay. Regardless of what I wanted, staying in Kenya for a full six months would not be possible if I couldn't afford it.

Enter, Jonathan and Andrea Dowell: the couple from Portland, Oregon, who walked into my life at the perfect time, but in the most unexpected of ways.

Late one night, while I was preparing for bed at St. Anne's, I became violently ill. I felt fine all day, ate dinner that night, and started feeling nauseous sometime after that. Now, as you know, I am no stranger to an upset stomach; but this time it seemed that the more I vomited, the worse I felt. Equipped with packets of electrolyte mix that I brought from the States, I did my best to sip on some fluids and get some rest.

Unfortunately, my body wasn't having any of that. For three straight hours, I ran back and forth to the toilet. There was no keeping down fluids, there were no moments of rest. I didn't have a thermometer, but my burning skin and aching joints told me that I had a fever. Feeling weak and severely dehydrated, I knew that I needed to get to a hospital. The only problem was that I had no way of getting there.

It was well after midnight. Chris and Sarah were out of town, visiting a child sponsorship program on the coast, and there was no tuk-tuk driver who worked in the middle of the night. The only staff at the guest house was the security guard, and I wasn't sure if he'd be able to help me. I felt too weak to walk down the stairs and ask him.

Feeling desperate and unwilling to wait for the morning, I dug out

149

my copy of the Kisumu Women's Bible Study contact list. It was given to me back in June, when Sarah suggested that I attend one of their meetings to connect with other expat women who were living in our area. Still not feeling ready to do a deep dive into Biblical text, I only attended their meeting once; the day that they happened to provide everyone an updated contact list.

Of the twenty-something names, I only recognized about three of them. I knew that Sally, an English woman in her sixties, lived with her husband just a few properties down from St. Anne's. She had invited Sarah over for tea one afternoon, and since I was staying with Sarah at the time, I was welcomed to tag along. Sally had been very kind to me then, and I prayed that she would offer me the same kindness at two o'clock in the morning.

The following hour is somewhat of a blur to me. Sally answered my phone call, and let me know that she and her husband would be willing to bring me to the hospital. Since driving around Kisumu in the middle of the night was somewhat of a safety concern, she contacted their private security company and requested an escort for their vehicle. I remember crawling down the stairs and laying on the floor in the lobby while I waited for them to arrive.

By the time we reached the hospital, I had nothing left in my body to get rid of. I continued to dry-heave and was certain that I was going to lose consciousness, but I wasn't afraid. I made it to the hospital, and I wasn't there alone. That's all I was concerned about.

As it turns out, I simply had a nasty stomach bug. I was given IV fluids, topped off with anti-nausea medication and something to ease my body aches. They also gave me some probiotics to bring home and drink twice a day. I was exhausted, but relieved to be feeling better.

"I don't like the thought of you recovering by yourself at St. Anne's," Sally told me on the way back from the hospital.

"Unfortunately, we've got a meeting out of town this weekend, so we won't be able to come and check on you."

In all of my time spent in Kenya so far, I don't think I had ever felt so lonely.

"That's okay, I'll just take a few days to rest and then I'll be fine."

"Do you know anyone else here besides us and the Nicholsons?"

"I've met others before, but I don't really know them."

We pulled up to St. Anne's and I slowly stretched my legs out of the car. The idea of going back up to my bed, after spending all of those miserable hours in it the night before, made me feel sick all over again.

"I'll tell you what I'm going to do, then," Sally continued.

"A woman named Andrea lives just down the road from here, as well. You might have met her before. She's quite lovely, and I'm sure she wouldn't mind coming to check in on you. Is it okay if I give her your number?"

I eagerly accepted Sally's suggestion to let another person check in on me. Though I knew that I would be physically okay, being sick in a foreign country, far from all of your loved ones, has a way of making you feel painfully alone.

Andrea Dowell texted me later that morning, and then came by the guest house. She asked how I was feeling, and if there was anything that I needed or wanted. I told her that I was craving pasta, and asked if she had any butter and parmesan cheese. Less than an hour later, Andrea returned with the butter, the cheese and an offer that I wasn't expecting.

"My husband, Jonathan, and I would love to have you stay with us for a few days, while you recover."

I hardly knew this woman, but I could have kissed her. Those were the sweetest words I had ever heard in my life.

"You would have your own room, on your own side of the house. It'll be nice and quiet, but you would also have the comfort of knowing that you weren't alone."

"You really wouldn't mind?" I asked, already mentally packing my bags.

"We wouldn't mind at all. You'd be very welcome."

For three glorious days, I recovered from my stomach virus at Jonathan and Andrea Dowell's house. I ate the American meals that Andrea cooked, and watched my favorite American shows on an actual television. Their shower was always hot when I turned it on, and their internet was hardly ever spotty.

In the midst of such luxury, I often found myself sitting in a place of guilt. I was recovering from this stomach virus the same way that I've always had the privilege of recovering from an illness: safe shelter, ample food and water, proper medications, hot showers, my favorite television shows, and the option to move back and forth between a comfortable bed and a comfortable couch. Only this time, there were people right across the street from me, who were suffering through illness without a single one of those things. There were human beings- many of whom were children- laying on concrete floors, with high fevers and no medication.

In my opinion, that gap is the most challenging space to find God. It's easy to acknowledge His love and provision when you're the one being provided for; but impossible to justify the claim of His eternal goodness, when such suffering exists right across the street.

151

Each night, while I was recovering at the Dowells, I would lay in bed and wiggle my fingers and toes; memorizing how the sheets felt on my skin and thanking God for always providing me with a safe place. Perhaps the most cherished piece of advice that Chris and Sarah Nicholson had ever given me over the years, was to lead with gratitude over guilt. Guilt has the tendency to paralyze, whereas gratitude propels you forward into a place of serving others. We may never have all of the world's answers, but the very least that we can always do, is be thankful for our blessings.

On my fourth night with Jonathan and Andrea, I planned on telling them that I would be heading back to St. Anne's in the morning. I was grateful for their hospitality, but feeling much better and didn't want them to think that I was taking advantage of their kindness. We sat down at the table for dinner, and prayed over our food. I was mere seconds away from thanking them again, and announcing my departure, when Jonathan looked up from his plate and said,

"Andrea and I have talked about it, and would like to offer you a place to stay for the remainder of your time in Kenya."

I dropped my fork and looked back and forth between the two of them.

"Are you serious?"

"We are very serious," Andrea answered. "We would love to have you here with us."

Jonathan continued, "We wouldn't charge you rent; only the cost of household expenses. So, if you feel ready to leave St. Anne's, then you are welcome here."

I couldn't believe what I was hearing, but I knew that it was an echo of God's voice. I felt more than ready to leave St. Anne's, and was about a month away from having no other financial option but to head back to the States early. All that time spent praying for God to reveal whether I was meant to stay, and I always hoped that His answer would come in the from an unexpected donation. Turns out, God revealed His intentions for me in the form of a stomach bug.

Chapter Fifteen

Dad wants to bring me to the Reservoir.

It's a nice day outside and he says that I should enjoy it, so I listen and follow him out to the car. I don't want to go because I don't really like walking, and I'm afraid that we will see a snake or a fox or some other kind of scary animal. But I also don't want to hurt Dad's feelings. He's trying so hard to help me feel better, and I don't want to disappoint him.

We get to the Reservoir and Dad starts skipping down the trail. He looks so happy and I wish I could be that happy, too. Sometimes he asks me why I feel bad and I tell him I don't know. Then he says that at nine years old, I shouldn't feel so sad all of the time. He tells me that I have a really wonderful life; and I know that he is right. I just don't know what's wrong with me.

As we walk, Dad keeps taking deep breaths of the fresh air, and telling me to do the same.

"Breathe in the fresh air, Jennifer! Breathe it in and enjoy it! It is a beautiful day!"

But I don't really know how to enjoy it. I'm trying, but I feel sad and a little bit anxious inside. Dad's good at making me laugh, so I wish he would try to do that, instead of making me go on this walk. I didn't even really eat today, so I don't have much energy.

Dad can see that I'm not going to cheer up at the Reservoir. He tells me that we at least have to make one full lap around the water, and then we can leave. By the time that our lap is almost finished, I'm starting to like being there. I want to tell Dad that, but then he might make me stay longer, and I still don't want to.

We get back in the car and drive home. I look out the window for the entire drive, and feel sad that our special day together is coming to an end. I just know that if Dad takes me back to the Reservoir someday, I'll do better next time. I'll enjoy the whole thing; rather than just the very end, right before it's time to go home.

~ ~ ~

Dear Sweet Girl,

When my friends and I moved to Tennessee after college, it took us a while to find jobs. In the meantime, we used our savings to explore the social scene in Nashville, and made friends with a group of guys who worked at a bar near our apartment.

One weekend, the guys invited us to spend a day out on their friend's boat. There was lots of alcohol, lots of marijuana, and a suggestion to go cliff jumping off of the rocks that surrounded the marina. Having lost all of our inhibitions, Jackie, Kellagh and I followed our new friends up to the top of the rocks.

The guys volunteered to jump first, so that we could see the proper way to do it. We were told to straighten our bodies like a pencil, and land feet-first, in order to avoid hitting the water with dangerous force. Apparently, if you jump from high enough and don't land well, the impact of hitting the water is equivalent to the impact of hitting a brick wall.

I remember standing at the edge of the rock and looking down. I remember thinking to myself that if I didn't jump right in that exact moment, I was going to chicken out. Not wanting to miss an opportunity to be brave- though it was a façade fueled by intoxication- I closed my eyes and jumped. I then panicked, in mid-air, and curled my body into the fetal position. That's how I landed.

I should have gone to the hospital, but I ignored my throbbing chest and the huge black spots that were forming on the backs of my legs. I assumed that I would heal in a couple of days, and be left with nothing but a ridiculous story to tell about something that I would never, ever do again.

To this day, I continue to have health problems because of that jump. I eventually sought the help of a Chiropractor; whose x-rays revealed a curve in my neck from the whiplash that I endured when I hit the water. I was given an MRI to ensure that there was no further damage, and had months of physical therapy to heal my neck and back muscles. I get chronic migraines, and sometimes I get dizzy spells or a low ringing in my ears. I was later diagnosed with an auto-immune disease that has no confirmed cause, but my doctor speculated that it could have been triggered by the damage done to my body when I jumped. If I could take back any decision I've ever made, it would be that one. For a long time, I couldn't revisit that memory without hating myself.

I was sitting on the Dowell's couch when I made the decision to move to Kenya. My neck was beginning to tighten with the pain that usually signals a migraine, and I was feeling a little bit dizzy. At this point, concerns over my physical health were the only thing standing in the way of me making a decision. Though I wasn't dealing with anything life threatening, I was unsure that I could commit to living in a place that didn't necessarily have all of the health care provisions that I was used to back home.

I spent weeks contemplating this, ever since God made it abundantly clear what His intentions were for me, by moving me into Jonathan and Andrea's house. He had called me to Kenya and was intending to keep me there. It was no longer just a fun and magical place for me to visit; being in Kenya had almost become essential to my heartbeat. God's grace allowed me to cast aside desires for what was easy and comfortable, and replace it with what felt like the purest way to live my life: in His love.

Sitting on the Dowell's couch, I picked up my phone and searched the internet for ways to manage the lasting effects of whiplash. I then set my phone down and did a series of stretches that I remembered from physical therapy. For years, I had avoided any engagement in ways that I could heal my body, because I was so angry at myself for damaging it in the first place. But with God's voice in my ear, I sat on the couch of the people who were strangers to me only a month before, in a country thousands of miles away from home, and stretched my neck and shoulders. Then I picked my phone back up, called Mom, and told her that I was moving to Kenya.

One of my least favorite things to do in this world, is to participate in a social situation where I'm forced to pretend that my own world isn't smack in the middle of turning upside down. You know those times where you've had to go to a big family celebration or a neighborhood dinner and act like Mom and Dad weren't just fighting for the last five hours? Or pretend that Dad was working late, when really, he had just moved out again? I hate to break it to you, Sweet Girl, but you're going to encounter quite a few more of those in your lifetime. The world doesn't always stop for our difficult days, but at least you get pretty good at throwing on a fake happy face.

I found out that Chris and Sarah were moving, as we were setting up their house for a neighborhood gathering. They weren't planning on telling me until after the party, but I knew in my gut that they had made a decision, and insisted that they tell me before the other guests arrived. The only thing that I hate more than putting on a fake smile, is anticipating difficult news.

Upon finishing the year in Kisumu, they would return to the States for a brief furlough, and then relocate to Malindi: a small town on the coast of Kenya. There was a child mentorship and sponsorship program that was in need of some direction, and its team felt that Chris and Sarah would be a good fit for the task. Knowing how much prayer and emotional processing was put into their decision to leave Ringroad, my first reaction was to be thankful that God was giving them another opportunity to serve His people in Kenya. However, I'm not going to lie and tell you that I wasn't also completely devastated that they were leaving.

"Go figure, you decide that you're leaving right after I decide to move here," I joked.

"You're going to do great," Sarah encouraged. "We have complete faith in you."

Being in Kisumu without The Nicholsons was impossible to imagine. They built such a beautiful life there, and over the course of two and a half years, I had the privilege of walking through it alongside of them. They were fiercely beloved by the Ringroad community, their local friends, and fellow expats. For so many, they were a pillar of hope, and a living example of God's unconditional love. There was no doubt in my mind that their impact would be lasting, but that wouldn't take away from the pain of watching them go.

On a brutally hot day in November, Chris and Sarah Nicholson stood in front of the students and staff at Ringroad Orphans Day School and announced their plan to relocate to the coast. I sat quietly on the office steps and watched them fight back tears, as they poured their deepest sentiments of love and gratitude over all who were a part of the Ringroad family. They assured the children that their reason for leaving was not a reflection of diminishing love for them, but rather a calling from God to spread that love to other children who were just like them. For the rest of the day, students flooded the office with hugs, tears, and Thank You letters.

In His infinite wisdom, God began preparing me for this season long before it fell upon us. I spent three full months living with Jonathan and Andrea, and was welcomed into their world with open, loving arms. Like Chris and Sarah, they were patient with me as I stumbled through the learning curve of navigating life in Kenya. They offered their wisdom when I asked for it, and stepped back when they felt I needed to assert my independence. I was incredibly grateful that I'd have them there with me as I transitioned into full-time ministry.

156

During my last week in Kisumu with the Nicholsons, I spent a night at their house. So many of my earliest and fondest memories of Kenya revolve around the time we spent together in their home, and I wanted to honor that with one final sleepover. We enjoyed a wonderful dinner together, and then I offered to help get the girls ready for bed. I was giving Ruth-Michael a bath when she looked up at me and said,

"Are you feeling sad, Jen?"

I had always been impressed by Ruth-Michael's emotional intelligence. She was only three years old at the time, but she was already developing a sense of empathy and understanding that felt well beyond her years.

"No, I'm okay, Baby Girl. Why did you ask if I'm feeling sad?"

Ruth-Michael looked down at the teapot that she was playing with in the bathtub. She filled it with water and spilled it back out, over and over again.

"Because everyone is sad that we are leaving Kisumu. People keep telling Mama and Papa how sad they are."

Watching Ruth-Michael play with her teapot, my eyes began to burn with the tears that I had been trying to suppress all night. Of course I was feeling sad; but I was also committed to making our time together about anything but my own sadness. I knew that Sarah and Chris were preparing their hearts for this next season, and my own grief almost felt selfish.

I didn't shy away from telling them how sad I was to see them go; I just didn't want my feelings to be the center of attention. As I explained to Ruth-Michael why the sadness people expressed wasn't necessarily a bad thing, I found that I was also sort of explaining it to myself.

"People are sad that you're leaving Kisumu because they love your family very much. But they also understand that God is leading you guys somewhere else, so that you can take all of the love that you found in Kisumu, and share it with even more people. Does that make sense?"

Ruth-Michael shrugged her little shoulders. "I don't know."

I smiled and told her to close her eyes, so that I could take the teapot and dump water on her head, before I added shampoo.

"People are feeling sad because you are moving away; but moving away is not a bad thing. Your family has helped many people to feel happy, and that's why everyone here loves you so much, and wants you to stay. But when you go to your new home, you will have a chance to spread more love and happiness than you could if you just stayed in one place."

I couldn't really tell how much of what I was saying resonated with Ruth-Michael, but at the age of twenty-seven, these words were just starting to resonate with me. In explaining to Ruth-Michael the beauty of what her family was doing, I, myself, began to embrace their decision in a way I hadn't truly known how to. God used Sweet three-year-old Ruth-Michael Nicholson, to give me the most perfect gift in further understanding His love.

I decided to return to the States just before Thanksgiving. My hope was to permanently move to Kenya at the beginning of the following year, so I wanted to spend the holidays with my family and begin fundraising for my ministry as soon as possible.

Visiting a developing country changes one's heart. Living there, as an outsider, deepens the imprint- for better or for worse. Some days I find myself walking around with an abundance of gratitude for the privilege that I live in; while other days, I'm angry at everyone who has the audacity to live their lives without acknowledging the human suffering that exists in the world. Is that fair? No. But I'm working on it.

Returning to the States after five months in Kenya, proved to be more of an adjustment than living in Kenya ever was. I didn't necessarily "forget" how to live in my own country, but I often felt like I was an outsider, who was going through the motions of acting as if I belonged there. My way of processing the world began running through a filter that included dozens of names and faces attached to extreme poverty, illness and abuse. Every single day that I woke up and lived my privileged American life, I carried with me the millions of ways that my life seemed to be unfair. I forgot to be thankful for things like the innumerable options for cereal at the grocery store, because I was too focused on the guilt of knowing that other people didn't have food to eat.

In the moments where I allowed myself to be still, and to hear God's voice, He reminded me that I am not being asked to harbor any guilt. What He wants is for me to be so thankful for my blessings that I use them to help other people. Just like Chris and Sarah taught me: guilt leaves you paralyzed, while gratitude prepares your heart to serve others. So much potential for good is wasted if a privileged life is lived in guilt.

Chapter Sixteen

We've been excited about this trip for weeks.

Sas, and I are going to be spending a whole week with her extended family up in Maine. Her aunt and uncle have a big, beautiful house on the lake, and Sas had always talks about how much she loves going up there to visit.

Having grown up together, I know and love Sas's family as if they are my own. Both of our families have extended relatives that come to visit us in Farmington, and we all love seeing each other. We even call each other's grandparents "Grandma and Grandpa."

Our parents have taken us on so many vacations together. We celebrate birthdays and holidays, have sleepovers on weekends and find ways to laugh together, even when life feels a little bit scary or confusing. Sas doesn't struggle with anxiety but she knows that I do, and she never makes me feel bad or embarrassed by it. She is a constant safe place for me.

Our trip to Maine is supposed to be a way of celebrating that we are about to go into our Junior year of high school. The end of sophomore year was a tough stretch for me, because my anxiety peaked again, and I was barely making it through an entire day of school. Even now, I don't want to do anything social. I'd be perfectly happy staying in the safety of my home, with my family. The problem is that staying home always ends up making me feel depressed. I want to have a desire to do things.

We are supposed to leave for Maine after lunch, but I haven't been able to get myself to eat anything all day. I spent the entire morning watching the clock, counting down the minutes until I have to say goodbye to my house and my family for one whole week. I decide to tell Mom that I don't want to go, after all.

Mom calls my Dad and asks him to come over. I'm so thankful for the way that they take care of me, but I am so sick of needing to be taken care of. Dad arrives and we all go over to Sas's house, where her family is waiting to load up the car and hit the road. I feel so miserable inside; not only because I'm anxious about leaving, but that I can't match the excitement of Sas and her family.

159

Her Aunt Leigh and and Uncle Brian hug me and tell me how happy they are that I am coming along, but I can't honestly tell them that I am happy, too.

It's always scary to tell people who don't already know about my anxiety. Even if they are people that I feel close to, I don't want them to start looking at me differently once they know how badly I struggle sometimes. I get nervous that it will be the only part of me that they see, and then it'll be too late to take it back.

Even though Sas knows my anxious tendencies, she doesn't know the extent. Aunt Leigh and Uncle Brian, don't know any of it. And so, instead of piling into the car and leaving for Maine right after lunch like we are supposed to, Mom, Dad and I sit down with Sas and her family, and tell them just how hard of a time I was having.

Mom and Dad start by talking briefly about my history with anxiety, and how I was starting to struggle with depression, as well. I do my best to articulate why I feel so anxious in this moment, but I'm not sure it's making sense. If I wasn't so used to it myself, it wouldn't make sense to me, either.

"It has nothing to do with you guys, I just don't ever want to leave the house anymore."

Everyone listens and tells me that they love and support me. They say that I can feel safe with them, and not be embarrassed. I guess that helped me to feel better, because now I'm ready to go to Maine. Sas and I get in the car with Aunt Leigh, Uncle Brian, and their two little girls, Jennie and Lexi. We have a long car ride ahead of us, and I still haven't eaten anything, but I finally feel like I can. I'm so glad that my anxiety didn't win this time.

~ ~ ~

Dear Sweet Girl,

On February 10th, 2016, myself and four tightly packed suitcases made the long journey back to Kisumu, Kenya. It's funny, because even though I seemed like the most unlikely person to make such a move, there

160

was never a moment where I questioned it. Much like when I joined Lipscomb's mission trip three years earlier, once my decision was made, I never looked back.

After thirty hours of travel, I was overjoyed to find Andrea waiting for me at the airport in Nairobi. Since I wasn't able to get a flight out to Kisumu until the following morning, I had asked Andrea to meet me in Nairobi so that I wouldn't have to spend the night there alone. Seeing her face gave me the comfort that I needed to remain level-headed, as I looked around the airport and slowly processed the idea that this particular arrival did not come with a subsequent departure date. It was there that I would be making a life for myself, and the United States that I would be visiting every so often.

I took a few days to settle in before I dove back into the work. The Dowells offered me their home again, and told me that I could take my time in searching for a house of my own. Being back in their space helped to anchor me as I attempted to get a sense of what my "new normal" would be, without The Nicholsons by my side. Being honest, if I hadn't had all nine months' worth of previous time spent in Kenya, there's no way that I would have felt comfortable enough to move there- with or without Chris and Sarah. There's also no way that God didn't know that. His timing was, and continues to be, at the very heart of this story; perfectly aligning the pieces of this most unassuming life.

I waited two whole days before I went to Ringroad. I know that doesn't sound like a long time, but the most I ever waited in the past was only a number of hours. It was important to me that I walked into the office feeling confident in my place there, and not like I was still hovering in the shadow of my beloved friends and mentors. Yes, I would always carry their example with me, but it was time that I saw Ringroad more as God's place, and less as Chris and Sarah's or anybody else's. It didn't belong to any of us- not me, not them, not the directors or the donors who built it- Ringroad was God's place, and it was up to each of us to understand our roles within it, as He intended them. When I thought about it that way, the transition felt much easier. Naturally, though, I still cried the first time I walked into the office, post-Nicholson's.

Aside from getting myself acclimated, seeing Anyango was a priority for me. I wasn't able to communicate with her while I was in the States, but I was able to send Mercy her financial support from Rhonda and Kathy each month. She emailed me once from a computer at St. Anne's and let me know that she received the money, but other than that, I didn't hear from her. It had been seven months since Caren passed away,

161

and I was excited to see Anyango and hear about the progress she was making both in school and at home with Mercy and the other children.

St. Anne's was just around the corner from The Dowell's house, so I walked there one afternoon to see Mercy and arrange a time for me to meet with Anyango. When I arrived there, all of the staff were so excited to see me, and quick to ask why I wasn't staying with them this time. I explained that my friends offered me a place to stay, and promised that I would continue to walk over and visit them when I had the chance. When Mercy saw me, her eyes lit up and a huge smile spread across her face.

"Aye! Jenny! How I've missed you, My Dear!"

In Kenya, it is customary to shake someone's hand when you are greeting them, but I ran over and gave Mercy a big hug.

"I'm so happy to be back!" I told her as I melted into her arms, overwhelmed with joy and gratitude for all that she had been doing for that precious girl of ours.

"I can't wait to see Anyango! How has she been doing?"

Mercy put her hands on my shoulders and pulled back from our embrace, so that she could look me in the eye.

"Oh, Jenny. It is a good girl that we have there. She is doing her studies and helping in the house with the other kids. She is really doing very well."

I was ecstatic to hear this, especially when I thought about what could have easily been the alternative. Being with Mercy was keeping Anyango off of the streets and allowing her to focus on getting her education. Maybe she had a chance for a bright future, after all.

Mercy and I made a plan for Anyango to meet me at St. Anne's the following Sunday after church. I wasn't completely opposed to visiting Mercy's house one day, but I was weary of going into a slum that I wasn't familiar with, and drawing too much attention to myself. It was easy for Anyango to get to St. Anne's, so it felt like a good mutual spot for us to meet.

Days passed, and I continued to ease myself back into the work at Ringroad. One of the first cases that I had upon my return, was a little boy named Frank, who suffered from Sickle Cell Anemia. He was not a Ringroad student, but he attended a school that was within the same sponsorship program, and resided at the children's home there. He was brought to us by one of the staff members at the home, since our location had a clinic on site.

Sickle Cell Anemia is a disease that effects the red blood cells; causing them to be misshapen and to die more quickly. Anemia is the lack of healthy red blood cells, and Sickle Cell Crisis is when the misshapen cells become stuck and block normal blood flow in the body, causing severe pain. When Frank was brought to our office, he was in Sickle Cell Crisis.

Evans and I knew that Frank would need a blood transfusion, which could not be done at our clinic. With sponsorship through the Texas-based non-profit, Christian Relief Fund, Frank would be able to receive the medical attention that he needed from the government hospital. Evans contacted CRF to request funding for the transfusion, while I brought Frank to his grandmother's house in Nyalenda. He would need a family member to accompany him to the hospital, and I wanted to be sure that they were clear on what exactly Sickle Cell Anemia is, and what they would be going to the hospital for. It wasn't the first time that Frank needed a blood transfusion, but he didn't always go to the hospital with the same person.

We arrived at his grandmother's house, and I asked my tuk-tuk driver, William, to come in and translate for me. Frank's English was fluent, but he was feeling too sick to speak and I didn't want to push him. He was barely able to walk through the doorway without stopping to catch his breath. As soon as he made it inside, he collapsed into a plastic chair.

The house reminded me a lot of Caren's. It was a one-room home with mud walls and a dirt floor. In the corner, there was a bed frame with a thin mattress on top that was so worn down, it could not have possibly offered any sort of comfort. Frank's grandmother was sitting on the bed, and silently turned her head towards the doorway at the sound of our entrance. I walked over and held out my hand to greet her.

"Shikamoo, Nyanya ya Frank. Habari ya asubuhi?" I said.

I didn't know much Swahili, but I was familiar with basic greetings and knew that I had gotten that one right. It translates to:

"Greetings, Grandmother of Frank. How are you this morning?"

She smiled in response to my effort to speak her language. She didn't have any teeth, and her soft, deeply wrinkled skin told the story of a lifetime's worth of hard work, suffering, and sacrifice. Her eyes were light gray and coated with a layer of milky white film. When she greeted me, she fixated them on the wall behind me.

"Frank? Is your grandmother blind?"

"Yes," Frank answered softly, as he shifted in his chair and winced in pain.

"How does she take care of herself then?"

"My aunt comes to help her."

163

I was relieved to know that she had help, but knew that she likely spent most of her time completely alone. This hurt my heart.

"So, it will be your aunt who brings you to the hospital?"

"Yes."

Frank's aunt lived just around the corner. We waited for her to come home, and then discussed why Frank needed to get to the hospital for a blood transfusion as soon as possible. I worked hard to tame the urgency that I felt on the inside, because I was learning to accept that the Kenyan culture was not built to absorb it. There are too many health crises and not enough educational or practical resources to manage them all. Therefore, any urgency or panic that I expressed would be left hanging in the air; adding space to a gaping hole that there are no resources to fill.

This was an incredibly difficult urge for me to fight. I saw Frank's little body curled up in pain, and all I wanted to do was pick him up and rush him to the hospital. I didn't want to wait for his aunt to get home, or to explain to her what Frank needed BEFORE he was able to go and get it. I did not want to hear her tell me that she would take him to the hospital AFTER she finished preparing lunch. As I went through the motions of doing those things, I fought the temptation to ignore what was encouraged of me and just take care of Frank myself. But the reality was, Frank would be okay to wait another hour or two, and it would ultimately do him a disservice if I ran around shouting about how unreasonable the waiting felt to me. He was able to manage his pain without uttering a single complaint, because he had been taught that there was no other choice. As badly as I wanted him to have some immediate relief, I also knew that Frank needed to sustain the ability to be patient and strong. After all, when they finally did reach the hospital, they wouldn't find any urgency there, either. It was important for Frank to be able to cope in those waiting periods.

Later that evening, I received word from Frank's aunt that he had been admitted to the hospital and was receiving his transfusion. I thanked her for taking care of him, and requested that she contact Evans to settle the payment of the medical bills. My heart was relieved, as I sat quietly on the floor of my bedroom and thanked God for allowing me to be a part of Frank's story. I also thanked Him for giving me the discernment to know my place, and to not overstep out of assumption that I knew better. At the end of the day, Frank would be thinking of how thankful he was for the opportunity to feel relief; not about how long he had to wait to get it.

Two days before my scheduled visit with Anyango, I received a phone call from her. It was right before dinner, and I was helping Jonathan set the table as Andrea pulled one of my favorite chicken recipes out of the oven.

"Hi. I am Anyango."

The sound of her soft voice brought me back to Caren's house, even though I knew that wasn't where she was calling me from.

"Hi Anyango! How are you?"

"I'm fine, and you?"

"I'm doing well, and I am so excited to see you soon!"

There was a pause on the other end, before Anyango responded with a "me, too."

Her hesitation, coupled with the fact that we were to meet in two days, led me to believe that something was wrong. She never would have called me just to shoot the breeze, especially so close to seeing each other in person.

"Are you okay?"

"Well, not really."

My heart sank and I lost my appetite, as my mind immediately went to worst-case scenarios. Her "not really" could have meant anything, but to me it meant that she was either pregnant, kicked out of school, or out on the streets.

"Okay, do you want to tell me what's going on?"

Another beat of hesitation. "Can we meet tomorrow instead of on Sunday? I want to tell you in person."

My heart was now racing. "Yes, that's fine, but can you at least tell me if you are in danger?"

"No, I'm not. I would just rather talk to you in person."

For nearly twenty-four hours, my brain swirled with possibilities that could have prompted Anyango to call me and ask to meet a day earlier than we had planned. What was so important that she couldn't wait until Sunday, but also couldn't tell me over the phone?

I walked over to St. Anne's and waited for her in the lobby. She told me that it was still okay for us to meet there, but she wasn't going to tell Mercy that she was coming. To me, this either meant that she and Mercy had a falling out, or that she got herself into trouble outside of the house and was afraid of Mercy's wrath. I let her know that Mercy would likely see us at St. Anne's and ask what she was doing there, but Anyango told me that was okay. She didn't care of Mercy knew she was there; she just didn't want to let her know ahead of time.

The girl who walked into the lobby shortly after I did, was not the same girl that I remembered leaving months earlier. She was wearing a sheer black skirt and a red button-up top. Her figure had filled out some, and she no longer appeared to be feeble or malnourished. Her hair was completely shaved off, her neck and shoulders held high in a display of confidence. I could not jump up to hug her fast enough.

"Anyango! I've missed you!"

For the first time ever, Anyango gave me a full smile back.

"Me too."

"You look so beautiful!"

"Thanks."

Violet, who was on duty at reception, came around the desk to greet Anyango, as well.

"Wow, you are looking really great," she said in English. Then she added a few more sentiments in Swahili, and turned to grab my hand.

"Jenny, this girl is really improving from the last time we saw her. She is looking so strong."

I couldn't have agreed more. Anyango may have come to discuss something serious, but there was life in her eyes, and a lightness to her that put me at ease. Whatever she needed to talk to me about, she was going to be okay. I asked if she wanted me to go and find Mercy, but she said no. She wanted to talk to me alone, first.

Violet gave me a key to the room that the staff uses when they need to take a rest. It had been a while, relatively speaking, since I used a room at the guest house, and the sights and smells hit me with a wave of nostalgia as I opened the door. It felt as if all of my time spent in those rooms- crying, loving, praying and processing- had prepared me for Anyango, and whatever she was about to share with me.

Once we were settled, I pushed past the formality of making small-talk, and asked Anyango to tell me what was wrong.

"I haven't been staying with Mercy since November. I've been staying with my aunt in Nyalenda."

I didn't understand. Mercy told me how well Anyango was doing at her house. She told me about her chores and her school work, and how well she helps to care for Mercy's other children.

"What do you mean you aren't staying with Mercy? She's told me how great things are working out with you being there."

"Well, I haven't been," Anyango said, bluntly. "She wasn't treating me well, so I left."

My head was spinning. "Can you tell me what you mean by that?"

166

Anyango spent the next few minutes telling me about her experience at Mercy's. She told me that Mercy would be away for long periods of time, and not leave money for Anyango to feed herself or the other children. She barely gave Anyango enough money to get more than a piece of flatbread, called chapati, for school lunch, and she forced her to do all of the household chores before she was allowed to eat, do her homework or go to sleep. When Mercy came home in a bad mood, she would yell derogatory things and tell her what a bad girl she was.

I felt sick to my stomach, as Anyango painted a horrifying picture of what life was like with the person that I left her with; the person that I trusted. Not knowing which claim to address first, I decided to go with the food. All of Mercy's alleged behaviors were inexcusable, but denying a child food felt particularly cruel; especially when money was being sent each month to ensure that child had enough to eat.

"I've been sending Mercy money for food each month. Did she tell you that?"

Anyango looked at me with an expression that gave me my answer.

"She told me that you promised to send money, but abandoned your promise as soon as you left Kenya last year."

My hands shook as I grabbed my phone and pulled up a financial statement from the app that I used to send Mercy money. I scrolled through all of my transactions, so that Anyango could see for herself that I had kept my promise. Not only was I mortified that money sent by friends of mine was being misused, but I was absolutely brokenhearted to learn that Anyango spent all of those months thinking that I abandoned her.

"Anyango, I am so sorry. Did you believe her?"

Shrugging her shoulders, Anyango replied, "I had no reason not to. I don't know you that well."

I wanted to scream. I wanted to storm up the stairs, find Mercy and scream in her face until she gave me an explanation and an apology. All that time, I thought that she was different; that she was offering to take in a child out of the kindness of her heart, and not for any sort of personal gain. How could I have been so naive?

"You're right, you don't know me that well. But I want you to know now that I would never, ever break a promise like that to you."

"Okay."

"And I am so sorry."

"It's okay."

When I asked whether Mercy got upset with Anyango when she decided to leave, Anyango told me that she was instructed not to tell me about it.

"She said that I'm only receiving school sponsorship because I am staying with her, and that if you found out that I am staying with my aunt, you would take my sponsorship away."

I knew what Mercy's fear was, and it had nothing to do with Anyango's school sponsorship. She didn't want to lose her monthly payment for Anyango's food and household needs. The payment that, apparently, she was keeping all for herself. Again, I wanted to scream…really, really loudly.

"So then why did you decide to tell me the truth?"

"My aunt told me that it was the right thing to do."

I needed to speak with Mercy, and asked Anyango if it was okay that I disclosed everything that she told me. When Anyango agreed, I asked if she wanted to leave the room once I called Mercy in, but she said that she didn't. She wanted to hear what Mercy had to say for herself.

Now, just like you, Little One, I have an enormous amount of sympathy for other human beings. I tend to forgive quickly, because I hate for people to feel any sort of guilt or shame; especially in front of other people, or when it seems they've learned their lesson. And, in this situation, I knew why Mercy did what she did. It was the act of a desperate person, who had lived her entire life in a cycle of poverty, and saw an opportunity for some small financial gain. I understood it, but it was going to take a whole lot of praying for me to sympathize and forgive. She wasn't just dishonoring me or Anyango's sponsors; her actions came at the expense of Anyango's health and well-being. That was what I could not tolerate.

When I called Mercy into the room, she saw Anyango and knew immediately why she was there. I could tell by the expression on her face, and the way she anxiously stood near the door. I confronted her with Anyango's claims and she didn't deny them. I asked her where the money was going to, and she told me that she had been saving it incase Anyango ever came back to her and told her that she needed something. I knew that she was lying, but asked that she go to the bank and withdraw it, anyway. She told me that she would need a few weeks.

I told her how disappointed I was, that I trusted her and considered her a friend. She responded by telling me that she doesn't want to lose me as a friend, because she may need to come to me for help one day, and she wouldn't want me to turn her away. It was a punch in the stomach to learn where Mercy placed all of the value in my friendship, while coming to the realization that she likely wasn't alone. Chances were, others who claimed me as a friend, only did so because of what they assumed I could offer them.

Needing to be freed from this conversation, I turned my attention back to Anyango and asked if she was okay at her aunt's house. When she told me that she was happy there, I thanked her for being honest, said we would be in touch, and walked her out to the front gate.

"We'll talk soon," I told her.

She hopped on the back of a motorbike, and I silently apologized again, as I watched her ride away.

Chapter Seventeen

I didn't know how I would feel about seeing a new therapist.

Rachel already knew everything about me, and I was really comfortable talking to her. Not that I couldn't feel comfortable with anyone else, but it's hard having to start from the beginning with someone new. Even if my existing file was passed on to her, I knew I'd still have to fill in a lot of blanks.

As it turns out, building a relationship with Michelle wasn't as hard as I thought it would be. She's very sweet and attentive, and understands everything that I'm saying without needing a long explanation. It seems like she just...understands me.

"I was thinking about starting a weekly support group with a few of my young female clients," she tells me after my session one day.

"If I do, would you be interested in joining?"

I love this idea. I've always wanted to meet other girls my age, who could relate to some of what I've been going through. At this point, it's hard for me to imagine that anyone's been dealing with anxiety for as long as I have. I practically came out of the womb with it.

"Yes, that would be great! Just tell me when, and I'll make sure my parents get me here."

Michelle arranges for our group sessions to be on Thursday evenings at 5pm. This actually works perfectly for me, because Thursdays are one of my nights with Dad and Sharon, and Michelle's office is really close to their house. I already have my individual sessions with her on Thursdays, but that doesn't cut into my time at Dad's because it's right after school. Now I'll have two therapy sessions back to back, and then get out in time to have dinner with the rest of the family.

When I tell Michelle how excited I am to start our group sessions, she tells me that she's not surprised.

"I have a feeling you all will be a great support system for one another," she said. "And I think you have a lot to offer the other girls."

This makes me feel so proud. If I can help other girls begin to conquer or cope with their anxieties, than maybe mine have their purpose. Maybe the reason why I was born this way was so that I could help others, with an understanding of what they're going through.

After my individual session the following Thursday, Michelle asks if I'm too tired to go right into our group session.

"I know you've been looking forward to starting this group, but now that it's here, do you still feel up for having one session after another?"

"I've been excited about this all day," I answered honestly.

Therapy, though it is healing, can also be very emotionally draining. Sometimes I do feel tired after spending an hour digging to the roots of my sadness and anxieties, but I've come to realize that this is where I feel most comfortable. Not only do I get to work through my own obstacles, but I get to learn how I might be able to help others do the same thing. The process of therapy almost feels like an artform; and I enjoy soaking all of it in.

Including me, there are five girls in our group. They all suffer from various levels of anxiety and depression, and two of them suffer from Obsessive Compulsive Disorder. One of them is in recovery from Anorexia and Bulimia. Some of them come from families with a history of mental illness or substance abuse. We may all have different stories, but there is a common thread that unifies us. Within five minutes of knowing one another, we share a bond that feels intense but natural at the same time. We all know what it feels like to be paralyzed by anxiety; and to be faced with the obstacle of explaining ourselves to people who don't understand. For the first time in my life, I understand that I am not alone in my feelings or struggles. I am not just being heard; I am being understood.

My struggles with food may not be related to how I feel about my appearance, but I understand the high that comes with gaining control from throwing up. My anxiety is not appeased by performing rituals like facing all of the clocks in my home a certain way, but man, do I understand what it feels like to have your mind race with irrational fears. I've never spent a day and a half in bed, but there have been plenty of times that I wanted to. There is a part of me that knows all of these girls, and can feel all of the pain that they describe.

Before our first session is over, I sense that my time in this group is going to give me more than a new layer to add to my support system. I decide that whatever I end up doing in this life, I will always make it a priority to help other people feel heard and understood. After tonight, I realize that absolutely nothing feels better than that.

172

Dear Sweet Girl,

I remember your dream of buying our old house back some day. You were adamant in your belief that you would never, ever feel at home anywhere else. It's a good thing that didn't turn out to be true, because you were ten years old at the time and still had a lot of life ahead of you. Also, that house is large, expensive, and you can't afford it. I'm so sorry to spoil your dream.

You do, however, find yourself an adorable little concrete home on a church compound, across from a slum in East Africa. It comes with hot water, simple furniture and a relentless ant problem. To you, this may sound like a total nightmare; but to me, it's where my life truly began.

I was actually surprised by how eager I was to find my own house in Kisumu. I loved living with Jonathan and Andrea, but knew that if I stayed there for too long, I'd never want to leave. After years of living with Mom and Paul in Tennessee, and intermittently traveling back and forth to Kenya, it was time that I settled into a place of my own. Andrea was also surprised by my desire to move out so quickly, but she was supportive and agreed to help me look for a place.

The house that I moved in to was the first and only one that I looked at. It was across the street from Nyalenda, and shared a compound with a church, a row of small offices, a dining hall, a couple of multi-purpose rooms, and a public transportation parking lot. The security was minimal, but the house came furnished and the rent was only three-hundred dollars a month. It was actually a two-family house, and my neighbors were an older American couple who worked on a sustainable clean water project in the area. If they felt safe on that compound, then I knew that I could, too.

I moved in to my new home in mid-March. I can't explain it, but I felt comfortable there right away. There was just enough furniture to make the space feel lived in, and I was able to decorate with the few personal items that I brought with me from the States. I had photos of friends and family, a pile of books for the coffee table, and some other knickknacks to scatter around. Even though there were a few plates and kitchen utensils left for me to use, I bought some of my own at the local super market. On my first night, I lit a candle, propped my feet up on the coffee table and stared at my living room wall in silence for about twenty minutes. I never felt so independent in my life.

In order to keep myself from becoming completely isolated, I popped over to the Dowells almost every day. Their house was in walking distance from mine, and I loved spending as much time with them as I could. Aside from serving as missionaries to Kisumu's population of street children, Jonathan and Andrea gave just as much of themselves to serve other missionaries and expats. Whether they were offering someone a place to stay, cooking them a meal, or hosting community Worship Night, the Dowells constantly and intentionally created space for others to feel safe, well cared for and free to nurture their faith. Being in their presence continued to help me feel grounded.

Once I had a chance to settle in and feel a sense of routine, I called Anyango and invited her to come by. I wanted to check on her again, but didn't feel comfortable meeting at St. Anne's anymore. I decided to have her come over for dinner on the same night that I had Caroline's daughter, Hellen, over. They were around the same age and I thought they might get along, since they had been through some of the same things.

Hellen was not at home when I met her mom years before, but one of my goals in coming back to Kenya was to find her and get her enrolled in the Christian Relief Fund's sponsorship program. I knew that if no one advocated for her to go back to school after her mom died, she would end up doing housework for one of her relatives, until she was picked up and taken away by a man. I didn't get to spend as much time with Caroline as I did with Caren, but I knew for sure that Caroline would want better things for her daughter.

The girls came to my house for dinner and a sleepover on Easter weekend. I had a spare bedroom with one bed in it, and the Property Manager was kind enough to lend me another one. I cooked pasta with meat sauce and green beans, because I didn't know how to cook Kenyan food. Though fluent in English, both Anyango and Hellen were painfully shy. We spent the first part of the evening drowning in silence.

After dinner, the girls offered to do the dishes while I changed into my pajamas. I came out of my bedroom to find them chatting away, as one washed and the other dried. They had music on in the background and they seemed to be enjoying each other's company. Not wanting to interrupt, I stood in the doorway and listened to them giggle and swap stories in Swahili. My heart was full.

When I had a moment alone with Anyango, I asked her how things were going at her aunt's place. She said that she was okay there, but that her aunt and her aunt's husband fought with one another often. I

174

asked her if she felt unsafe, and she said that she didn't. I thought about the possibility of enrolling her in CRF's sponsorship program with Hellen, but that meant she would need to change schools. Even though she was no longer staying with Mercy, she liked the school in Mercy's neighborhood and continued to go there after she moved out.

Like most primary schools in Kenya, Shauri Moyo was a day school. Typically, only secondary schools offer boarding, but there were a few CRF-sponsored primary schools with an option to board in a neighboring children's home. I suggested this, but ultimately Anyango decided to stay at Shauri Moyo and continue living with her aunt. I told her that was fine, and that she could come and visit me whenever she needed a break from the fighting at her aunt's place.

Hellen enrolled in the sponsorship program as a boarder. She began ninth grade at a CRF school that was relatively close to my house, and occasionally came to stay with me on the weekends. Whenever Hellen was visiting, Anyango came over so that they could spend time together. I enjoyed having the two of them around and seeing them slowly come out of their shells. I would watch them together and imagine both of their Mamas sitting up in Heaven, smiling down on their daughters.

On a Sunday afternoon in late April, Hellen was gathering her things to go back to school. Anyango typically left my house when Hellen did, but on this day, she didn't seem to be in much of a hurry. Though she was always relatively quiet, she appeared to be more distant than she had been in a while. It almost reminded me of her demeanor right after Caren passed away.

"You okay?" I asked, as she sat on her bed and watched Hellen get ready to leave.

"Yeah."

I figured that was as much as I'd get out of her for the time being, so I went into my room to put my laundry away and give the girls a few more minutes together before they went their separate ways again. But it wasn't five minutes before Anyango appeared in my doorway and asked if we could talk.

"My aunt's husband is really abusing her, so she is looking for another place for us to live."

I couldn't tell if Anyango was more upset that her aunt was being abused, or that they had to find a new home. Either way, I could tell that she felt the weight of the chaos.

There are moments in life where we act on impulse, and moments that we seize because we know they come from the Lord. If we aren't

175

paying attention, it can be hard to tell the difference, but nothing is more magical than knowing when God is planting a seed. My decision to jump off of the cliff with my friends, was impulsive; as were most of my tattoos. Deciding to move to Kenya was a response to God's calling; as was the decision to move Anyango into my home.

"If it's okay with you and your aunt, I'd like to have you stay here with me. Is that something you would consider?"

"Yes," Anyango responded, gently. "I would like to stay here with you."

In the moment, it may have seemed like I was acting on impulse. Here was this girl that I loved, who continued to find herself stuck in a cycle of heartbreak and chaos that she had no control over. Mature as she was, she was still just a child who needed nurturing and stability. It was easy to look into her troubled eyes and offer to take her in. But it wasn't an impulse.

Anyango's circumstances weren't unique for a place like Kisumu, Kenya, but my calling to be a bigger part of her story, was. I had built relationships with the students at Ringroad, and other children within the community. I loved them all deeply, but rarely felt that my role in their lives was meant to move beyond the ability to serve them in a professional capacity. On occasion, I would step in to support a family's urgent needs, but I was careful not to offer more of myself than I was capable of giving.

God prepared my heart to step into a deeper role with Anyango, long before I met her. Of course, I didn't know this until she and Caren became a part of my life; but from the moment that they did, I knew it to be true. Every time I looked at either one of them, I felt a gentle pull that let me know I was staring into the face of my greater purpose. After Caren died, I sensed that God was equipping me to care for Anyango in all of the ways that she needed. I was prepared to say "yes," to whatever He was asking of me in this situation; I just didn't know it until I heard Him ask.

176

Chapter Eighteen

Dolls are my favorite.

I have lots of toys and I love all of them; but nothing makes me happier than getting a new doll. I love pretending that I am a mom and that they are my real babies. I even make lists of names, and spend lots of time choosing the perfect one. Sometimes I name a doll before I get her, but most of the time I wait and see what she looks like first.

The best kinds of dolls are the ones that do things like real babies do. I have one named Victoria who came with a pretend potty that she actually uses. I fill her bottle with water and when she drinks it, the pee comes out. My doll named Emily has a spoon with food on it, that disappears when you touch it to her mouth. It's like she is really eating her food. Then I have Tiffany, who looks and smells like an actual newborn. She has wrinkly skin and eyes that are kind of squinted closed. I've seen lots of newborn babies in real life, like my little cousins, and I know that Tiffany looks just like them.

Today we are at the toy store, and I already know that I'm getting another doll. Mom and Dad think I have enough of them and that I should consider another toy, but dolls make me the happiest. I don't think I could ever have too many of them. The only problem is that it's always hard for me to choose one. I don't know if all of the dolls get picked eventually, but in my mind, I tell myself that they do. It would make me really sad if some of the dolls were never chosen.

I look at all of the dolls on the shelf, and finally decide that I want the one that cries. I've had dolls that make noises before, but not one that actually cries. I think I want to name her Ashley, and I can't wait to bring her home. The box says that she cries when there is a loud noise, so I'm going to be careful about keeping my room quiet. If I want her to stop crying, I'm supposed to pick her up and rock her.

We get home and Dad puts Ashley's batteries in. To make sure she works properly, he claps his hands really loud. Ashley starts crying so I pick her up, just like the instructions say. She stops crying, and I put her in the doll crib that I have in the corner of my room.

I think it's going to be easy to keep Ashley quiet, but it isn't. Every time I bring her out of my room and there's a noise, she cries. Dad has the football game on and I accidentally put Ashley too close to the TV when the crowd makes cheering noises, so she cries. Jake gets upset because Mom puts him in time out for something; and when he starts screaming, Ashley starts crying. I love having dolls who act like real babies, but this feels like too much for me. I won't be able to play with any other dolls if all of my attention is on keeping Ashley quiet. I can't just let her cry...so what am I supposed to do?

Dad suggests we take her batteries out, so that Ashley can just be like a regular doll. I tell him that it's too late, and that I don't think I can take care of her anymore. Even if she isn't crying, I still know that she is able to. That makes me feel really sad, and I think I made a very big mistake.

I let Dad remove her batteries, and then I lay Ashley in the corner of my parents' bedroom. Mom says they will return her, but I'll have to wait until the next time I earn a special treat, to get another doll. Even though I'm sad about that, I agree. I just want that poor, crying doll to be out of our house.

~ ~ ~

Dear Sweet Girl,

Let me tell you a few things about motherhood. First of all, there is more than one way to get there. I know the path you wish to take some day, and that is still very much a possibility. Carrying and birthing a child is something that's been on your heart since you were old enough to know that women are capable of doing so. When you imagine your future, you dream about that more than anything else. You know motherhood to be your calling, and you aren't wrong. But you will become a mother long before you have a chance to birth a child.

The second thing that you should know about motherhood, is that it changes you in the most beautifully confusing way. Your entire life becomes devoted to a human being that depends on you for things you didn't know you had to offer. Whether you start your journey with a biological child or an adopted child; a newborn or a newly sixteen-year-old, the second you become somebody's mother, your entire world becomes this insane mixture of the easiest and hardest things you'll ever to do. The simplest, but the messiest.

You would do anything for your child, but constantly question whether or not you're doing the right thing. You reach deep down and find enough of yourself to give, even when every single part of you is screaming that there is nothing left. You love this human so intensely and completely, that not even their most disappointing or frustrating actions are capable of running your love dry. Their joys and victories set your heart on fire, and their pain cuts you like a knife. They are your world.

Taking Anyango in, meant more to me than providing her with food and shelter. The second she moved her belongings into my house, I was ready and willing to be everything that the mother of a teenager needs to be. Even though I didn't fully understand what that would look like for someone like Anyango, I was prepared to learn as I went. A lot of her needs were likely to be different than that of an American teenager, but I was confident enough in God's voice to surrender to the challenge.

My first test in parenthood came pretty immediately. As an eighth-grade student, Anyango was preparing to take the Kenya Certificate of Primary Education exams, or, the KCPE. Most schools require their exam candidates to spend extra hours at school, revising their papers and studying with their teachers. They like for their candidates to spend as much time preparing as humanly possible, even if it comes at the cost of physical and emotional rest.

Since we lived in a different part of Kisumu than the location of her school, Anyango needed to wake up and leave the house very early in the morning. She also got home extra late; which meant that she both left and returned in the dark. As a woman raised in the western world, who had a clear vision of how she planned on raising her own children someday, learning to be okay with Anyango's school routine proved to be a huge challenge for me.

She left home in the dark, walked to the main road and hopped on a motorbike that brought her to school. Then she sat in class for twelve hours, hopped on someone else's motorbike, which brought her back to our side of town, and walked home in the dark. I didn't want to let her do it, but this was the routine that students in her culture followed. She was used to seeing those streets in the dark, and finding random motorbike drivers to bring her from one place to another. Eventually we compromised and I had her take tuk-tuks to school, because they are safer, but making those types of decisions quickly became a constant in my life: What parts of her culture and what parts of mine were best to draw upon for Anyango's overall well-being? As soon as I realized that I was okay asking myself that question on her behalf for the rest of my life, I truly felt like I was her mother.

It didn't take long for the two of us to settle into our own routine. Every night when Anyango came home from school, she would quickly

179

change out of her uniform and wash up for dinner. I always had dinner ready for her, and she would tell me all about her day as we ate together. Afterwards, Anyango did the dishes and then worked on her homework. Sometimes, I'd do my own work while she did hers. At bedtime, we prayed in her room together, and then I'd give her a kiss goodnight. She settled into our routine so smoothly that it became hard to remember what life was like beforehand. It felt like it had always been the two of us.

Mom desperately wanted me to get a dog. You know how she adores German Shepherds, and finds comfort in their loyal and protective nature. I wasn't completely opposed to the idea, but I was hesitant to add the extra expense and responsibility. In less than two months, I had moved into a new home- in a foreign country- and unofficially adopted a teenage daughter. My days were spent caring for the students at Ringroad, and my evenings were devoted to nurturing Anyango's needs. Even finding time to spend with my friends was becoming a challenge; and adding a new puppy to the mix wasn't going to make anything easier.

I told Mom that I would not actively look for a dog, but if I happened to come across an advertisement for German Shepherd puppies, I would consider it a sign and go take a look. Less than two weeks later, a fellow expat posted her brand-new litter of German Shepherd puppies on social media. There were eight puppies, and they were all waiting to be adopted.

Simon joined our little family in May. When Anyango left for school that morning, I let her know that she may come home to find a new puppy in the house.

"It isn't definite," I told her. "I'm just going to look."

To which Anyango replied, "You know you're going to get one."

I spent two hours across town, torturing myself over which of the seven remaining puppies I should choose. The litter was a German Shepherd-Rottweiler mix, and some of the puppies looked more like one breed than the other. I ultimately decided that I wanted mine to look more like a Shepherd, so that narrowed my options down to two puppies. I chose the one who kept breaking away from the rest of the litter and finding places to hide on his own. I had a soft spot for his seemingly shy disposition.

The name Simon was not randomly chosen. I knew that I wanted to use an "S" name to honor Grandpa Tep, whose actual name was Sanford. I'm not sure if you know this, but in Jewish tradition, we don't name our children after loved ones who are still living. When choosing a name, we include the names or initials of loved ones who have passed away. Simon is a Hebrew name that means, "To Be Heard." Not only did I like the fact that it is a Hebrew name, but the meaning of it resonated deeply with me. The belief that everyone deserves to be heard, is one of my strongest personal values. I realize that upholding Jewish naming traditions doesn't apply to family pets, but it shouldn't surprise you that I put as much thought into it as I did.

I held Simon in my lap all the way home, as we bounced down the dirt roads in the back of a tuk-tuk. He didn't appear to be afraid, but I kept telling him it was going to be okay, anyway. When we finally reached my house, I set him down on the concrete floor of my living room, and let him explore his new surroundings. I didn't have any puppy supplies, and I had no idea what to do with him. He chewed the corner of my coffee table, and peed and pooped on the floor multiple times before Anyango even got home from school. I knew that I was likely in over my head, but I continued to be up for the challenge.

Simon took to Anyango immediately. On his first night with us, she held him in her lap and marveled over how tiny he was. In the Kenyan culture, dogs are seen either out on the streets, or being used strictly for protection. It is not typical for them to be treated as part of the family, like it is in the States, which is why the idea of bonding with an animal was so foreign to Anyango. She thought he was cute, but she didn't know how to attach to him.

Simon, on the other hand, stuck to Anyango like glue. He followed her around the house, and used his paws to push her bedroom door open. When she left for school in the morning, he would lay on her dirty laundry that was left on the floor. Regardless of Anyango's reluctance to bond with an animal, knowing that Simon was already exhibiting such strong loyalty to her, gave me more peace of mind than I expected.

Unlike the routine that Anyango and I settled into when it was just the two of us, it was much more difficult to get into a good rhythm with Simon. As hard as I tried to get him on a bathroom schedule outside, he had accidents in the house multiple times a day. He chewed on everything that was within his reach, and howled when I locked him in the kitchen for bed time. I didn't have a crate, so I would quarantine him in a corner of the kitchen with propped-up suitcases at night, or whenever we left the house. He figured out how to wiggle his way around them by day four.

Somehow, I was able to train him to do his business on the newspapers that I laid on the floor when neither Anyango or I were around to take him out. Though I was proud of him for learning, I was still having to clean up a mess every single time I came home. It began to feel like the majority of my waking hours were spent squatting over urine-soaked newspapers and heaps of dog feces, with disinfectant spray in one hand and paper towels in the other. The jury is still out on whether the bulk of the paper towels were used to wipe up his mess, or to wipe away my tears of frustration.

About a week after bringing Simon home, I placed him in his make-shift-suitcase-crate, and left the house knowing that he would likely knock them down and free himself before I got back from work. Doing my best not to let my discouragement set the tone for my day, I kissed him goodbye, and cheerfully met my tuk-tuk driver outside. We set out for Ringroad, but before I reached the gate, I received a call from Anyango's teacher.

"Lavin is very sick today. You must pick her up and bring her to the hospital."

It took me a moment to register that he was talking about Anyango. At school, she went by her first name, which is Lavin. While her family preferred to call her by her middle name, and that was how I was introduced to her, the name Anyango is her tribal name and it is shared by thousands of other people who are a part of the same tribe. If students went by their tribal names in class, it would lead to lots of confusion because too many of them share the same ones. I still wasn't completely adjusted to switching back and forth between her two names.

I was also confused by this phone call because Anyango seemed fine when she left the house that morning. She didn't have any trouble getting out of bed or ready for school, and she was in normal spirits when she left the house. I asked her teacher what seemed to be the problem, and he told me that she was presenting with symptoms of Malaria. Even though I didn't know how this was possible, given that I had just seen her a couple of hours ago, I panicked all the way to Shauri Moyo.

When I walked into the Head Teacher's office, I found Anyango sitting in a chair, shaking uncontrollably. She was surrounded by a group of her friends, all of whom were holding wet cloths up to her skin, in an attempt to deescalate her fever. I knelt down in front of her and put my hand up to her cheek, and then her arm. It didn't feel like she had a fever to me, but her teeth were chattering and she was shaking so aggressively, that I knew I could have been wrong. A teacher and a few of her classmates helped stand Anyango up and guide her over to the tuk-tuk. I decided to bring her back to Ringroad with me, so that they could see her at our clinic, while I gathered a few things from my office. If Anyango was going to be sick at home, I wanted to be home with her.

She tested negative for Malaria. They ran multiple blood tests and a urine culture to see if she tested positive for any other sort of virus or infection, but she didn't. A temperature check confirmed my initial guess that she did not have a fever. By the time we got back in the tuk-tuk to head home, Anyango's shaking had subsided. It was my feeling that she may have had a panic attack, but I didn't think it was an appropriate time for me to try and investigate that. I wanted to get her settled in at home and allow her to rest, before I started asking any questions that might be triggering for her.

For the entirety of the day, I think Anyango spoke less than ten words to me. I had become so used to her growing confidence at home, that this regression threw me for quite a loop. Not only would she barely answer me when I asked if she wanted something to eat or if she was feeling any better, she wouldn't look me in the eye, either. Still sensing that this wasn't an appropriate time to ask any emotionally charged questions, I decided to give her some space and assumed that she would emerge from her bed, eventually.

Well after dark, Anyango finally came out of her room. I was in the living room attempting to get some work done, after managing Simon all afternoon, when she walked in and told me that she wanted to eat pork for dinner. We didn't have any pork in the house, and I told her that it was too late for her to walk over to Nyalenda and buy some off of the street. I knew Anyango didn't understand my rule about her being out after dark, because she grew up having the freedom to go where she wanted, when she wanted. Nyalenda may not have been completely safe for me to wander around alone at night, but it was where Anyango came from and she saw no reason why I wouldn't let her go there after a certain time of day.

Even so, I assumed that she would concede and find something in the kitchen to eat. Instead, she told me that the only thing she wanted was pork, and that if she couldn't have that, she wouldn't eat anything at all. To say that I was thrown off-guard is an understatement. Her attitude in that moment was so unexpected, and so unwarranted, that I could have exploded.

"Are you kidding me? You haven't eaten all day and you're going to starve yourself all night just because I won't let you go get pork?"

"Yup."

"Do you see that I have a kitchen full of food for you to eat? Or care enough to show some appreciation that I'm the one who provides for you?"

183

Anyango didn't say a word, her eyes diverted to a spot on the wall that was on the opposite side of the room from where I was sitting.

"Look at me," I demanded.

Anyango turned to look me in the eye, but immediately shifted her gaze to the floor.

"I have been taking care of you all day. I left work, picked you up from school, brought you to the clinic, and stayed home with you all afternoon. I have done everything I can to take care of you today, just like I do every day, and I'm happy to do it because I love you."

My voice was raised, and a tear rolled down Anyango's cheek.

"But instead of giving me a single 'thank you,' or expressing your gratitude one time, you're going to hold it against me that we don't have the one food in this house that you're craving?"

I wanted to yell louder and longer, but I didn't. My patients were worn thin and I was exhausted from taking care of a sick child and an untrained puppy all day, but I was also aware that my parenting style was new to Anyango. She never lived a life with rules about where she went, or the expectation for her to express gratitude. She wasn't used to being taken care of when she was sick, or being able to take advantage of having options for meals. I understood the disconnect, but I was also very angry.

Still looking down at the ground, Anyango quietly whispered, "sorry," and then turned around and went back to her room. I took a moment to catch my breath, before I shifted my focus towards Simon; who had disappeared into the kitchen at some point during that exchange. I walked in to find him rummaging through the pantry, with urine and feces left all over the floor. Without any attempt to calm myself down, I picked Simon up, yelled in his face, and locked him out of the kitchen so that I could clean up his mess. He cried and scratched at the kitchen door, as I cried into another paper towel and disinfected the spots left by his bodily fluids.

Once I was finished, I went into my room, sat on the floor and sobbed. I wept loudly and uncontrollably, as Simon sat beside me and licked my leg in an attempt to be consoling. I picked him up and apologized for yelling; then I held him in my arms and rocked him back and forth as I continued to weep. There was a knock at my door, and I told Anyango she could come in, not caring whether she heard me cry or not. This normally would have been something that I tried to keep from her, but a part of me wanted to her to see how worn down I was. Maybe that would spark some gratitude.

"Why are you crying?" She asked, when she found me sitting on the floor.

"I'm okay. Go back to your room and I'll come talk to you about it in a few minutes."

Anyango did as she was told, and I took a moment to collect myself. My plan was to explain to her why I was hurt and frustrated by her attitude, and then go over what I expected of her in the future. I also wanted to let her know that I understood the situation was new for both of us, and we were still learning how to navigate it.

I opened the bedroom door, and Anyango was laying on her bed, with her face buried in a pillow. When I gently said her name, she didn't respond, so I leaned over and tapped her shoulder. She removed the pillow from her face, revealing that she had begun crying just as hard as I was; only she was attempting to hide it from me.

For the next hour, I laid on Anyango's bed and held her in my arms. She was inconsolable for longer than I expected her to be, but I continued to do my best to soothe her. I reassured her that while I had been feeling frustrated and a little bit overwhelmed, what happened between us did not make me love her any less or regret my decision to take her in. Once she finally calmed down enough to speak, she told me that she was upset because she knew that she was the reason why I was so upset.

We continued to talk and explain to each other where we were both coming from. I let Anyango know that I'm happy to do everything I can for her, but need her to be a little bit more mindful about expressing her gratitude. Anyango said that she was more thankful to me than I could ever possibly know, but that she wasn't used to expressing her feelings out loud. She agreed to try her best as we moved forward.

"I get really quiet when I'm sick because I hate being sick so much. When I don't feel good, I don't talk, so that's why I didn't talk to you today."

"I understand. But do you see how I could have interpreted that as you being upset with me or ungrateful that I was trying to take care of you?"

"Yeah, I see."

It was clear that both of us felt ready to move forward, so I ended the conversation. For the rest of the night, we chatted normally and Anyango's spirits slowly began to rise. Simon, who was desperately wanting our attention, came to the side of Anyango's bed and stood up on his back legs. I pulled him onto the bed, and we laughed as he crawled all over both of us and tugged at the blankets. His little tail was forever wagging; his joy sparked by simply being close to us. I wouldn't have traded that moment for anything.

I often asked myself how Anyango found the strength to wake up in the morning. She was living a comfortable life in my home, but that didn't erase the scars left by what she had experienced in her past. As she grew more familiar with me, she began to process the events prior to, and immediately following, her mom's death. She shared all that she could remember about finding Caren's body in the middle of the night, and then retrieving it from the morgue days later.

I continued to refer back to Violet's advice about encouraging Anyango to stay strong because she didn't have a choice. And while that made sense for Anyango at the time that Violet suggested it, I found it to be true that a person has more space to grieve when they aren't spending the entirety of their days fighting to have their most basic needs met. Anyango was no longer in a position where she was concerned for her physical survival, therefore her emotional trauma was beginning to surface.

Every once in a while, when I would walk into Anyango's room to wake her for school, I'd find her already sitting up in bed. She'd have a blank stare on her face, and occasionally, tears in her eyes. Her nightmares were so vivid and intense, that she woke up consumed and paralyzed by them. On those days, she wasn't able to go to school. I'd encourage her to talk about her nightmares so that we could process through them together, and she would eventually release them enough to carry through the rest of the day.

All things considered, Anyango appeared to be thriving. She was doing well in school, and found a group of friends that she connected to. At home, she was typically cheerful and always willing to help me around the house. She was hesitant to admit it, but she also began bonding with Simon. Aside from helping me to take care of him, I would catch her petting or talking to him, without me encouraging her to. Eventually, he was tall enough to climb onto her bed by himself, and she always let him.

Sometimes, when she had a break from her eternal study sessions at school, Anyango would join me at the Dowell's house for Worship Night or a family dinner. She was slowly becoming more comfortable around other westerners, and began picking up on some of our mannerisms or expressions. She knew how to interpret the sarcastic banter that Andrea and I often had, and she found Andrea to be quite amusing. It was a joy for me to watch her learn to interact with people who were different from what she was used to, but who welcomed her with love and open arms.

At the same time, I felt strongly convicted in the importance of Anyango maintaining her cultural roots. From simply keeping Kenyan food as a part of our diet, to ensuring that she was able to visit her relatives in her home village outside of Kisumu, I never wanted her to forget or neglect where she comes from. Luckily, Anyango felt the same way, but it was miraculous to me how seamlessly she transitioned back and forth between such different worlds. Granted, we were still living in her home country; but she was simultaneously experiencing two completely different ways of living.

Much like my reservations toward her school routine, I struggled to make peace with how she spent her time in the village. I recognized the importance of her maintaining a connection there, but I hated the idea of her sleeping on the ground, going to the bathroom outside and bathing in the river. They had no electricity, and their food was prepared outside in a tiny pot that sat on top of burning coals. In order to even find food, she had to walk miles into the town center nearly every day.

No refrigerator, no microwave, no lights. No bed, no shower, no toilet. I continuously reminded myself that just because I imagined that way of life to be miserably uncomfortable, it didn't mean that Anyango felt the same way. In fact, she always came home from the village with a smile on her face, and often shared some of her favorite memories from growing up there. When she was little, they hardly had any food and she had no shoes, but she remembers being happy.

The day after the first anniversary of her mother's passing, Anyango did not wake up in the morning. We had a nice day celebrating Caren's memory, by eating lunch down on Lake Victoria and reflecting on her life. Anyango was a bit quieter and more introspective on that day, but it was nothing that I didn't expect; considering all that she had been through. At bedtime, we prayed as we always did, and I kissed her goodnight. I sensed that she was ready for the day to be over, but she did not appear to be overly distraught or in a place of deep grieving.

The next day was a Monday, and I went into Anyango's room to wake her for school. That early in the morning, it wasn't unusual for me to have to call her name multiple times before she responded. But on this particular morning, as I gently shook her shoulders and continued to call her name, I knew that something wasn't right. I lifted one of her arms, but it was dead-weight; flopping back down onto the bed as soon as I let it go. Panic set in as I checked for breathing and a pulse. Although I'm sure I felt relief when I found both, all that I remember is screaming and begging

Anyango to wake up. Then, I pleaded with God not to take her away from me.

I opened one of her eyelids, but her eyes didn't move to focus on mine. They were distant and still. My mind raced as I considered the possibilities of what happened over night to my precious girl: a stroke? A brain aneurism? A neurological bacterial infection? A drug over-dose?

Kenya does not have the same type of emergency response system that we do in the States, so my phone call was to Andrea. It was only 5:30 in the morning, but I knew that she would have her phone on, and that she and Jonathan wouldn't hesitate to jump in their car and come right over. I called and spoke words to her, but I don't remember any of them. It felt like I was existing outside of my own body and watching a nightmare that could not have possibly been real life. I felt beyond helpless as I watched Anyango lay motionless in her bed without any signs that could point to what was wrong or how I could begin to make it better.

I unlocked the front door and then shut Simon in the kitchen so that he wouldn't get in Jonathan and Andrea's way. He immediately began slamming his body against the kitchen door and letting out high-pitched, torturous cries that seared through my bones. I didn't understand what was happening, but I knew that I couldn't withstand any of it. I was overcome by the chaos and the helplessness that I felt, as I continued to beg God for Anyango's life.

The Dowells arrived at my house in less than five minutes. I stood back and watched them examine her; checking first for breath and a pulse, like I did. Jonathan had Emergency Response Technician training, which gave me some sense of peace. Even though he had no equipment available to him or an ambulance standing by, he knew enough to do an initial evaluation before we brought her to the hospital. Andrea took out her cell phone and shined its flashlight into Anyango's eyes.

"Oh, this is good," she said. "Come look, Jen. This is a good sign."

I walked over to Anyango's bed; my entire body numb.

"When I shine the light in her eyes, her pupils respond to it. Can you see that? That's really good."

"What does that mean?" I asked, hearing my own words but unable to identify with them. They were simply falling out of my mouth and into the air.

"It means she has brain activity. Her brain is functioning."

This was good news, and I knew it; but I couldn't understand why Anyango continued to remain unconscious.

"Why isn't she waking up, then? There has to be a reason."

"They call this 'Hysteria' here," Andrea explained.

"We see it at our Children's Home a lot, with girls who have experienced traumatic events. They kind of mentally 'check out' for a bit, but they always come back. In fact, Anyango can probably hear us and everything. She's just shutting herself down, to avoid the trauma that she doesn't want to process. But she will wake up, I promise."

With this unofficial diagnosis came a whole new list of questions, but I felt myself beginning to calm down. Andrea's confidence in knowing what we were dealing with, allowed me to breathe for the first time in what felt like hours. When I asked how Hysteria is typically handled, Jonathan said that there isn't anything to do but wait. Eventually, the girls wake up on their own.

"If you still want to get her looked at, we will absolutely take you to the hospital, but we're pretty sure that this is an episode of Hysteria."

Both Jonathan and Andrea appeared confident in what they were saying- and I believed them- but I wanted to bring Anyango to the hospital, just in case.

Jonathan carried her out to the car, and we headed for one of the best hospitals in town. Anyango was laying across my lap, and I gently stroked her head with one hand, as I held hers with the other. I prayed that she would wake up during the drive, but she didn't. Her body was warm, but limp. We pulled up to the Emergency entrance of Aga Khan Hospital, and Andrea got out of the car to ring the bell. Seconds later, a couple of nurses emerged from the building and came over to the car window. Jonathan and Andrea explained our situation to them, because I didn't feel capable. It was less than an hour earlier that I had woken up and expected to begin a typical Monday morning by waking Anyango for school.

After checking her vitals, the nurses confirmed Hysteria.

"Has this girl experience some kind of trauma recently?" one of them asked.

"Yes, she has. It was the year anniversary of her mother's passing yesterday, and that day was very traumatizing for her."

The nurse nodded his head and looked over at Anyango, who was now laying on one of the triage beds. She was still unconscious.

"Did she see her mother pass?"

"She was the one who took care of her mother when she was sick. It was just the two of them living in the house, and she woke up in the middle of the night to find her mother deceased."

"Mmm. That is a trauma."

"Yes, it is."

A doctor came into the triage bay to examine Anyango further. He checked her vitals again, shined a light in her eyes, and told me that all we could do was wait for her to wake up. I told the Dowells that they could go, and that I would call them if anything changed. The nurse instructed me to go to the reception desk to formally check Anyango in. I was afraid to leave her alone, in case she woke up and didn't know where she was, but I did as I was told.

Within thirty minutes of being at the hospital, Anyango finally opened her eyes. She didn't say a word, but that familiar single tear rolled down her cheek.

"Hi, baby," I whispered. "Do you know where we are?"

She didn't answer or look at me.

"We're at the hospital, but you aren't sick. You just had a little trouble waking up this morning."

Another tear dripped down her cheek and she turned her head to face the doorway.

"Hey, Anyango. Look at me, baby."

Anyango did as she was told.

"I need to know that you understand what I'm saying to you. Can you answer me with your words?"

"I understand." Her voice cracked and her eyes welled up completely.

Soon afterwards, she was discharged from the hospital and we rode home in a tuk-tuk. Anyango didn't say anything the entire way, and she crawled back into bed as soon as we reached the house. Simon was finally potty-trained, and I felt so guilty for making him wait all morning to go outside. I hadn't even let him out of the kitchen before we left for the hospital, because I was in such a panic. I let him out as soon as we got home, and gave him some TLC before I went in Anyango's room to check on her. She was laying on her side, but her eyes were open.

"Can I come lay with you for a little bit?"

"Yes."

I leaned against her bed frame, and put one of her pillows on top of my lap.

"Here," I said, patting my hand over the pillow.

Anyango slid her body closer to me and laid her head down. Like I had done in the car, I held her hand and gently stroked her head. I was afraid that if she fell back to sleep, she would have another episode; but at least I'd know what to do next time. The most important thing I could do in that moment, was to let Anyango know that she was safe. As a mother, that is my most important job.

Chapter Nineteen

I've waited a long time for this.

Ever since I learned that they make medication for people like me, I've known that I wanted to try it some day. Now that I'm sixteen, Mom and Dad feel okay about me going to talk to a Psychiatrist. I honestly couldn't be happier, because I know that I need the extra help.

All of my therapists have always been women, but this guy seems pretty nice. His office is filled with posters and charts about the way chemicals transfer in our brains. Apparently, my problem is that I don't have sufficient Serotonin levels in in my brain. This is a chemical that helps to regulate our mood, and when it is absorbed too quickly in our neurological system, we can experience things like anxiety and depression.

"So basically what the medication is thought to do, is slow the rate at which your brain absorbs the Serotonin."

Listening to this doctor explain how my new medication will work, makes me feel more validated than I ever have in my life. Don't get me wrong; I love going to therapy, and I'm thankful for all of the people who support me without judgement. But having someone acknowledge that what I experience is a medical condition, and not just something that I can make go away by learning how to change my thought process, is everything to me right now. I'm so thankful for this doctor that I could kiss him.

Before he decides to write me the prescription, he asks me a bunch of questions. I'm used to answering questions about my anxiety and where I think it comes from, because I've grown up talking about it in therapy. This is appointment feels a little bit different from therapy, though, and I know exactly which details are relevant and which ones I can skip over. This doctor doesn't need to know about the guy I like at school, or why there's been some tension lately within my group of friends. What's important for him to know is that I threw up four times last week, just to be sure that I could control my anxiety before I let it control me.

"When I get anxious enough, I feel sick to my stomach and then I throw up. I learned when I was little that throwing up makes me feel better, so now I make myself do it. I do it before my body decides to do it on its own."

"How often do you initiate the vomiting?"

191

"Not every day or anything like that; just before I go into a situation that I think might make me feel anxious."

"Can you give me an example?"

"If I'm going somewhere that I've never been to before, so i don't know what to expect. I'd rather throw up and go to that place on an empty stomach, than feel anxious when I get there and throw up in front of other people without being able to control it."

"So you've come to see the vomiting as a way of gaining control over your anxiety."

"Yes."

The Doctor confirms that starting medication is the right way to go for me. He explains that it can be effective for people whose anxious, depressive or obsessive thoughts and behaviors have begun to affect their Activities of Daily Living. That's exactly what's happening with me: I feel so anxious that doing things like getting out of bed, showering and eating feel like much bigger tasks than they are supposed to. I shouldn't have to work so hard to do basic things.

Even though I'm told that it will be a few weeks before I truly feel a difference, I cannot wait to take my first pill at bed time. I swallow it and imagine it dissolving down my throat; being absobed by my blood stream and heading straight for my brain. I imagine how much relief my brain will feel once it finally has a chance to slow down. Being given this medication is probably the best thing that's ever happened to me.

I wake up in the middle of the night to pee. My body feels shaky and weak. When I stand up I feel dizzy; and I think I might throw up. The doctor told me that it might take my body a few days to adjust, but I did not realize I would feel this bad.

I lie awake and wonder if I'll feel better in the morning. We're going on a family trip to Maine, and I really don't want to be dealing with medication side effects the entire time. This pill is supposed to help make sure that I can enjoy things like going on vacation with my family. We're going to a place in Maine that I've never been to before, so I've already been feeling anxious about it. If I feel like this the whole time, it's only going to make things worse.

Maybe it's better if I wait. I've gone my entire life without this medicine; I can survive another week.

~ ~ ~

Dear Sweet Girl,

Now is probably a good time to dive a little bit deeper into where I stood with God. It had been over a year since Grandpa Tep passed away, and I had lived a lot of life since then. I trusted God enough to move to a developing country, partner with an organization that sponsors hundreds of children in Kisumu, alone, and become responsible for raising a grieving teenage girl and a cheeky, spirited puppy. Surely, I would not have done any of these things without the ability to acknowledge God's presence in my life; but my faith in Him was far from perfect.

Every day, I felt like I was playing a game of Heads or Tails; only my two options were "Miracle" or "Tragedy." Don't get me wrong, there were plenty of days at Ringroad where nothing eventful happened. I met with students, assessed their needs, and found the appropriate community resources. Then I'd go home, play with Simon, take some time to relax, catch up with family and friends, make dinner for Anyango, and commence our nightly routine. Those "simple days" were my favorite; but they were never the ones that I was expecting.

I knew that at any given moment, God could call me into a situation that resulted in either a miracle or a tragedy. A child may recover from a near-fatal illness, or we may have to lay another one to rest. A missing female student could find her way back to Ringroad after months of unexplained absence, or she could drop out of school after finding herself pregnant at the tender age of fourteen. We may find a new home for a child who endured years of domestic abuse, or we may discover that the extent of abuse has pushed one of our children out onto the streets and into a life of drug use.

Like many people who find themselves grappling with their faith, it was easier for me to see God in the miracles than it was in the tragedies. I didn't know how to thank Him for His healing and provision, without blaming Him for the world's suffering and despair. How could I tell a roomful of impoverished children that God was good all of the time, when so many of them were in the midst of experiencing the most unfathomable levels of human suffering? Just because I was witnessing God work in my life, didn't mean that I felt qualified to tell others that He was working in theirs.

In my moments of stillness and reflection, I got the sense that God likes it when I ask questions. My lack of understanding was not a roadblock for Him, but rather an opportunity to reveal the deeper layers

193

of who He is and how He works. I also felt Him continuously reminding me that it isn't my job to fix all of the world's brokenness. My role in His story is to love the people that He has called me to love; and to give of myself what He has equipped me to give. As long as I did that, He would take care of the rest.

Little Nissi Patience was the first child that I was introduced to in Kenya. She was the youngest Ringroad student to accompany Chris and Sarah to the airport when they retrieved our group from Lipscomb; and the one who gave me my yellow "Welcome to Kenya" rose.

Nissi was in the first grade when she met us at the airport; and she was now in grade four. She worked extremely hard in school, and always scored at the top of her class. She was kind to everyone, and never gave her teachers a single problem. Watching her grow over the years was a true joy for me, especially because of our history.

During her fourth-grade final exam week, Nissi became very sick. Like the little warrior that she is, she sat through all of her exams with a fever, and didn't complain to anyone. On closing day of school, I received word from her best friend, Rose, that she was admitted into the District Hospital. I thanked Rose for letting me know, and decided that I would go and visit Nissi if she wasn't released from the hospital by the following day.

Lo and behold, I ended up at the Kisumu District Hospital. Many of my days were spent in hospitals with our students, but District was one of my least favorite. It was always over-crowded, and severely under-resourced. This was true of most hospitals in the area, but there was something about District that made me feel extra uneasy inside. I think it was because the overflow of patients made for a likely chance that you would come across a dire situation in any nook or cranny of the premises. If a dying person needed to lay out on the front lawn while they waited to be seen, then so be it.

Nissi was admitted into the Pediatric Ward. Like all of the other wards, Pediatric had rows of beds lining its walls from one end of the building to the other. There were no private rooms, or even curtains to separate the patients. If a situation was delicate enough, the nurses would bring out a tiny space divider that barely wrapped around a single bed. The air smelled like a mixture of wounded flesh, bodily fluids and sterilizer; and the screaming was constant.

As I walked down the ward and searched for Nissi, I tried my hardest to block out all of my surroundings. The sights, smells and sounds that come from a roomful of sick and dying children, are powerful enough

194

to puncture your soul beyond any sort of earthly repair. I didn't feel capable of protecting myself from such damage, but if those children were strong enough to fight, then I needed to be strong enough to bear witness to it.

I found Nissi halfway down one of the rows. She was curled up in the fetal position and her breathing was extremely labored. I gently held my hand up to her cheek and was alarmed by the heat that radiated off of her skin. She had no IV, no oxygen and she was barely conscious.

Both of her parents were standing at her bedside. Her mama was running a damp cloth over Nissi's body, and her dad was whispering words of encouragement. After I greeted them, I asked for an update on Nissi's condition, but her parents didn't have much information to give. She had already been in the hospital for days, and even though she was clearly having respiratory issues, she was still waiting to receive a chest x-ray. She wasn't able to eat or drink anything, and they couldn't recall the last time that a nurse came by to dispense medication for her fever, because it had been so long.

I sat down on the edge of the bed.

"Nissi?"

Nissi opened her eyes at the sound of her name.

"Mmm?"

Though she didn't say a word, the sound of her tiny voice pulled at my heartstrings. She mustered up all of her strength to utter a simple noise, and I knew that she was fighting a lot harder than she was letting on. When a nurse finally began making her way down Nissi's row, I called her over to ask for an update since Nissi's parents were still so unclear on her condition.

"Can you please tell me how this child is being treated? What have the doctors found, and what medication has she been given?"

The nurse looked at Nissi's chart and told me that she was given a fever reducer and was waiting to receive and x-ray.

"What about an IV?" I asked, with an urgency that I knew wouldn't be well-received. "She hasn't had anything to eat or drink in days."

Here's the thing: I knew how overworked the nurses were and how few resources they had to work with. I knew that this particular nurse's complete lack of emotion- which translated to me as a lack of compassion- was the result of a need to protect herself from crumbling under the stress of watching children die every day, and not being able to do anything about it. I knew all of this, and continuously made an effort to temper my own sense of urgency when it came to managing the health

195

of our sickest students; You know, like I had done when Frank needed his blood transfusion. In that situation, my demand for urgent and immediate action would have likely done more harm than good.

With Nissi, however, I knew that we were watching her die right in front of us. She was running an extremely high fever, barely breathing or conscious, and hadn't had fluids in days. My efforts to respect the process of the Kenyan healthcare system were crucial in sustaining an effective ministry; but doing everything that I could to help save little Nissi's life, was going to have to trump all of those other efforts.

I needed permission from the Christian Relief Fund to move Nissi to a private hospital where she could receive higher quality care, since CRF and their donors would be the ones to cover her medical expenses. Even though it was only seven o'clock in the morning back in Texas, I decided to take a chance and call the personal number of Emily Bell; the Director over the Kenyan Child Sponsorship Program. By the grace of God, Emily answered her phone, and gave me immediate permission to transfer Nissi to another hospital.

My relief was abundant, but temporary, as I quickly realized that discharging Nissi from District was not going to be an easy task. When I approached the administrative staff and asked them to begin the discharge process, I was met with a lot of push-back. They recognized that Nissi's condition was dire, and felt she needed to remain under their care; in spite of the fact that they had yet to take any adequate steps in treating her. I explained that I would be transferring her to a different hospital, but the staff did not take kindly to this, because it was an indirect way of telling them that they weren't doing their jobs. It was not my intention to make them feel inadequate, but my interference in their process had done just that. Had I not felt that we were racing against the clock for Nissi's life, I would have been much more sensitive in my approach. But God, forgive me, there just wasn't time.

For what felt like hours, the District staff dragged their feet in processing Nissi's paperwork. They sent me on a wild goose chase around the hospital; collecting signatures from doctors and administrative staff, and paying the medical bills that Nissi had accumulated over the three days that she received virtually no treatment. I was so desperate to get her out of there, that I attempted to bribe a nurse with the equivalent of twenty dollars, to help me speed up the process. She took the money, and then told me that there was nothing she could do.

"You have to be patient," she said.

While waiting for permission to take Nissi and leave, I stood at her bedside with her parents. Diagonally across from us, was a baby girl

196

sitting up in her bed, all alone. She appeared to be physically and intellectually disabled, and no one was paying her any attention. Nissi's mama caught me looking in the baby's direction and sensed that I was curious about her.

"That baby was abandoned by her family because she has a lot of problems. They brought her here and then left her, so now the nurses just give her porridge to drink and leave her sitting in the bed alone all day."

Sweet Girl, there are not words adequate enough to describe such a heartbreak. I remember looking at the abandoned, disabled baby, and at the children in the beds surrounding her. As I saw each of their faces and heard their cries, I wondered how this world could possibly keep spinning, while carrying such unimaginable heaviness. I marched up to the nurses' station and demanded that they give us permission to leave, or I was going to take Nissi without it. I called William, who was waiting with his tuk-tuk outside of the hospital gate, and asked him to come inside and help me by being another voice in my corner. We needed to get Nissi help, and I needed to remove myself from the Pediatric Ward, as soon as possible. My heart was dangerously close to caving in on itself, and preventing me from serving in the way that I knew I was called to.

We took two separate tuk-tuks to Aga Khan Hospital. Nissi and I rode with William, and her parents followed. The whole way there, I held Nissi in my arms and begged her to be strong. I told her that we were on the way to getting the help that she needed, and all she had to do was hang on until we got there.

"They're going to take care of you," I kept telling her. "I just need you to stay strong a little bit longer for me."

Nissi made tiny noises, to let me know that she heard my words. Her skin was so hot that I could feel the heat through her clothing and my own, as she laid across my lap. I prayed fiercely for God to spare her precious, young little life.

We reached Aga Khan and William rang the Emergency bell. The responding nurse took one look at Nissi and sprang into action; calling another nurse outside with a wheelchair, and demanding the immediate preparation of IV fluids. In all of my time spent in Kenyan hospitals- Aga Khan included- this was the fastest I had ever seen medical staff respond to a patient.

Once Nissi was placed on her IV drip and the chaos began to die down, I noticed that the responding nurse was someone that I knew. Nurse Gloria had been one of the staff who took care of me, when I came through the Emergency Room with my stomach bug. Seeing her familiar face under such intense circumstances, almost made me start weeping right

197

there in the triage bay. Instead, I breathed a huge sigh of relief, knowing that Nissi was now in good hands. I decided to save my weeping for later, once I was in the privacy of my own home.

Nissi was admitted into Aga Khan with a severe case of Double-Pneumonia. Nurse Gloria said that she may not have made it through the night, had we not brought her in for treatment when we did.

"Thank God you were there for her," she told me.

Later, when I called the CRF office to give Emily an update on Nissi's condition, she also thanked God that I had been there. When I called Sarah Nicholson to process through the day with her, she said the same thing.

"I'm so thankful that you were there for her. God really used you in a big way today."

I desperately wanted to bask in God's goodness along with the other women, but I found myself unable. I chose, instead, to focus on all of the children who wouldn't be saved. The children, like that abandoned baby girl, who had no one to advocate for them, or to offer them sufficient medical resources. There's no question that Nissi's life was worth saving, but why did she get to be the lucky one? Why had God chosen to save Nissi, and why had He chosen to use me in the process?

With these questions, came a much bigger, more significant question: Do our actions have any effect on God's intended outcome?

If I considered visiting Nissi at District Hospital, but then decided to wait one more day instead, it's very likely that she would have passed away before I got there. Would this have been God's will all along? Or would it have meant that God was asking me to visit her a day earlier, and I neglected to hear or acknowledge the will that He was speaking into me?

I knew that this was a question that I needed to sit with and seek the Lord's guidance in, but instead I began spiraling into the world of "what if's," rather than leaning into the opportunity for growth within Him.

What if I was meant to do more in the Pediatric Ward that day than move Nissi to a better hospital? What if the abandoned baby girl caught my eye because God was asking me to advocate for her somehow, and I neglected to listen? Hospitals in Kenya have protocol in place to deal with abandoned children, but what if my voice could have made a difference in the outcome of that innocent baby's future?

What if there was a child in the ward whose family only needed ten or twenty more dollars to cover the expenses for that child's care? If I had paid more attention, would I have heard God calling me to give what I had to them? Or was it His will to send me into that ward strictly for

Nissi's sake? The dilemma of contemplating when I should or could have done more, was one that existed since my life in Kenya began. But it wasn't until I helped to save Nissi's life, that I realized the danger of not knowing how to process that question.

Not long after my experience with Nissi, I found myself at District Hospital, once again. This time, I was there with one of our high school students; who we'll call Millie, for the sake of her dignity. Millie had attended Ringroad as a primary school student, and went on to attend a CRF-sponsored high school that was close by. Although I hadn't seen her in a while, I remembered her from Ringroad, and recognized her name when it was brought to my attention.

"Millie was sent home from her school because she is having mental problems," one of the teachers at Ringroad told me.

"I've seen her around Nyalenda, and it's like she's gone mad or something. She's talking to herself and yelling at people; saying they are all out to get her. She thinks people are working together to put a curse on her."

At first, I took these claims in stride. Although it sounded like she was presenting with signs of Paranoid Schizophrenia, there could have been other reasons why Millie was acting out. It may have been her way of coping with some type of trauma, or she could have started using drugs or alcohol. Even though she was a boarding student and hardly ever left her school's campus, there was still a possibility that she found access to harmful substances. I also considered the possibility that she became involved in a cult that practiced Witchcraft, as this is not uncommon in Kenyan culture.

Regardless of the reason behind Millie's behavior, I agreed to meet with her and see if we could get her some help. I requested that someone from her family accompany her to my office, so that they could be held accountable for helping to manage Millie's health. Since both of her parents were deceased, Millie came with her older brother, Emanuel.

As soon as they walked through the gates at Ringroad, I knew that something wasn't right. Millie's hair was unkept, and she was wearing dirty clothes that hung off of her body and almost exposed one of her breasts. Before she made her way over to my office, she wandered around campus with a lethargic shuffle and a blank stare on her face; walking into classrooms to greet teachers without their permission or any regard for the students that they were teaching. It took more than one staff member to effectively lead her in my direction, because she wanted to be left alone and free to go wherever she chose.

Luckily, Millie felt comfortable talking to me because she remembered me as someone who had always been kind to her. She told me how everyone at her school was conspiring against her because they wanted to see her fail, and that she had every right to get up and leave class whenever she wanted to, in order to avoid their negativity. She said that the only time she yells at someone is if they yell at her first; and she is constantly being yelled at.

"You believe what I'm telling you, don't you, Jen?" she asked, as she locked her eyes firmly with mine.

"I believe that what you are telling me is your truth," I responded.

"But I want you to answer a couple of questions for me, just to make sure that I'm able to help you in the correct way. Is that okay?"

Millie nodded, never breaking eye contact with me. I went on to ask if her if she ever has trouble concentrating in class, or gets distracted by the yelling that she hears, while she is trying to do her homework or campus chores. She answered yes to both.

"Do you have trouble sleeping at night?"

"Yes."

"When one of your teachers, or the principal, tells you to stop disturbing your peers, do you understand why they are telling you that? Do you understand what you have done to make them tell you to stop?"

"No. I've never done anything wrong, Jen. I told you, they are all trying to get to me. They talk behind my back and to my face about destroying me and my life. I don't do anything wrong to deserve such treatment."

"You are right, you don't deserve such treatment."

I continued to be sure and validate Millie's feelings. No matter what had transpired between her, her peers and the school staff, there was no wrong answer when it came to her explanation of what her own perspective looked like. It may have been detached from everybody else's reality, but she still had the right to share her own truth.

With CRF's sponsorship, I was able to take Millie to see a Psychiatrist at Aga Khan Hospital. She was resistant at first, because she didn't understand why she was the one who had to be evaluated by a doctor, when it was everyone else that was causing trouble. I did my best to explain that the doctor could help her to better process the things that were going on around her. He could offer medication that would not change the circumstances of her life, but might make her distractions and anxieties more manageable. Reluctantly, Millie agreed to go for an evaluation, and to try the medication that was subsequently prescribed to her for Paranoid Schizophrenia.

The following weeks were filled with phone calls and visits pertaining to Millie and her fight against mental illness. Her school called me because the medication was making her too drowsy to participate in class. I went out to the school in order to see for myself, and then called the Psychiatrist. He asked me to bring her in for a follow-up visit, so I did. Then he adjusted her medication.

Days later, I received another call from Millie's school to let me know that she stopped taking her medication, because she didn't like the way it made her feel. I went out to her school, again, and witnessed the rage and paranoia that she exhibited towards the people around her. When she was suspended from school again, I received a call from Emanuel, telling me that she had become unmanageable at home. He then brought her to Ringroad and begged us to "do something with her," because she was out of control.

"She is disturbing our neighbors, the way she walks around shouting and talking about prophets who are going to come visit us."

He looked defeated and exhausted.

"I don't know how I can help her because she refuses to listen to me. She won't take her medication."

Unfortunately, as you know, there is no cut and dry solution when it comes to treating mental illness. People respond differently to the various types of medications that are available; and effective treatment plans often include other therapies to accompany a pharmaceutical one. Having a strong support system is also extremely important. If you surround yourself with people who care about your well-being and have taken the time to learn about your diagnosis, they will be the ones to offer encouragement, and know when it's time to reach out for additional help.

Fearing that she was becoming a danger to herself and to those around her, I decided to bring Millie back to Aga Khan for another evaluation. Her doctor worked at multiple hospitals in the Kisumu area, and we happened to show up to Aga Khan on a day that he was somewhere else. There was no one there to cover for him and we were desperate, so her doctor agreed to come in once he was finished at his other location.

For this visit, I asked both her brother, and Ringroad's resident Pastor, George, to accompany Millie and I. Since she was so resistant to going back to the hospital, I felt it was best to have an additional person with us who could help keep Millie calm, while also helping to manage the logistics of getting her the treatment that she needed. Pastor George's steady demeanor and unwavering faith made him the perfect person to bring along. He is the kind of man that one could always seek safety in; a man who could find the world on fire and still be a source of comfort and peace to those around him. To this day, he is one of the most steadfast and Godly men I know.

Given Millie's erratic behavior and her refusal to get back on medication, it was recommended to us that she be committed into a Psychiatric Ward. I had suspected that this would be the case, but I was brokenhearted to learn that she was being sent to the Psychiatric Ward at Kisumu District Hospital. We were instructed to bring her to District ourselves, and told that her doctor would make his rounds there later in the evening; as he had multiple patients who were receiving treatment there.

"Why are we going there, Jen?" Millie asked me over and over.

"You promised you were going to help me, and now you're bringing me to another place that I don't want to go to."

As she spoke, her tone shifted between anger and fear.

"Please don't make me go there, Jen. Just let me go home. Please, Jen, just let me go home!"

I was screaming on the inside, but I couldn't allow for my own despair to show, or cloud my ability to take proper action. My focus in that moment was to help Millie feel safe, and trust that every step we were taking was towards help her to feel better. My prior experience as a Social Worker in outpatient mental health, reminded me of how incredibly difficult it is to earn or keep a person's trust, while inflicted such extreme psychological stress. You may be acting on behalf of their safety and well-being, but the terror and trauma felt by a patient in the midst of a psychotic episode is very real; especially when you are acting against their will.

We arrived at District Hospital just behind a middle-aged woman who had been in a car accident. She was wheeled to one of the reception desks, as she shouted in pain and fear. Her clothes were half-torn off of her body, and she was bleeding in multiple places. Even though she was sitting in front of a receptionist, no one seemed to be in a hurry to help or soothe her.

Millie kept her eyes on the car accident victim, as the four of us took our seats and waited to be called up to reception.

"I don't need this place, Jen. I have control of my own life, and I want to go home. I will go whether you want me to or not. I will get up and leave right now."

"Millie, I understand that you don't want to be here, but I also know that it's important for you to start feeling better. Your brother, Pastor George and I want to make sure that when you go home, you're feeling your absolute best."

"But those voices are not disturbing me today, Jen. I can just go home and if they disturb me again, I'll tell you and we can come back here."

I came incredibly close to telling Millie that we could leave; to allowing her to go home, and making her promise me that she would call the next time she was triggered by audio hallucinations. I so badly wanted to appease her, but I knew that bringing her home wasn't the right thing to do. Asking a vulnerable person- who often feels out of control of her own thoughts and actions- to make a promise that she likely could not keep, is both unreasonable and unethical. It had become clear that Millie needed a proper medication regiment; and I'd never forgive myself if something happened to her, or to someone else, because I let her go home without one.

When it was finally Millie's turn to see a receptionist, I asked Emanuel to speak on her behalf. All of the hospital staff spoke English, but I wanted to be sure that Millie's brother was clear on how to advocate for her. The hope was that someday, Millie would be able to advocate for herself; but it was important that she have someone who could step in for her when she wasn't capable. Emaunel showed the receptionist a list of medications that Millie had been prescribed, but refused, along with the request from her doctor to receive a Psychiatric Evaluation.

"All patients need to receive a blood test before they are seen by a doctor."

She pointed to a crowded corner across the hospital lobby.

"You can go pay there, and then wait in line for the blood test."

The line to make a payment was long; The line to receive blood work was even longer. Losing her final shred of patience, Millie shouted and stormed outside. I looked around and saw a handful of people were nursing their own wounds while they waited to be tended to. All of the babies in the lobby suddenly seemed to be crying at once, and the woman in the wheelchair was still being ignored. The heat was stifling, and the mounted wall fans were doing nothing to provide any sort of relief. The entire scene felt unbearably overwhelming to me, but I knew that my angst could not compare to that of Millie's. She was afraid, over-stimulated and exhausted.

"Excuse me." I got the receptionist's attention and immediately regretted it.

"I'm so sorry to bother you, but the patient that we came with has been having a really hard day. She does not have the proper medication and she is very overwhelmed. Is there a quiet room that she can rest in, while she waits to receive her blood test?"

I heard the words come out of my mouth and almost wanted to laugh at myself.

Look around, Jen. There are no quiet places in here. There's no privacy. There's no time to coddle a patient in distress.

The receptionist confirmed the absurdity of my question with the expression on her face.

"Your patient must wait in line for the blood test. There isn't any other option."

I turned around to find that Millie had come back inside. She was slumped over in a chair; tired and defeated.

"Hey, Millie?"

She looked up at me with her beautiful, big brown eyes. There was a softness in them that I hadn't seen all day.

"I know that you're angry, and that you don't want to be here. But do you trust that Emanuel, Pastor George and I are only trying to help you?"

"Yes, I trust you. I don't understand why you're doing this, Jen. But I trust you. And them."

I knelt down in front of her chair.

"You know, we wouldn't spend all day trying to help you feel better if we didn't care about you. Sometimes, we need people to help us do the things that we aren't able to do on our own; and that is okay."

Millie nodded. "I understand, Jen."

I confirmed with Emanuel and Pastor George that they were okay to wait at the hospital with Millie. I had done what I felt I was being asked to do, and knew that if I stayed, I would offer nothing but the sense of urgency that almost never proved to be helpful. Pastor George let me know that he would call me after he left the hospital.

My entire body ached. I walked into my house, sat on the living room floor, and wept. I grieved for Millie, and for the life of additional obstacles that she now had ahead of her. I imagined what the Psychiatric Ward at a place like District Hospital must look like; the concrete walls and rows of beds filled with people who felt scared, alone and confused. Some would be screaming, and some would be catatonically still. All would be heavily medicated and stripped of the dignity that we, as human beings, strive so hard to hold on to.

I'm so sorry, Millie.

Lord, please protect her.

I picked up my phone and called Sarah Nicholson. She knew Millie, and she knew District Hospital. She would be able to empathize with my heartache and my discouragement, as I struggled to process the level of human suffering that exists in a place like that.

At the sound of Sarah's voice, I allowed myself to continue grieving deeply, and unapologetically. She listened without any sort of agenda; giving me permission to hold the brokenness, rather than trying to remind me that God's love supersedes all that is broken. She knew that in this moment, I needed nothing more from her than space to grieve.

"I'm so sorry, Jen. I know how hard this can be."

Of all the wonderful people in my life, Sarah is among the very few who actually do know how hard a day like this was. I often find myself debating how much of my life in Kenya to share with my loved ones back in the States. I never fear that they aren't going to be supportive, but I fear that they won't give me the exact response that I feel I need. I also understand that no matter how many details I give, I won't ever truly capture the emotion behind any of it. Even as I sit here and write these words to you, they feel grossly insufficient relative to my actual experience.

On days like I had with Nissi and Millie, I tend to step back on personal communication, altogether. Once I've given myself time to process, I do choose to share some of these stories with the people who follow my journey on a public platform. It feels easier for me to convey my experiences to the masses; rather than individually, with loved ones who bear the burden of finding the right thing to say in response. There's a handful of people that I've gone deeper with, but most of the time, "How was your day?" feels like too loaded of a question to answer honestly.

Two weeks after I left Millie at District, she walked through my office door at Ringroad. She was wearing her school uniform and had a big smile plastered across her face.

"Hi, Jen!"

The room filled with God's presence, as I stood up from my desk and marveled over how healthy and happy this precious girl looked.

"Millie! How are you? How are you feeling?"

"I'm good. I feel better now."

"You're going back to school today?"

"Yes. But I must go back to the doctor for a check-up once a month."

I knew that Millie still had a long road ahead of her, but she now had the footing to begin engaging in her daily activities, once again. As it turns out, God does use places like Kisumu District Hospital, to give people exactly what they need.

I've had plenty of days where being a mother to Anyango felt like the only thing I knew how to do. And, on days when I didn't even know how to do that, she was often the only person that I was willing to make an effort for.

When she came to me and asked if I would visit her family's homestead, I had mixed feelings. I wanted to see the village where Anyango and her family come from, but I was always hesitant to visit places where my presence would cause more of a stir than usual. Being singled out in Nyalenda was becoming less of a problem for me, and I wasn't sure how well I'd handle the commotion that inevitably followed me to new surroundings. The more rural that a place is in Kenya, the less likely its residents are to have interacted with a white person before. I was not concerned for my safety, but I dreaded the attention.

Ultimately, my desire to get a deeper look into where my daughter comes from, trumped any reservations that I had. Caren was laid to rest on the family's property, so I also I wanted to pay my respects to the woman who profoundly changed my life.

We traveled to the rural village of Seme, via tuk-tuk. I had asked Solomon, one of my most trusted tuk-tuk drivers, to bring us out there and join us in spending the day at Anyango's homestead. Upon our arrival, we were greeted by her grandfather, Johannes, his wife and many other extended relatives. They were all giddy with excitement, but too shy to address me directly. I've never felt so unworthy of a pedestal in my life.

The truth is, Anyango ended up with me because no one, on either side of her family, wanted to take her after Caren died. Some of them probably would have let her in, like Aunt Judy had, but they weren't actually willing to care for her. At times it's hard for me to forgive that, but there's an unconditional respect I have for the place and the people who gave me my daughter. I am not in a position to judge the actions or decisions of any human being; let alone the ones who've experienced hardships that I likely never will. All that I am being called to do, is love with an understanding that it isn't up to me to have someone else's answers. As Anyango's family continued to fawn over my existence, I turned inward and released their praises back to God. He was the only one who deserved them.

Although I had spotted Caren's burial site as soon as we arrived, I waited to walk over there until after our official greetings were finished. I didn't want to be rude or dismissive to anyone else, but I ached to kneel down beside Caren's resting place and feel a sense of her peace. After all, she and I were now eternally connected.

I received a tour of the family land, and met a couple of their neighbors. Anyango and her little cousins brought me down to the river where people bathe and do their laundry. Fresh fruits hung from the trees, and small piles of wood had been collected for building fires and homes. Their material possessions were scarce, but their land was abundantly full of promise. I never wish to minimize the privilege of convenience; however, I am continuously in awe of the way that Kenyan people utilize their corner of this earth. Even though it stems from necessity over choice, there is something so beautifully humbling about seeing God's people rely on His creation.

Anyango's family prepared lunch for all of us, and they watched with joy and wonder as I ate. I am always a bit weary when it comes to eating food in a village or slum, but I try to never turn it down completely. The sacrifice that is made just to feed a visitor is one that should never go unappreciated. I enjoyed some fried eggs, ugali (boiled maize meal) and greens.

We spent a bit longer together after we ate, and then it was time for Solomon and I to make the two-hour journey back to Kisumu town. Anyango had asked me if she could spend the night with her family in Seme, and I told her that would be fine. Seeing where she stayed when she was away from me, made it easier to let her go. There was a different sort of light in her eyes, that I had never seen until we visited Seme together. She had this ease about her, as she settled back into her roots. I prayed that she would never lose that.

Chapter Twenty

Dad's office is at our house.

We're supposed to pretend he isn't home during the day so that he can concentrate on his work, but I like to go in there and say hi to him whenever I'm allowed. If he isn't on the phone with a client, he lets me come in. Then, if he isn't too busy, we play "pretend." I get to be the boss and sit in Dad's chair, and he sits on the other side of the desk and pretends that he is my client. I don't know his job at all, so I just make up things to say and Dad thinks it's funny.

Sometimes, if I promise to be really quiet, he lets me bring in my toys and play under his desk. Our dog, Rueben, likes to lie under Dad's desk, and I like to lie with him while I play with my dolls or stuffed animals. If Dad gets a phone call when I'm already in here, he doesn't kick me out. He lets me stay under his desk, as long as I don't make any noise.

I like listening to Dad when he talks on the phone. He talks about business things that I don't understand, but I think that's kind of cool. I imagine Dad as a little kid and wonder how old he was when he first started to understand things. I know that he had to learn everything he talks about on the phone. All of it sounds pretty complicated, but it makes perfect sense to him. He talks about things like insurance policies and business proposals. I don't know what those things are, but I see that they make him really happy. He has a ton of awards hanging on the walls, so I knew that he's good at it, too.

I wonder what I will be good at some day. I wonder what I'll learn about when I grow up, that I'm too young to understand now. Whatever it is, I hope I love it as much as Dad loves whatever it is that he's talking about.

~ ~ ~

Dear Sweet Girl,

At the beginning of this story, I told you about the time that my friend, Sarah van Edema, and I drove half-way across the country. Now, if it's okay with you, I'd like to tell you a little bit more about that day.

Sarah and I were driving from Connecticut to Tennessee, about a year and a half after I moved to Tennessee...the first time. As I shared with you earlier, my college friends and I moved down to Nashville after we graduated from college. We were in search of a fresh start; in a brand-new place that was nothing like where we came from. And while we did manage to carve out new lives for ourselves, we each had our reasons for ultimately moving back up north.

Out of the three of us, I was the last to move back home. I quit my job as a Social Worker because I was so unhappy being on the road all of the time. I did have a main office; however, the majority of my visits were done at clients' homes, and my days were often spent driving from one location to another. I had made friends, both in and outside of work, yet I struggled to feel as comfortable in Nashville as I felt I should by then.

Mom and Paul had recently moved to their new home just outside of Nashville, and they offered for me to come and live with them while I figured out what I wanted to do next. I told them that I appreciated their offer, but didn't think Tennessee was the right place for me anymore.

"Do you think you feel that way because Kellagh and Jackie moved home? Or do you truly feel that you aren't meant to be here?" Mom asked me.

"I just feel that if I were going to love being here, I would know by now. I've been in Tennessee for a year and a half and I still don't completely feel at home. Maybe I'm just meant to move back to Connecticut."

"You've talked about going to Graduate School," Mom pressed.

"Paul and I would be happy to have you stay with us if you want to enroll in a full-time graduate program."

I did want to go to graduate school, and I would have loved to stay near Mom and Paul, but not badly enough to stay in Tennessee. So, respecting my wishes, Mom helped me pack up my apartment. Then we

210

pack up my car, and she and Paul drove me all the way back to Connecticut. They dropped me off at Dad and Sharon's house, kissed me goodbye, and told me that if I changed my mind, their offer still stood.

I was so excited to be back near Dad, Sharon and their entire side of the family. I loved being able to call up friends from high school and college and arrange to meet them for lunch or drinks. I applied for a couple of social service jobs in the area, and Sas and I started looking into apartments to rent together. All of these things made me happy, but I couldn't get this tiny voice out of my head that was telling me I had made a mistake. What if I had given up on Tennessee too soon? What if I should have taken Mom and Paul up on their offer?

Less than three weeks after I moved back to Connecticut, I called Sarah van Edema and asked if she would help me drive back down to Tennessee. You may think that you don't know Sarah yet, but you actually do. As a matter of fact, you've known her and her family for years. They live across the street from the house Mom moved you into after the divorce. You are neighbors, but in time, you and Sarah become the best of friends. You talk to each other almost every day- all the way through college and beyond. She is your sounding board, your cheerleader, and the one who hops in the car with you in the wee hours of a chilly morning in March, to help you drive back to the State that you just moved away from.

Once the sun came up and we were able to focus on other things besides the seemingly extended period of darkness, Sarah asked me what my plan was upon my return.

"Do you think you'll enroll in grad school right away? Or will you try to look for a job first?"

"I think I'll enroll in school first, because there are so many steps involved. Once I do that, I'll start looking for part-time jobs that I can work around my school schedule."

Well, Sweet Girl, you probably know where I'm going with this. I didn't end up at Lipscomb University because I lived in Tennessee; I ended up there because I moved *back* to Tennessee. I joined Lipscomb, traveled with them to Kenya and fell in love. Because of that, I desired to seek God, found Him in Grandpa Tep's passing, traveled back to Kenya with a conviction to visit bed-ridden patients, and was introduced to Caren and her daughter, Anyango. Today, with Caren's spirit imprinted on my

211

heart, I acknowledge the four-year anniversary of Anyango calling me "Mom."

Just like I told you, we can make our own plans, and dream about what our futures will look like, but we don't always know what we truly want or need. Sometimes our definition of what makes sense, is challenged or disrupted in a beautifully unexpected way, and that's how you know it's a "God Thing."

When the opportunity to travel to Kenya was first presented to me, I turned it down. Remember? I was too afraid to travel so far from home, with people that I didn't know. Once I decided to go, I fell in love with Kenya. I vowed that I would continue to visit, but didn't know if I could ever see myself living there. Sure enough, I began to see myself living there; but not without the Nicholsons. And what happened after that? The Nicholsons moved to the other side of the country.

In the spirit of continuing to set expectations for myself that God would inevitably challenge, I declared that I would be willing to live in Kenya without the Nicholsons nearby, but only if I stayed in Kisumu. I knew Kisumu well and I was comfortable there, so why attempt to go anywhere else?

But you see, here's the thing: When you commit to serving God's people, you're committing to go wherever He calls you; regardless of where you feel the happiest or the most comfortable. I always felt that the comfort of my surroundings would play a role in the way that my life played out because…well…you know. Clearly, God's gotten a real kick out of my assumptions.

After four years of mission work in Kisumu- over a year of which I did full-time- I called Chris and Sarah to ask them how they knew when it was time to move on.

"Well, we felt like we had served our purpose at Ringroad, and that they were running smoothly enough for us to move on and serve in another community. Sarah answered. "Is that how you feel?"

"I do. I feel like maybe it's time to be in a community that doesn't have the same level of support that Ringroad does."

"Would you consider coming out to Malindi?" asked Chris. "We may know of an opportunity for you here."

On July 17th, 2017, Anyango, Simon and I loaded up in a private van and headed across the country. Despite the pain of saying goodbye to the Ringroad students and the Dowells, I felt at peace with my decision to relocate us to the coastal town of Malindi. Of course, before we left Kisumu, I received permission from Anyango's family to take her with me. She was hesitant to start at a new school in a new town, but her desire was to go wherever I went.

We traveled through the entire night; our driver only stopping when we needed to use a bathroom or walk Simon. In the early morning hours, as the sun began to peak over the flat, green terrain, I looked out my window and thanked God for giving me this life. And, just as He intended, the sun rose in perfect timing and gave us another day.

Epilogue

Dear Sweet Girl,

Someday, when I'm ready, I'll tell you all about Malindi. It's different from Kisumu in a lot of ways, so my cultural learning curve was nearly as steep as it was the first time around. It is in Malindi that I dove deeper into learning about who God is, where Anyango and I strengthened and grew in our relationship, and where I explored what it means to be a white, privileged, American female- living abroad- during an extremely tumultuous time in my own country's political history.

What I will tell you now, is that I still don't have all of the answers. I see heartache on a daily basis, and constantly ask God to reveal Himself in the midst of it all. I ask Him what my role is supposed to be; and I thank Him for His grace, as I question whether or not I'm fulfilling it well.

When it comes to you, Sweet Girl, I want you to know that I am sorry it took me so long to seek you. Once I learned how to free myself of the world that you passed on to me, it was easier to stop acknowledging you all together. I've never forgotten where I come from, but reflecting back on your pain can be exhausting sometimes. It makes me sad to think of the hours, days, and years you spent trapped under your own irrational fears and unrelenting sadness.

You've been given such a beautiful life, and I wish it wasn't going to take you as long as it does to fully enjoy it. With that being said, please know that I understand it isn't your fault. You were born with psychological challenges that are very real, and can often be hard to understand. The important thing is that you do get to a place where you are able to live a full life; and use the experiences that you've had to nurture and care for others.

Sometimes I wonder what it would have been like for you to read these words and know this story, back when it was still your time. There's no telling how you would have received it, but I actually don't think it would have helped you much. This is the type of story that you need to grow into. What an amazing blessing it will be for you to take this story and use it to inspire others someday.

You were born with the privilege of access. All your life, you've had access to food, shelter, quality education, and any type of medical care that you've ever needed. You've also had- and will always have- a support system that is wide and unconditional. It is access to these things that is going to lead you down a path of serving others who have far fewer resources. Painful as it is to watch sometimes, it is always going to be worth it to advocate for the life of another human being.

So now, here we are. You live in the world of "hindsight," and I'm able to share this story because of the journey that God carried you through. Thank you for being exactly who you are, so that I could become exactly who I am. I love you much more deeply than I've ever been able to let on in the past.

I look forward to diving further into my journey with you, because there is so much more that I want you to know. There are so many more beautiful, heartbreaking, humbling stories that God leads me through, and desires for me to share. But at this time, Dear One, I've got another sweet girl in my life who also deserves a letter...

217

Arriving in Kisumu for the first time

Children playing at Ringroad Orphans Day School

The Nicholson Family (Chris, Sarah, Iddy, Ruth-Michael and Abby-Jones) and I

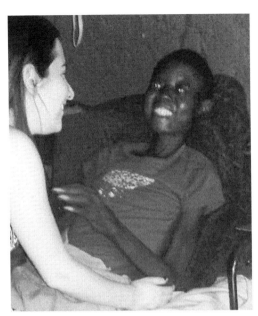

Caren and I and Caren's home in Nyalenda

Nissi recovering at the hospital

Joanie and I

Our family: Anyango, Simon and I

Dear Anyango,

How do I begin a letter to the person who exists as the brightest light in my life? Each time I express how deeply I love you. I feel that my words or actions fall short of what you deserve. If there's one thing that I learned from writing this book, it's that I will never do our story justice. It's too perfectly layered with God's grace and provision; His faultless intention and unconditional love. Our story is really His story, but I'm thankful for the chance to tell it as best as I can; inadequate as it may be.

Over the years, you've made reference to me "saving your life." And, when other people hear about us, they say the same thing: "Look at how you saved her life." But, did I really, though?

I can acknowledge that I've made certain opportunities available to you. I won't hesitate to tell you, or anybody else, that I've put every single part of who I am into learning what it takes to be the best mother to you that I can be. But saving your life? I will never take credit for that; because I am not the one who did.

With or without me, you are one of the most capable human beings that God placed on this earth. Your work ethic is untouchable and your willingness to help others is a beautiful thing. You are strong, intuitive, passionate, and motivated to set a better example than many of the ones that you were given. You've been created to do big things and make a big impact; and I'm just thankful that I get to be a part of your story.

Every once in a while, I flash back to the day that I came to visit you after your mom died. I can see you sitting outside, up against the mud siding of your house, with your knees tucked into your chest and tears rolling down your cheeks. It's hard to imagine that the young women you are today, was once that scared, sad little girl. I thank God and your Mama every day for growing you into the person that you've become.

It's no secret that this world doesn't always feel like a safe or fair place. You've witnessed injustice that will likely never be understood in this lifetime; but my biggest wish for you is that you never, ever let that hold you back. Embrace who you are, and where you come from. Recognize the beauty of your skin, and carry yourself as the strong, proud black woman that you are. Serve as a role model to the young girls who look up to you, and educate the people who've never known your country to be more than just a place of human suffering. You, my sweetest girl, are capable of it all; and no one can ever take that away.

Thank you for allowing me to love and parent you the way that my heart has led me to. I know that I don't always get it right, but I promise you that I always try. There have been days that my sole purpose for getting out of bed was to be the mother that you deserve to have. Thank you for recognizing when I'm feeling overwhelmed, and for finding ways to help my life feel a little bit more manageable. Thank you for your patience in helping me to better understand your culture. Thank you for loving me as well as you do.

Like we've said many times, God knew that we needed each other. I believe down to my soul, that my life was not meant to exist without yours. You will forever be my first child; the one who taught me what motherhood feels like, and confirmed why it's been something that I've dreamt of since I was a little girl. I can't wait to see all that you accomplish in this next season. I promise to always be your Number One cheerleader, and your Number One safe place.

I love you forever and ever.

-Mom

A Note from the Author

Although many chapters of our story remain to be told, I would like to acknowledge Anyango's acceptance into Lipscomb University's 2019 Summer Scholars Program, and subsequent acceptance as a freshman student for their 2020-2021 academic year. This book was written prior to many important events in our lives, and Anyango's journey to America and university is one that deserves to be written in perfect detail, in its own time.

To my readers, and to a certain little girl who desperately wants to know how her life turns out: the story continues, so please stay tuned!

Acknowledgements and Gratitude

This book is a love letter to a lot of people. Those who are mentioned in the telling of this story, and many who are not, played significant roles in helping me to become who I am today. I've been blessed my entire life by a support system that is stronger and wider than I feel I deserve.

With that being said, I'd like to take this opportunity to thank the individuals and groups of people who make up the base of that support system. I would first like to thank **Michael Kiggins, Paul van Gogh** and **Ali Friedman McCormick** for handling my manuscript with such care and respect throughout the editing process. Writing a book is a very personal, vulnerable experience; and parts of this were more difficult to write than others. Thank you for providing me with constructive feedback, while protecting the dignity of my story. Your hard work in helping me to produce the best final draft possible is greatly appreciated.

Mom and Dad- How do I begin to thank the people who brought me in to this world; the ones who have unconditionally loved, supported and encouraged me from the moment that I was born? You've each given me a lifetime of opportunities that have allowed for me to grow and thrive in so many ways.

Mom, you are my #1 safe place. Thank you for constantly making my health and happiness a priority, and for the years of nursing an ache of mine that I couldn't quite put my finger on. You've never given up on me or made me feel like a burden. You embrace who I am and bring out the dreamer in me. I nurture Anyango the way that I do because I've had you as an example.

Dad, you are my #1 cheerleader. Thank you for always encouraging me to step outside of my comfort zone, and for imparting your wisdom and values on me- both as a parent, and as an equal. I am constantly pushing myself to try new things in life, because that's what you taught me to do. In raising Anyango, I've done my best to stress the importance of humbleness and gratitude, because of the way that you raised me.

227

Jakey- My brother, my friend, my ally. I'd always hoped that we would grow up to be close, but I never could have imagined just how full our relationship would become. When we were little, I knew that it was my job as your big sister to nurture and protect you. And now, it has been my honor to watch you grow into the type of man who nurtures and protects those who matter most. I'm so thankful to be one of those people. I'm also thankful to you for giving me the sister that I've always dreamed of having.

Allie Pallie, thank you for embracing our family as your own, and for becoming an equal part of the familial support system that I cherish so deeply. Your patience and your gentle nature often keep me grounded.

Paul and Sharon- Thank you for stepping into your roles as step-parents to Jake and I so seamlessly. You both have been family for nearly two decades, and have seized countless opportunities to deepen your parental relationship with me in ways that not all blended families are able to do.

Paul, thank you for coming alongside Mom in her desire to nurture my health and support my dreams. You are quick to celebrate my victories; and offer patience and understanding in the midst of my struggles. Your calm demeanor brings me peace in times of chaos, and it is my honor to learn from you each time you teach me something new; whether that be how to properly file my taxes, or how to communicate well in times of stress.

Sharon, thank you for coming alongside Dad and supporting his conviction to raise us with humble and down-to-earth values. You've never made me feel less than one of your own, and you don't ever hesitate to offer your time or compassion to me, or to others in my life who may need it. I'm thankful for the way that you cheer me on, and always make sure that I have everything that I need in order to feel safe, comfortable, and loved.

Austin, Thijs and Stef- My brothers from other mothers. As the oldest and the only sister on both sides of the family, it has been my privilege to share life with the three of you and watch you grow into kind, intelligent, motivated, adults.

Austin, some of my favorite memories from growing up involves getting to take care of you. You were my baby doll, my smiley little sidekick and the one who always tried to push my buttons but never got away with it. I am so proud of the young man that you are becoming, as you explore your passions and make plans for your future.

Thijs and Stef, we started our relationship as brother and sister with a slight language barrier, but quickly connected and grew into a family of dysfunctional siblings that I cherish more than you know. I admire your passion for learning, and both of your abilities to absorb culture (and literally all other information that exists). I always have a blast exploring new cities and countries with you. Thank you, to all three of my step-brothers, for loving me and treating me with respect.

Sarah and Chris Nicholson- So much of who I am- as a missionary, a person of faith, and a parent to an adopted child- is because of the example that you both set for me. You opened my eyes to the beauties and challenges of living as an expat in a developing country, and showed me the value in building connections and making time to sit with people of different cultural and religious backgrounds. It has been my honor to learn from you, serve beside you, and tackle daily life with you over the past seven years (give or take a few gaps in time here and there). Thank you for trusting me in and outside of ministry, and for allowing me to share in your victories and your challenges. You, Iddy, Ruth-Michael, and Abby-Jones will forever be family to Anyango and I.

Jonathan and Andrea Dowell- I suppose I should start by thanking you for saving my life, post-stomach bug. Thank you for opening up your home, and allowing me to seek refuge in a place that is always full of acceptance and free of judgement. You took me under your wing, and made space for my endless questions and silly neuroses. You embody the phrase, "come as you are," and your commitment to serving others is a beautiful gift that I have witnessed, over and over again. The way that you care for those in each of your many communities, prepared you for your role as parents ; another part of your lives that I am thankful to have witnessed. Thank you for letting me in, for loving me and for being an example that I am proud to carry with me.

Ringroad Family- First and foremost, thank you to the Directors, teachers and support staff for your commitment to the students in your program. For many of the students, you serve as the only positive adult role models that they've been exposed to. Thank you for spending your days as educators and advocates for your community's most vulnerable population. Thank you for welcoming me into your family and giving me the opportunity to love and educate the children, alongside of you. Thank you for your patience and understanding as I learned to navigate through our cultural differences, and for offering me grace when I didn't get it right. Finally, thank you to all of the children who were students at Ringroad during my time there. Your strength, resilience, and spirit are unmatched. I learned much more from you than you ever could have learned from me.

Christian Relief Fund (CRF)- The opportunity to partner with you in Kisumu was a blessing. I am grateful to your team for trusting me with your sponsored children, for supporting my ministry and for all of the ways that you give in Kenya and around the world. Thank you for putting up with my endless emails and phone calls, and for helping me to sustain my work in every way that you possibly could. I am forever indebted to you for allowing me to be small part of the CRF family.

Ministry Supporters- As I've said in all of my newsletters, your role in this work is equally as important as mine. Every student, every patient, every community that I've ever touched; is one that your generosity has touched, as well. None of this would have been possible without your supportive giving, prayers and encouragement. On behalf of my entire Kenyan family, I'd like to thank you for having faith in my mission.

Extended Relatives and Family Friends- Whether I've known you for a short while or for my entire life, thank you for your love and support. From the Aunts, Uncles and cousins that I share cherished memories with, to the women who stepped up and served as second-mothers to Jake and I at various points in our lives, I am thankful to have a support system the extends beyond immediate family.

Friends- From middle school, high school, college and beyond; thank you to the girlfriends who have continued to love me unconditionally over the years. You've shared in my joys, been my sounding board in times of sorrow, supported my mission and patiently encouraged me as I've moved from one season of life to another. You all know who you are, and I am grateful every day for your support.

My wonderful therapists- Wherever you are in your careers and in your lives, I'd like to thank you for giving me safe space to process my thoughts and emotions. Each one of you played a role in helping me to understand what it means to suffer from chronic anxiety and depression. Not only did you provide me with effective coping skills, but you encouraged me to use my own experiences to help others who might be going through similar things. Thank you for listening without judgement, and for giving me space to grow as a child, a teenager, and a young adult. I owe so much of my life to what I learned from each of you.

Made in the USA
Columbia, SC
30 August 2020

17892373R00128